MUSTANG'S LAST RIDE

THE CLOSURE OF THE MUSTANG RANCH BORDELLO

Bill Valentine

Nevada Undercover Publishers
Carson City, Nevada

Copyright © 2001 Bill Valentine

Published by
Nevada Undercover Publishers
P.O. Box 1384
Carson City, NV 89702
775 885 2420

ISBN 0-9714553-0-9

Printed in the United States of America

Cover and Book Design by Jonathan Gullery

All rights reserved. No part of this book
may be reproduced, stored in a retrieval
system, or transmitted in any form or by
any means, electronic, mechanical, photo
copying, recording or otherwise, without
the prior permission of Bill Valentine,
Nevada Undercover, Carson City, Nevada, USA.

About The Author

During his twenty-year career with the Nevada Department of Prisons, one of Sgt. Valentine's major responsibilities was the identification and tracking of prison gang members, prison gangs, and related criminal groups. In so doing, he compiled vast amounts of intelligence data over the years.

For many of these years, Sgt. Valentine gave freely of his time in instructing others in gang identification and management. He has been a featured speaker at many national gang seminars, and has written many articles on the subject.. He has been seen frequently on local television discussion groups, along with others who share a common interest in suppressing active criminal groups.

His first book, "Gang Intelligence Manual," was published in September, 1995, by Paladin Press, Boulder, CO. Following this, in February, 1998, he produced a two-part law enforcement video titled, "Reading Gang Tattoos." This video is currently being distributed by Calibre Press, Carrollton, TX. In November, 2000, his third work, a book titled, "Gangs and Their Tattoos," was published by Paladin Press. These three works are currently available.

In addition to tracking prison gang members for many years, Sgt. Valentine also followed the decades long, sordid career, of erstwhile brothel owner, Joe Conforte. Conforte, once known to the public as a wealthy, generous, jewel-bedecked, cigar-smoking, flesh peddler, is the erstwhile owner of the Mustang Ranch, a legal bordello located outside of Reno, Nevada. Conforte, now a fugitive from justice, is thought to be living in Brazil.

During Valentine's tenure in the Nevada Department of Prisons, the Mustang Ranch and Joe Conforte were an ongoing topic among inmates. Many knew of the bordello first hand. Those that didn't, liked to boast they did. They did the same with Conforte's name. Most of the inmates knew of him--his flamboyance. Others boasted they knew him well. Still, a few others left no doubt about their close association, and allegiance, to the brothel owner. These tightlipped, con-wise inmates, had the right answers, though unlike the braggarts, were selective in who they spoke to.

And it was in this environment, that Sgt. Valentine became acquainted with many of the persons and events described in this book. And it was here that the idea developed to bring this story to the public's attention.

Acknowledgments

Nevada State Historical Society

Nevada State Library and Archives

Storey County Court Records
Washoe County District Court Records
U.S. District Court Records, Reno Nevada

Matt R. Penrose. Pots O' Gold. A Carlisle & Company of Nevada and Binders, Reno, NV. ©1935

Las Vegas Sun, Las Vegas, Nevada
Carson City Daily Appeal, 1924, Carson City, Nevada
The New York Times
Reno Gazette-Journal, Reno, Nevada

A Special Thank You To The Nevada Appeal, Carson City, Nevada, For Allowing Me To Reprint Articles In This Work

A Special Thank You To The Gold Hill News, Virginia City, Nevada, For Allowing Me to Rerprint The Interview The Paper Did With Joe Conforte, in June, 1976

Willard Ross Brymer Sr. (April 7, 1945–June 27, 2000). Though our uniforms were of a different color while in prison, we sensed a mutual respect, though neither ever crossed the line.

Willard Ross Brymer Jr., Reno, Nevada.
We too, were thrust together behind the walls. In a confined area such as a prison, every person is known by their reputation. Ross Jr., was known as a strapping youngster who never backed down from anything. Yet like his father, Ross Jr. always returned respect to those who gave.

DEDICATION

This work is dedicated to my wife, Jessie, of many, many years. Without her patience and understanding, I doubt that you would be reading this. Thank you Dear.

FORWARD

On Monday, August 9, 1999, a task force of federal law enforcement officers converged upon the grounds of the Mustang Ranch, a world renowned legal brothel, that lie just outside of Reno, Nevada, in Storey County.

The officers carried with them, court documents that would effectively transfer ownership of the brothel from one, Joseph Conforte, to the federal government. This action was designed to shut down the brothel forever. The loss of revenue for tiny Storey County would be disastrous.

Conforte, an infamous character and fugitive from justice now living in Brazil, was well known by law enforcement officials as well as pleasure seekers. And because of his penchant for skirting the law, the cops had been tracking him for decades.

Born in Augustia, Italy, on January 16, 1926, Conforte arrived in this country while still a a child. He grew up street smart in Oakland, California, and at age 30, migrated to the Reno area. In Reno, he took a job as a cab driver, and not long after, was procuring girls for the local patronage, a task he knew well, and for which he had been arrested in Oakland.

It wasn't long before he had built up a sizable clientele, so much so, that he opened up an illegal bordello run out of a shabby trailer, parked on the boundaries of three counties, Washoe, Storey, and Lyon. Business was brisk. And because prostitution in these counties was illegal at the time, payoffs, too, were brisk. Being mobile, when the authorities in one county tried to squeeze him excessively, he simply moved the trailer across the county lines.

The local newspapers regarded Conforte as good copy, and as such, was accorded generous coverage. Having his name spread across the papers so often, only added to the notoriety and mystique. This of course increased his business dramatically. Local citizenry, who of course knew he was operating illegally, for the most part, looked the other way.

Though his payoffs to local law enforcement officials were often talked about, there were some law officers who sneered at his influence peddling and dogged him repeatedly. Their efforts resulted in convictions for which he did time in both state and federal prisons.

Though he was a convicted felon, and a brothel operator, the federal government, in their infinite wisdom, at one time spent hundreds of thousands of dollars to induce him to cross over and testify against one of their own, a federal court judge. Conforte must have inwardly felt this was the epitome of his career, being proselytized by an agency of the federal government.

When this blew up in their faces, the feds again went after their quarry with a vengeance.

Conforte, no longer a state's witness, was again fair game. He could also be the hunter.

An Argentine heavyweight boxer who had arrived in this country seeking a championship title fight, was to end up on the steps of the Mustang Ranch, his life blood ebbing onto the ground, because of his association with the notorious brothel owner.

Though Conforte liked to boast of bringing happiness and pleasure to millions of persons during a career that spanned four decades, he left many broken people in his wake.

Bill Valentine

CONTENTS

CHAPTER 1	JOE CONFORTE	1
CHAPTER 2	NEVADA STATE PRISON	33
CHAPTER 3	PRISON GAMBLERS	43
CHAPTER 4	A LEGAL BORDELLO	49
CHAPTER 5	CORRUPTION IN SPARKS	59
CHAPTER 6	THE SICILIAN CONNECTION	65
CHAPTER 7	OSCAR BONAVENA	71
CHAPTER 8	WILLARD ROSS BRYMER	95
CHAPTER 9	THE LONG ARM OF THE LAW	107
CHAPTER 10	QUESTIONS LINGER	117
CHAPTER 11	THE FISH TANK	125
CHAPTER 12	GEE JON AND LETHAL GAS	155
CHAPTER 13	THE EXECUTION OF JESSE BISHOP	..166
CHAPTER 14	WHITE SANDY BEACHES	189
CHAPTER 15	JUDGE HARRY CLAIBORNE	205
CHAPTER 16	BORDELLO FOR SALE	251
CHAPTER 17	THE LAST RIDE	269
EPILOGUE		289
NOTES		295

ILLUSTRATIONS

1. Mustang Ranch Closed
2. Nevada State Prison Cellhouse Under Construction
3. Aerial View Of The Nevada State Prison
4. Nevada State Prison, East Facing Lower Yard
5. Nevada State Prison, West Facing Lower Yard
6. Nevada State Prison Culinary
7. "Modern Cell." Nevada State Prison
8. Disciplinary Segregation Cells, Nevada State Prison
9. Disciplinary Detention Cell, C-Block, Nevada State Prison
10. Leonard Fristoe, Intake Photo
11. Leonard Fristoe On The Prison Yard
12. Leonard Fristoe After Capture 46 Years Later
13. Leonard Fristoe Arrest Warrant
14. The Author On Patrol Inspecting C-Block
15. Prison "Brass," Nevada State Prison Medium Of Exchange
16. Low Ball Card Table, Nevada State Prison Casino
17. Fully Functional Craps Table, Nevada State Prison
18. Baseball And Pari Mutual Betting, Nevada State Prison
19. Inmate Joe Conforte At The Craps Table
20. Outside Of The Mustang Gate, The Scene Of The Slaying
21. One-Lane Bridge Over The Truckee River That Leads Into And Away From The Mustang Ranch
22. Group Photo Taken At A Lake Tahoe Hotel-Casino During A Frank Sinatra Performance
23. Century Old Storey County Courthouse And Jail
24. Cabin In The Sky Restaurant
25. Nevada State Prison Intake Photo Of Gee Jon
26. Entrance To The Disciplinary Cave, Nevada State Prison
27. View Taken Inside The Cave

28. Sketch Of The "Killing Machine"
29. Improvised Structure Used For The First Lethal Gas Execution
30. Building Constructed Specifically For Use As A Lethal Gas Chamber, Nevada State Prison
31. Witnessing A Lethal Gas Execution
32. Prison Photo Of Jesse Bishop
33. Modern Gas Chamber With Two Side-By-Side Steel Chairs
34. Entrance Into The Lethal Gas Chamber Through The Air-Lock Door
35. Ross Brymer Shown Being Taken Down By Officers In The Parking Lot Of The Nevada State Prison
36. Ross Brymer Shown With Willie Nelson
37. Ross Brymer Shown With Another Musician

Chapter One

JOE CONFORTE

Northern Nevada law enforcement personnel know him as Joseph Conforte, aka" Joe Konforte, purveyor of sex, both legal and illegal, who was born in Augustia, Sicily, January 10, 1926, and who is now naturalized. Last known local address is listed as 3115 Sullivan Lane, Sparks, Nevada. With graying black hair, and brown eyes, Conforte's height is listed as 5 ft. 6 in. (when not wearing elevator shoes), and weighing 165 lbs. He is a known felon, a fugitive from justice, now thought to be living in Rio de Janiero, Brazil.

Today marked the end of an icon. Monday, August 9, 1999, spelled doom for the world famous Mustang Ranch, which for over 30 years had been an operating bordello in northern Nevada, eight miles east of Reno. Saddened by the turn of events, many of the working girls sat quietly chatting, many of whom were chain smoking cigarettes and sipping drinks. Others, fearful of what lie ahead, were openly sobbing, matching the dreariness of the overcast day. Heavy clouds above threatened at any time, to unleash their own sorrowful tears.

Pebbles, the matronly general manager of the bordello for the past 30 years, not yet ready to admit defeat, strode outside past the electronic gate to greet the gathering crowd. After pleasantries were exchanged, she tossed her hair to the wind and jumped atop a waiting horse. Armed guards manning the two prison style guntowers above, shouted down to her.

"Mustang's last ride, Mustang's last ride…" and the crowd of journalists and curious onlookers who had gathered outside, roared their approval as Pebbles galloped around the parking lot.

Inside the two buildings (the bordello was actually two adjacent buildings, Mustang 1 and Mustang 2), throngs of the curious were being led through tours of the working rooms, which numbered over one hundred. Some of the cribs were no larger than a prison cell, furnished with only a bed and wash basin. Others were much larger, some extravagantly decorated, with framed paintings on the walls and mirrored ceilings. The expansive orgy room featured a king size bed, a large screen television complete with porno movies, mirrors, and a Jacuzzi. For customers with a more kinky persuasion, the torture room could be had for about one thousand dollars a night.

Ambling through the hallways, the tour viewed other rooms installed for the comfort of the employees: beauty parlors, tanning rooms, massage parlors, and the never-stop laundry rooms. An employee's cafeteria jutted out from one hallway where the help could get anything from steak and eggs, to vegetarian dishes. Outside, a swimming pool and tennis court provided a welcome diversion for the off duty girls. Surrounding the entire complex, were ten-foot high security fences.

The fencing in front of the buildings was made from ten-foot high, spear-tipped, vertical iron bars welded into place every six-inches. A matching electronic gate provided secure entry into, and exit from the buildings. The sides and back of the buildings were enclosed within ten-foot high chain-link fencing.

Beyond the fences and gun-towers, ample space provided parking for scores of vehicles, including motor homes, and 18-wheelers. A helicopter pad was there to accommodate the frequent high-rollers. At night, the entire area was ablaze with neon lights, which served as a beacon to entice the big spenders.

In its heyday, the johns (men only customers) were admitted past the electronic gate and into the parlor where they would be greeted by the hostess (and not the madam who was usually out of sight). The hostess could be a pretty young woman or a matronly grandma type, or anything in between. She was not a prostitute; her job was to make the john feel welcome. And she was selected on the basis of having a friendly demeanor augmented by a flashy smile.

Once the john felt comfortable, he was told he could approach the girls who were lounging on sofas and chairs, or he could move over to the bar and sip a drink and exchange words with a few of the girls or with the bartender. It wasn't required of him to have sex with one of the girls, but it was expected he would. He was told right up front that no kissing was allowed. He was not here for romance; he was here for business. And business varied. A sign over the bar read, "Ask About Our Orgy Room."

After a couple of drinks, the john could advise the hostess he would like to inspect the merchandise. Depending upon the time of day or night, the peak tourist season, and other factors, there could be as many as 50-60 girls on duty, or as few as a handful. The line-up[1] was next, where the girls rose to their feet and recited their working names.

The john could now strike up a deal for sex, or he could engage one or more of the girls of his choice in conversation. It then became the responsibility of the girls to entice him into one of the back rooms, and to see how much money he would be willing to spend. After these formalities, the two—or in some cases, three— would then disappear into one of the working rooms. This could be either a cramped room with a small bed, or a mirrored room, or torture room, depending upon the john's persuasion and his bankroll.

Negotiations took place under a heater vent in the ceiling, which actually concealed a two way intercom connected to the manager's office. This was in effect to keep the girls honest since it was the girls who negotiated the price, and usually, the house's split exceeded what the girls got. After concluding negotiations and the money had changed hands, the activities began. The madam, waiting in the lounge, would start a timer.

During a recent interview, one of the girls explained, "The average time spent with a good customer could bring in as much as $600 dollars, but after expenses and the split, the girl may realize only $200 dollars."

Compared to the house's take, this may seem like a paltry sum for the woman who must give up her body, emotions, heart and soul repeatedly. However; the expected work period of the average girl was three weeks on and one week off. A good worker could turn more than a hundred tricks during her three-week work period, and earn thousands of dollars in so doing. And most of the girls spent freely, living in luxury, buying expensive clothing, facials, and hair styles. Some turned the cash over to their boy friends, husbands or children. Medical expenses ate up a lot, especially with the aging girls. Breast implants, tummy tucks, liposuction procedures, cheek and lip implants and other plastic surgeries were necessary for some of the girls striving to retain the allure.

The john inside the Mustang, could feel relatively safe in his encounters. Licensed prostitutes don't call wives, or make trouble. Protected sex has always been enforced by the Nevada Division of Health. Since March, 1986, AIDS testing of every licensed prostitute has been mandatory, as is the use of condoms in every sexual encounter. Girls not adhering to this mandate are fired. Blood tests for HIV and syphilis are conducted on each girl once a month. Testing for gonorrhea, venereal warts and herpes, are required weekly.

Unfortunately, many unlicensed prostitutes work the streets and hotel casinos unlawfully. Some of these girls have become AIDS carriers and have passed this onto some of their tricks (one freelance hooker with AIDS was arrested for the third time on January 26, 1998, just nine hours after being released on the same charge).

Why does a girl become a licensed prostitute? Excitement, glamour, money? These are valid reasons. Mustang Ranch prostitutes together, over the years, have said they found a family, much the way gang members do. Many had come from dysfunctional families and were throw-a-ways; many had drug and alcohol problems, many had been on welfare and had boy friends or husbands who were doing time. These girls appreciated the three weeks on and one week off schedule which gave them the security of a home. Reminiscing, one hooker said there was a kind of sorority feeling among the girls.

"We were family. We covered for each other," she explained. "For many of those girls who had suffered at the hands of their boyfriends or street pimps, it was the closest thing to home and family they would ever know."

During the Reno Air Races, Hot August Nights, or other special events, the girls sometimes worked 14-16 hours a day making good money. Happy days.

But those days were forever lost; the brothel would never see the millennium. Because of criminal activity associated with the ranch, and an unrelenting pursuit of one Joe Conforte—a balding, pudgy fugitive from justice now in his early seventies—who was the alleged hidden owner of the Mustang Ranch—the courts had placed the bordello into the hands of the federal government. Today, Monday, the 9th of August, 1999, marked the end.

Armed with a court order of closure by U.S. District Judge, Howard McKibben, federal agents, supported by local law enforcement personnel began converging on the parking lot, preparing to enforce the judge's rulings, much to the dismay of most of the curious onlookers who had gathered nearby.

The closure foreshadowed the unemployment of approximately 80-90 hookers (who actually were independent operators), and 75-80 salaried support persons, including security personnel, maids, cooks, bartenders, chauffeurs and related workers.

Following the closure, 45 Mustang prostitutes applied for work at the Moonlight Ranch, a Lyon County bordello. After being interviewed by the madam, only five were hired. The brothel's manager remarked that only the best were to work at the Moonlight. "We're going to be classier than the Mustang," he quipped.

Tiny Storey County, where the Mustang is located, also prepared for its loss of revenue which is about $250,000 annually. Approximately 4 percent of Storey's annual budget has been paid by Conforte in the form of licensing fees, and business and property taxes, for the past 30 years (and this allegedly includes periods when prostitution was illegal in the county).

Stories continue to circulate in Virginia City, the county seat, alleging a long history of payoffs from Conforte to local officials. Prostitution in Storey County had been illegal from 1955 until 1971.[2] Yet as far back as the mid 1950s, when the 29 year old Conforte arrived in Reno from California and took a job as a cab driver, he was procuring girls in a three county area, Washoe, Storey and Lyon (a thing for which he had done jail time, in California).

His next venture with pandering came when he raised enough money to open the Triangle River Ranch, which was an illegal whorehouse on wheels—literally. The Triangle consisted of a few mobile homes without a permanent address. Sally Burgess, a local resident, was hired on as madam and general overseer.

Based near Wadsworth, at the tri-county junction, the homes were frequently moved between Storey, Lyon and Washoe counties—depending upon the amount of heat generated by local politicians. Joe passed money around freely during this period of structuring. Currency wrapped cigars were offered as gifts to police, politicians and other influential persons.

One who didn't accept these tokes was William "Bill" Raggio,[3] Washoe County District Attorney (now a state senator), who set his sights on Joe Conforte. In 1959, Raggio began to build a case and filed a total of three vagrancy[4] charges against Conforte. Conforte retaliated by allegedly trying to set up the rigid District Attorney by using an 18 year old girl to lure the D.A. into a compromising situation.

On November 20, 1959, a felony arrest warrant was signed by Raggio. The felony complaint alleged that Conforte had threatened to involve Raggio in a "sex-trap" with a minor girl, provided the D.A. did not drop misdemeanor charges previously filed against the brothel owner. One of the investigators from the D.A.'s office, along with two deputies from the Washoe County Sheriff's Office were dispatched to look for Conforte. Crossing over into neighboring Lyon County, the three lawmen spotted the brothel owner near one of the illegal cat houses. He was subsequently arrested under protest and booked into the Washoe County jail and held in lieu of $50,000 bail.

The next day, District Attorney Raggio issued a public statement outlining the attempted extortion by Joe Conforte. Appearing unruffled, Raggio explained that on November 18, 1959, Joe Conforte had approached him demanding that Raggio drop all charges against him. If he failed to do so, Conforte allegedly threatened to make public a questionable affair between Raggio and an 18-year old girl. Further, Conforte was allegedly said to have demanded a public apology from Raggio, and assurances that the district attorney's office would no longer harass the brothel owner.

Raggio alleged that Conforte boasted of having connections statewide, and that he could influence actions and decisions from offices as high as the attorney general, on down through political offices on the local level.

Raggio emphasized that he would not be intimidated. He stressed that it was his duty as district attorney, to see that "scum and filth" could not influence the actions of public officers. Raggio explained that the young girl had come into his office on the pretext of obtaining a divorce. He said that right away, his instinct told him that something was amiss. He felt that she was not what she professed to be. After a short period of time in which they discussed the technicalities of divorce law, Raggio said the young girl excused herself. A meeting was then scheduled for the next day.

Suspicious, Raggio went on to say that the next day prior to the girl's arrival, he invited a male friend of his to be present so that there would be a third person—a witness—present in the event his suspicions were confirmed. When the girl arrived, Raggio said the three of them engaged in small talk in his office for a short period of time. From there, the threesome agreed to continue the conversation in a cocktail lounge while having drinks. They then left his office and proceeded to the Riverside Hotel.

After a few drinks, Raggio said the girl's demeanor and conversation soon became intimate and suggestive. And at one point she hinted that it would be more comfortable if Raggio's male friend left.

This last remark left little doubt about the girl's intentions, Raggio said, and he and his friend bid the girl farewell and left the room together. Raggio said in his prepared statement that she was later observed checking out of the hotel with Conforte. This revelation confirmed Raggio's suspicions.

Raggio said that he intended to prosecute the perpetrators of the attempted extortion vigorously, "to insure that no such tactics can ever again be used in the county to influence the actions of public officials, or the judiciary."

Following the statement released by Raggio, Conforte appeared that afternoon before the justice of the peace, who reduced the bail to $15,000, which was put up by a local bail bondsman. Conforte walked out of the jail and went straight to see his attorney.

The first legal question raised was the act of crossing over jurisdictional boundaries by the Washoe lawmen. The Lyon County District Attorney, stated flatly, it is "illegal" for law enforcement officers to roam from county to county at their own discretion conducting searches for persons suspected of committing crimes.

"I wouldn't think of ordering our deputies or investigators to go into Washoe County under similar circumstances," he said.

Washoe County Sheriff, C. W. Young, conceded his deputies had crossed over to the other county to make the arrest.

Raggio defended the officers actions by citing state law:

"If a warrant is issued by any other magistrate, it may be directed generally to any sheriff, constable, marshal, policeman or other peace officer of the county in which it is issued, and be executed by such officer in any part of the state, or if the defendant be in another county, it may be executed by any peace officer in the state."

There was little to add to that statement by Raggio, but he, along with other concerned persons who had been trying to shut down the brothel owner, expressed mild surprise at the support Conforte was apparently being offered by other law enforcement personnel. From all appearances, Conforte's influence passed over county lines with impunity.

With the subsequent finger pointing and suspicions directed at public figures, many were unavailable for comment, however, the Nevada State Attorney General, Roger Foley, released a guarded statement saying that Conforte wielded no influence with him.

"I don't know the man from Adam except by reputation," he declared.

Conforte was ordered to appear for arraignment on December 17, 1959. At that time, a trial by jury was set for June 27, 1960.

It was expected that Conforte would keep a low profile until the trial date, however; it wasn't to be. Two days after the arraignment, the bawdy house again came under fire, when four teenage college students, partying inside, refused several orders given by Sally Burgess to leave. A boisterous argument followed in which the boys were to find out that Sally had a mean streak.

As the boys continued to challenge her role as madam, the scuffle spilled outside onto the bottle littered ground in front of the brothel. Screaming profanities, Sally brought out a .38 caliber revolver and fired one shot at the feet of one of the boys.

The 19-year old screamed out in pain, as the close-range slug tore through his shoe and foot. Soon, sirens were heard wailing in the distance and Sally quickly closed down the brothel for the night. Subsequent warrants for her arrest were filed, and she was ordered to surrender herself to Storey County authorities.

Storey County District Attorney, Robert Moore, when contacted, denied knowing the brothel was in operation. He said if it were true, he would do whatever was necessary to shut it down permanently. It would qualify as a public nuisance.

In the meantime, Conforte continued peddling sex in the brothel as well as its annex, which was a red and white structure, just across the county line, in Lyon County.

His attorney, Gordon Rice began preparing for the defense of the upcoming extortion trial. A trial that was expected to last for about one week, and one in which inconsistencies, untruths, and surprises would dominate.

HOUSE WARMING

As early as 1957, Conforte was challenging Storey County authorities, who were trying to regulate his illegal bawdy houses. After a series of closed door meetings, the Storey County Sheriff, the district attorney, and city clerk, elected to put on a show of force. They unanimously labeled the Triangle River Ranch, an illegal brothel, and a public nuisance. They followed up on this by getting a court order forcing Conforte to destroy the ranch.

The brothel owner slow-played the order and continued operating. This unwillingness by Conforte to comply, actually did not seem to disturb the Storey County hierarchy, as one would expect. Could the currency wrapped cigars have had anything to do with it?.

One person though, Bill Raggio of Washoe County resented the indifference shown by Storey County. He continued to harass Conforte whenever the brothel owner ventured into Reno or Sparks. And now, after Conforte had allegedly tried to set him up, he reacted with vengeance. He began putting into motion the necessary gears which would force Conforte to comply with the earlier Storey County order to close the Triangle (even though he had no jurisdiction in that county).

Raggio sought out the Storey County D.A., Robert Moore. The two district attorneys held a series of meetings, and Raggio convinced the other that they should act on closing the Triangle. They took their plea to the first judicial district court.

On March 18, District Judge, Richard R. Hanna, signed a court order authorizing the destruction of the bawdy house, on the basis that the premises "were unlawfully used for the purpose of maintaining a house of prostitution."

In the early afternoon of March 23, law officers from Storey and Washoe County, along with a pumper truck from the Sparks Fire Department, converged on the structure of the Triangle River Ranch that lie in Storey County.

Outside of the high chain-link fence surrounding the place,

the lawmen shouted towards the front of the house demanding entrance. When no response could be reached, they hooked a chain from the fire truck to the chain-link fence, and pulled it down.

Once inside the fence, all power lines were disabled, and the invading party kicked open the front door. The only people inside were two cowering maids who were advised to keep out of the way. A thorough search of the entire house and grounds was then ordered by the Storey County D.A.

Searching through the various rooms, the lawmen removed assorted weapons including firearms, along with knives, black jacks and other impact weapons. Other contraband found was "french" movies and still photos. All contraband was inventoried and held for evidence.

In some of the rooms, the lawmen removed feminine attire, men's clothing, dolls, and paintings. In one large room, hanging on a wall were pictures of Joe Conforte and Sally Burgess. Above a large king size bed, an oil painting, a nudie, hung suspended above the headboard. A hi-fi, concealing a small safe was found and turned over to sheriff's investigators.

In many of the cribs, the searching party picked up "Bills of Health" signed by a local physician. These certificates verified that the girl whose name appeared on the paper, were "free of infectious and communicable diseases" at the time of examination.

Each crib was found to have been wired with a microphone and wiring that led back out to the manager's office where a recording device was discovered.

When the searching law officers could turn up no further evidence or contraband, the two trembling maids were summoned and told they had a short time to remove any personal items, or remaining furniture. They were instructed to be quick as the place was going to be razed.

They hurriedly carried what items they could across the line to the other half of the bordello in Lyon County, and deposited them in the hands of the scantily-clad prostitutes who had come out of their cribs to see what was going on.

At 3:25 p.m., the waiting firemen took over. After another thorough search of the premises, and satisfied that the one-story house was vacant, the firemen, methodically moved around the structure and set it ablaze. Within minutes, flames erupted out through the windows and then quickly spread to the roof.

Billowing smoke and flames burst through the plywood reinforced roofing sending timbers and other flaming debris crashing down below.

Bill Raggio, and the Storey County D.A., Robert Moore, along with the other spectators were forced backward by the intense heat as the one-story structure grew into an enormous fireball, and then slowly receded into glowing cinders and smoldering ashes. The clear blue, high-desert skies, silently rebelled at the balloon-shaped black cloud rising furiously from the cauldron like a giant genie released.

Shortly after 5:30 p.m., the firemen manning the pumper truck, opened the hose valves and directed streams of water from the 1800 gallon holding tank, onto what was left of the one-time illegal bawdy house.

Bill Raggio and the Storey County D.A., grinned widely, slapped each other on the back, and roared with approval. Prostitutes, 500 yards away in Lyon County, also voiced their approval—for with the demise of the competition, they expected to be increasingly busier.

Conspicuously absent, was Joe Conforte, who had missed the court-ordered house warming—done in his honor.

Conforte's lawyer though, Gordon Rice, wasted no time in acting. On Thursday, the day following the fire, Rice filed an action in Washoe District Court, seeking $50,000 general and punitive damages from Raggio; Storey County Sheriff, Cecil Morrison, and Storey County District Attorney; Robert Morrison. The complainant, was identified as Eleanor J. Anderson, (thought to be in reality, Sally Burgess).

When Raggio was interviewed by the papers, he told the reporters, that he, Bill Raggio, had undertaken the job of ridding the area of Joe Conforte, upon himself.

"You have to understand Conforte had flouted the law, and it was necessary to do what was done. Nobody would take the guy on…Things were getting out of hand."

TRIAL BY JURY

Jury selection on the extortion charge against Conforte began on Monday, June 27, 1960, following a meeting in the judge's chambers attended by Conforte's attorney, Gordon Rice, and the two special prosecutors, Harold O. Taber, and John Bartlett. Rice demanded witness exclusion from the courtroom, and the judge granted the motion. This meant that since Raggio was a material witness, he and the other witnesses could only be present in the courtroom while they were on the witness stand. Raggio, and four other witnesses were then sworn in and ordered to leave the room, Jury selection then proceeded.

The jury selection proceedings hit several snags as Conforte's attorney quizzed each prospective juror on their feelings about illegal prostitution, and their opinion of the defendant. Dressed in a conservative dark suit, Conforte smiled occasionally at the prospects who indicated approval of his lifestyle, while he continued to scan the prospective juror list—a paper he'd been handed, and which contained the names of 56 prospective jurors.

Many of the prospective jurors, were excused by stipulation of counsel, after admitting bias because of the recent publicity surrounding the defendant, and others after expressing disdain at the actions of Raggio and Storey County officials who had recently torched the Triangle River Ranch. Before final selection, the state had used three of it's preemptory challenges, and the defense, all four. Finally, after hours of intensive questioning, at about 5:00 p.m., the jury had been seated: eight women and four men—who now were in for a shock.

District Judge, Jon Collins, startled everyone when, at around 5:30 p.m., he abruptly announced a court-order placing all jurors in custody[5] of county officials for the duration of the trial. What this meant was that the jurors would have to spend their days in court, and their nights in seclusion, in special rooms at the Riverside Hotel, under the watchful eye of five court appointed security personnel.

Judge Collins instructed the jury that all contact with families, friends, and other persons was now suspended. Articles of clothing, personal hygiene, and any other necessary items, would be obtained for them, but as of now, they were all locked into the trial until its completion.

Following the first day's events, the jury members, along with one alternate, were escorted to the Riverside Hotel, and encouraged to make an effort to become comfortable, since they would probably be spending about one week there. Trial would start the next day, Tuesday, the 28 of June, 1960.

Tuesday morning, nearly 100 clamoring spectators pushed their way into the crowded courtroom, while the two star witnesses—sisters, Elsie Mae, and Jacqueline Lee Hitson, were ushered into separate rooms. Tensions between the two were all too obvious. Elsie Mae, age 20, was there to testify in defense of the 34 year old brothel owner, while her sister, 18 year old Jackie Lee—who was pregnant, was there as a prosecution witness.

Opening statements by the special prosecutor, John Bartlett, were made to the jury, and said in essence, that Jackie's pregnancy, was all part of a devious plot by Conforte, to oust District Attorney, Bill Raggio from office. Bartlett said that Conforte had deliberately sent her out of town—to Seattle, to get pregnant.

Attorney Rice, jumped to his feet to object to the "irrelevant pregnancy statements." He was however, overruled by the judge. He then stated he would withdraw the objection, "as long as we are able to produce evidence that Bill Raggio is the father of her child. We want to be able to show that the facts are not true in the scheme alleged by the state."

Bartlett concluded by saying the state would attempt to prove that Jackie was induced by Conforte to try and frame Raggio on the charges of furnishing alcoholic beverages to a minor for the purpose of seducing her. If successful, this scheme would effectively place the D.A. in Conforte's front pocket, and the charges of vagrancy that Raggio had filed against Conforte, would have to be thrown out. If this had worked, Conforte would be calling the shots; and he could put in his "own man."

In Rice's opening address, he advised those present that Conforte would take the stand and explain that his attempts to have a previous vagrancy charge dismissed, was done as a "return of a favor." To further explain, he said, "Conforte's request was in return for a previous incident when he was able to do Bill Raggio a favor by getting a certain person out of Reno."

Rice then went on to explain that the conflict between the flesh peddler and the D.A., was a "personal feud—no crime was committed in this case."

Speaking of the 18 year old, pregnant witness, he told the jury that he would tear down her testimony because, "she will testify to anything, depending [on] who has her in custody."

Rice then emphasized that he wanted lie detector tests to be administered to all participants, at which time the prosecuting D.A., jumped to his feet to object. The judge sustained the objection.

The first witness called, was Jackie Lee Hitson, the 18 year old who had tried to lure Bill Raggio into a compromising position. Jackie Lee, pretty, with nice features, and dressed demurely in a navy blue maternity dress, appeared troubled as the oath was administered and she was seated.

The prosecutor got right to the point and asked her if she'd ever had an affair with Bill Raggio. She unequivocally denied this, and then related how Conforte had given her $100 dollars to set up the D. A. This scheme, she said, was wholly for the purpose of removing Bill Raggio from his elected office. She testified under oath that Conforte, along with her sister, Elsie Mae, had coached her into how this could be done. First she had to use a fictitious name, and second, she had to pose as being twenty-two years old.

The scheme, she related, began playing out on Friday the 13th, a bleak November day, when she first entered Raggio's office. She had been well coached by Conforte and her sister on how to entice the D.A. into a sexual liaison. Prior to going to his office, she had spent considerable time doing her hair, her make-up, and dressing in such a way as to arouse his interest.

Had she been successful, she said, this would have given Conforte undeniable leverage over the office of the district attorney. Upon entering Raggio's office, she introduced herself as, "Jackie Newton." Following the script laid out by Conforte, she confided to the D.A., that she had recently made a big mistake in her young life by marrying a man while the two had been on a drinking binge in Tijuana, Mexico. Now, after sobering up, she needed desperately to get out of the marriage. Could he help her?

Next, Bartlett asked her if she had ever consumed alcoholic beverages with Raggio. She replied that during the office meeting, she'd been offered a drink, and the next day, she, and Raggio, along with a Reno public relations man, identified as Harry Spencer, had gone to the Riverside Hotel, and had several drinks in the Corner Bar. When quizzed as to how a teenage girl could be served alcoholic drinks, she replied that the time she had spent primping herself prior to the meeting, gave her the appearance of a woman in her twenties.

"Okay, Miss. Hitson, and what happened next?"

"The three of us went upstairs to my room in the Riverside, that I'd previously rented"

Had she and Raggio ever been alone in the room?

She replied emphatically, "no!" When Raggio was with her in the hotel room, she said it was always in the company of Harry Spencer.

Was Bill Raggio the father of her unborn child? With an air of contempt in her voice, she gazed at Conforte scornfully. Another emphatic, "no!" She went on to say the child had been conceived after Conforte had sent her to Seattle. Again leering at the brothel owner, she explained that during her stay in Seattle, someone had slipped knockout drops in her drink, and after she passed out, her child had been fathered by a Seattle "pimp!" Again she glared at Conforte.

"Your witness."

During cross examination, Conforte's attorney, Rice spent, two hours trying to cross her up, or otherwise discredit her testimony, which at times moved her to tears. At one time during a heated attack, she blurted out that when she'd told Conforte she hadn't been able to entice the D.A. into intimacy, Conforte scolded her and told her that in order to tie the child to Raggio, she would have to lie and say they had been intimate.

Rice then tried a different attack. Since the witness had already cast doubt on her own credibility because of her alluding to binge drinking, he hammered away at her background, trying to tear down her recall. He questioned her about her friends. Who had she been staying with in Reno? Where did she spend last year? In San Francisco? Who were her friends in San Francisco? What were their names? Their addresses?

She winced, knowing this line of questioning could place her acquaintances in jeopardy. She had come to know Conforte well, and was all too aware of his pledges of vengeance against those who had challenged him—and his devious methods—after all, he already had a list of the juror's names he kept fumbling with, and now his attorney wanted her to give up the names of her friends—and their addresses! Was he determined to push her to the limits of her composure? Had he no compassion for the child she was carrying? She writhed in the chair and dabbed at the mascara trickling down her cheeks.

Prosecutor Bartlett jumped up objecting that the questioning was irrelevant to the criminal charge. Staring at the defense table, he said, "It is apparent why she doesn't want to name her friends and give up their addresses."

Now, the outcry from Attorney Rice shook the courtroom when he jumped to his feet, objecting to the statement made by Bartlett that implied retribution by Conforte against the teenagers friends.

With both men on their feet and shouting at once, Judge Collins banged down his gavel and overruled the prosecutor.

"Indeed," the judge bellowed, "her credibility in this matter is highly important. Proceed!"

Rice again changed tactics and brought up the name of a practicing Reno attorney. Had she consulted the attorney recently saying she wanted to sign a paternity complaint, or a criminal complaint of statutory rape against Raggio?

Yes she had, she admitted. But only after Conforte had set up the meeting and had told her what to say.

After three hours of grueling testimony and cross examination, Jackie Lee Hitson was exhausted. She was excused. Up Next: Bill Raggio.

After being sworn in, Raggio sat down and faced the jury. Under questioning, he then admitted drinking with the 18 year old girl in the Corner Bar of the Riverside Hotel. He went on to explain that she had first come into his office on November 13, on the pretext of getting a divorce. She told him she was 22 years old, and she looked it, he said.

He denied ever being alone with her in her hotel room.

"I certainly don't deny I purchased her a drink," Raggio said, and was emphatic when he looked at the jury and stated he couldn't believe she was a minor. However; because of her demeanor, and the puzzling way she first appeared at his office, he became suspicious of her motives.

The next day, Saturday, the girl once again appeared at his office. After exchanging small talk, and on the pretext of feeling "faint," she asked for a drink. He said he complied and mixed her a scotch highball. But in his mind, something was not right. Who was she—really? What was her actual motive? He explained to the jury that he was becoming suspicious of the girl and felt he should investigate further.

Later on in the day, Raggio, along with Harry Spencer, whom he had contacted earlier, slipped over to the Corner Bar in the Riverside Hotel with the girl. At first, the three engaged in small talk, but then, he explained to the jury, her conversation became intimate. She soon invited the two men upstairs to see her room.

Upstairs, Jackie began making indirect suggestions that Spencer should go back downstairs leaving the two alone. Raggio, who said he was happily married, told the jury he had become uncomfortable in her presence and suggested that they should leave. Raggio and Spencer then left the girl in the hotel room, and went back downstairs.

Raggio went on to say that he knew something was not right. He felt he was being set up, but did not know by whom. After pondering on this for the next few days, it became only too clear to him, the day he received a phone call from Joe Conforte asking for a meeting.

Conforte suggested a meeting between the two in the office of Frank Peterson, a local attorney Conforte had hired to defend him against the vagrancy charges.

On November the 18th, at 9:30 in the evening, Conforte and Raggio met alone in the attorney's office. Eyeing each other with mistrust, Conforte suggested they frisk each other to confirm neither was wearing a bug. Neither man was wired.

Cautious that a bug could still be present, Conforte started out prudently. He tried to convince Raggio that the eighteen year old girl's mother had come to him disclosing a story her daughter had related, alleging the district attorney had plied the girl with booze, and then had allegedly raped her. Could Conforte intercede and do something?

Do what? Raggio asked.

Conforte again scanned the room as if looking for a possible bug, and then, apparently satisfied there was none, spoke in a bolder tone.

"I want this vagrancy charge against me dropped, and I want a public apology right there in the courtroom."

Raggio said he was taken aback by the sudden boldness of the brothel owner's demands. Conforte obviously had no respect for the office of the District Attorney.

"And what if I refuse," Raggio challenged Conforte.

Conforte replied that a charge of furnishing liquor-to-a-minor, and a complaint of statutory rape would be filed against the district attorney.

Raggio said he pressed Conforte to reveal who had the power of office, or motivation, to file felony complaints against the district attorney.

"The attorney general (Roger Foley) would do it," Raggio quoted Conforte as saying. "He'd love to do it. It would make him governor."

Again quoting Conforte, Raggio said the brothel owner was chuckling inwardly as he continued to threaten the D.A.

"Roger will do it. He wants to be governor. He'll do it. He'll do it."

"You mean you have Roger Foley in your pocket too?"

Conforte's response indicated he had something sordid on Foley's brother, who was district attorney of Clark County.

What did Conforte expect of Raggio? The D.A. wanted to know.

"I want you to throw out the case [vagrancy] and I want a public apology that you picked me up erroneously," Raggio quoted Conforte.

Raggio said he then asked Conforte what assurance there was that the dreamed-up sexual adventure with the teenager would be forgotten if the vagrancy charges were dropped.

Raggio said Conforte grinned and shifted the soggy Havana in his mouth.

"If the case goes through tomorrow, you won't see the girl again,." Conforte promised. [But] when you do see her, it will be in court," Conforte said. "The publicity alone will sink you," Conforte warned.

Raggio was reminded that his political career rested solely in the hands of the politically connected brothel owner, and to a lesser extent, in the hands of the teenage girl. The girl would do whatever she was told, Conforte reminded the D.A. Again quoting Conforte, Raggio said the brothel owner at times changed up from his boldness, to whine like a child.

"All I want is to be left alone," Conforte whimpered. "I want to be friends. I want to be treated like a human being."

Conforte then brought up the name of a physician, a Dr. Bryan,[6] who formerly practiced in Sparks, and who was appealing a liquor-to-minor charge; a charge Conforte suggested could be dropped by Raggio.

According to Raggio, Conforte said, "Dr. Bryan is a friend of mine. I help my friends. He checks my girls."

Raggio said he was reluctant to discuss Dr. Bryan's case with Conforte. Yet, he said, Conforte warned him repeatedly, that he would be finished politically if he didn't do as the brothel owner demanded. And, Conforte reminded the district attorney, the papers would love to learn the details of the sordid affair Raggio had with the teenage girl in the Riverside Hotel.. Helping Dr. Bryan would be just another way to help Conforte.

Though he didn't say it outright, Raggio told the court, Conforte hinted of a payoff once the vagrancy charge was dropped and other Conforte demands were met..

Raggio told the court the two continued sparring like this for most of the meeting. He said Conforte was alternately relaxing and making demands, and at other times, becoming increasingly more apprehensive about the possibility of the office being wired.

"Well, was it wired?" The prosecutor asked Raggio.

"Yes it was!" stated Raggio, a statement which jolted the courtroom, and caused Conforte and his attorney, Rice, to stiffen and stare into each other's face.

"Please explain."

Raggio then related how he had become suspicious of Jackie Lee, especially after she had invited him up to her room in the Riverside Hotel. His suspicions were confirmed a few days later, he told the jury, when Conforte called him requesting a meeting. It was then that he put the two together.

Next, he went to see District Judge, Grant Bowen, and asked the judge to approve installation of a recording device in the office where he and Conforte were going to meet,

"And did you indeed record your conversations?"

Again Raggio jarred the courtroom when he faced the jury and told them the threats of extortion made by Conforte were on tape. He went on to say he had hired a private investigator, Harold Lipset, from San Francisco, to bug the office. Lipset, he said, had set up the tape recording apparatus in an office directly above that of attorney Peterson.

On cross examination, Rice attacked Raggio's credibility, by showing a pattern of persecution against the brothel owner by the district attorney. Hadn't the D.A. arrested Conforte twice in one evening for vagrancy? Furthermore, hadn't he also spoken with casino owners downtown trying to persuade them to place Conforte's name in their black books?[7]

Raggio responded by saying this was true, however; he was not alone in doing this. He said former Reno Police Chief, William Gregory, and City Attorney, Roy Lee Torvinen, had also worked with him in attempts to keep Conforte out of town.

Special prosecutor, Harold Taber, jumped up to object to Rice's line of questioning. This line of questioning, he told the court, suggested there was a blockade against the defendant by city officials. And, said Taber, this was not true.

Rice however, argued successfully that he was trying to establish a pattern of "...a deep seated feeling against Joe Conforte by witness," and he added, he was also "...testing Raggio's credibility as a witness."

Judge Collins then interceded and recessed the trial until he could explore the possibility of introducing the playback of the entire contents of the tapes before the jury. The jury filed out of the courtroom and headed back to their quarters at the Riverside Hotel.

Wednesday morning, Judge Collins called to the stand, Hal Lipset, the private investigator who had bugged attorney Peterson's office. Lipset explained to the jury how he had placed two sensitive microphones in an office on the floor directly above Peterson's, on November 18, 1959. The amplified mikes were placed in such a manner, that they were capable of tuning in to all sounds in the office below.

The late night meeting between Raggio and Conforte, had lasted approximately one and one-half hours, Lipset testified. All conversation between the two had been recorded. After he had made the tapes, Lipset told the jury, they were booked into evidence (and were now going to be heard by the jury).

Judge Collins then recessed the court until the jurors could be fitted with ear pieces with which to listen to the tapes.

By early afternoon, the twelve jurors were wired and ready to listen to the profanity rich conversations, which, prosecutors

Bartlett and Taber assured the jury, would substantiate Raggio's allegations. When each of the jurors had been properly fitted with the earphones, the tapes began.

As the members of the jury adjusted their headphones, they listened in chilling detail as Conforte spewed out unprintable profanity. He was heard to demand that the district attorney drop the vagrancy charges lodged against him. If he didn't, Conforte warned, the papers would get the story of how the district attorney had plied the young girl with liquor, and after she passed out, had raped her.

The tapes went on to corroborate Raggio's earlier testimony that Conforte had said the girl's mother had contacted him and confided that her teenage daughter had been plied with liquor and then raped by Raggio. Conforte was heard on the tapes telling Raggio that the girl's mother sought his (Conforte's) help in bringing the district attorney to justice.

On the tapes, the jurors heard Conforte continue to threaten Raggio with loss of his credibility and probable loss of his office, if the story were given to the papers. Substantiating Raggio's earlier testimony, the jurors heard Conforte bring up the name of Roger Foley, the Nevada State Attorney General, who Conforte said, would love to file a paternity complaint,

Conforte also was heard to say he wanted the charge of furnishing liquor-to-minor offense, that had been filed against Dr. William J. Bryan, dismissed. Dr. Bryan, who had since relocated, was a personal friend of his, Conforte explained, and he wanted to "get him off the hook."

The jurors heard Conforte tell Raggio that the good doctor, prior to moving out of the area, had been used to check the girls at the "ranches" for diseases.

The jurors listened as Conforte repeatedly threatened to go to the papers with the trumped-up charges against Raggio, of contributing to the delinquency, and statutory rape of the teenage girl.

They listened intently as Raggio played along and asked Conforte what he expected in return for squashing the affair.

"If this thing [dismissal of the charges] goes through tomorrow, you'll never hear from me again. I swear on my mother." Conforte added that he always told the truth when he swore on his mother.

When the topic of the vagrancy charges against Conforte were discussed, the jurors were not surprised at Conforte's obviously veiled threats.

"When you stick a knife in a tiger, he's going to turn around and bite you," Conforte warned.

"You hurt me (referring to the vagrancy charges), and when I get hurt, I'm going to hit back with everything...if you were any kind of politician, you would never have stepped on me. I have too many friends."

Conforte continued to bring up Raggios supposed affair with the girl and said that if any publicity associated with the affair were to be made public, Raggio would be finished.

The remainder of the tapes continued with Conforte warning Raggio several times that the brothel owner had "many friends, in high places." He boasted that he had friends, in the Washoe County Sheriff's Office, as well as other law enforcement agencies. At one time he even boasted of having friends inside Raggio's district attorney's office.

At no time, though, did Conforte admit to being the person who had set up the D.A. with the underage girl.

At the conclusion of the taped conversations, the state rested its case.

Later on that afternoon, during cross examination, Rice hammered away at Raggio, trying to convince the jury the D.A. had acted solely out of spite and bitterness against Conforte. Prancing up and down before the jurors, he insisted there was no evidence of any criminal activity.

Thursday morning, the crowded courtroom was served another dish of turmoil. Rumors of impending harm in store for the jurors was arcing through the courtroom like uncontrolled lightning. Mixed together, the ingredients, were: a gossipy housewife, a worried husband, and an uncertain deputy sheriff.

The entire morning was devoted to the judge's attempts to either confirm or refute the rumors. The jurors eagerly blurted out that some of them were afraid of retaliation. Conforte, in the role of nice guy, admitted that he too, had heard rumors of the jury being threatened (even though, they had been in virtual lockup since the trial started).

Judge Collins polled the jury to see if any of them had been influenced by the rumors, and then had his investigators track down the source. The rumor apparently had been perpetrated quite by accident by a local woman.

The rumors had started the night before when this lady went to market, and engaged a butcher in conversation about the trial. By coincidence, the butcher's wife, was a member of the Conforte jury. Out of concern, the lady cautioned the butcher: "Bill, I see your wife's name in the paper. You'd better be careful; you might be visited by one of the 'gang.'"

Summoned to explain to the judge what she meant, she replied that it was only idle chatter, with no basis.

The butcher, a man named Thomas, also was summoned and took the oath as a special witness.

On the stand, Thomas related how, after the lady had alarmed him with her remarks, had returned home with a growing apprehension.

"I can't deny that she put a thought in my mind," he said. He thought it would be a good idea to arm himself, but when he searched for his handgun, he couldn't find it. However, he was sure his wife (who was locked up in the Riverside Hotel as a juror) knew where he had hidden it. So he phoned the Washoe County Sheriff's Office and asked them to contact her about the location of the gun.

Following this event, a deputy sheriff was then dispatched to the hotel and told to contact the juror with a written message: "Mrs. Thomas's husband wants to know what she did with the gun."

When called to the stand to testify, the deputy acknowledged that he may have said something like, " Mr. Thomas may have received a threat call, or something like that."

The next witness, was a second deputy, one who had been assigned to guarding the jurors. He told the court that after the jurors had finished supper and returned to their rooms, he took Mrs. Thomas aside and whispered, "Your husband wants to know where you put his gun."

"Why," she wanted to know, obviously startled.

Speaking in a low voice so other jurors wouldn't hear, he said, "There's been a threat made."

Grasping at what he regarded as a definite advantage, Attorney Rice jumped up and shouted that this entire incident was extremely prejudicial to his client. He then demanded a motion for a mistrial.

Judge Collins reserved his ruling on the motion and then instructed the deputies guarding the jury to return them all back to the hotel, with the exception of Mrs. Thomas.

The judge wanted to ensure himself that this would have no influence on the juror's ability to reach an objective decision. He also wanted to hear it from her directly that no threats had been made to her. This she acknowledged, and added that none had been made to her family.

"I will be fair in my decision regardless of any consequences," she assured Judge Collins.

The judge then summoned the other eleven jurors and quizzed each, one-by-one. Each juror assured the judge they could be fair and impartial in reaching a verdict. Satisfied, the judge denied the motion for a mistrial.

Judge Collins told the defense they could present their case at 1:30 p.m.

The first witness called by defense attorney, Gordon Rice, was Jackie Lee's sister, twenty-year old, Elsie Mae Hitson. She was put on the stand for one reason, to refute her sister's earlier prosecutorial testimony, and to vindicate Conforte.

Dressed sharply in an aqua-blue linen suit, stylish hat, and conservative jewelry, Elsie Mae admitted under oath that she had been working as a prostitute since age 16.

She related how she had been summoned to appear before a federal grand jury in Sacramento the year before. She said that during her appearance, she refused to answer specific questions, and was detained until bail could be arranged. The person who was responsible for her being subpoenaed was the Washoe County District Attorney, William Raggio.

She must have been under some kind of Conforte spell, because she stated flatly that it was she, and not Conforte who had coached her sister on how to lure the district attorney into a sex-trap. Her motive was nothing more than pure revenge, a way to frame Raggio for the grief he had caused her when she was prostituting. She said that she talked her sister into luring Raggio into buying her drinks so he could be charged with a liquor-to-minor, violation.

"Make sure when you go see him," she instructed, "he gives

or buys you a drink so I can take it to the attorney general."

Under cross examination, she appeared fidgety as Bartlett quizzed her in depth. "You intended to frame the district attorney...solely for your own personal revenge? You had no real dealings with Joe Conforte?"

"That's correct," she replied, and stressed that Conforte had been totally unaware of the plan.

Elsie Mae then went on to say she had concealed herself in the closet of the hotel room previously rented by eighteen-year Jackie Lee so she could eavesdrop when her sister and the others came in.

The first one to enter, she said, was Jackie Lee, at which time Elsie Mae came out of the closet. Jackie Lee told her she'd had about ten drinks. Elsie said, at this time she wanted to sober up her sister, when she heard a loud rap on the door. She again retreated back to the closet, where she heard her sister open the door and greet a man named Harry.

It wasn't long, she said, when she heard another rap on the door. This time, she heard her sister greet someone called Bill. More drinks were ordered from room service.

Quoting Bill, she said he announced, "I don't want to be seen. I'm an important man." Bill indicated he wanted to hide in the bathroom so as not to be seen by the bellboy.

Under cross examination, Bartlett put her to the test.

"When you were hiding in the closet and you wanted to protect your sister, why didn't you step out?

"I was afraid. I knew it was the district attorney," she lamented.

Bartlett changed the subject and pressed her for details of her background. Hadn't she in fact, worked as a prostitute at the Triangle River Ranch, for Joe Conforte?

She shot back that, yes she had worked at the Triangle, but while there, had worked for Sally Burgess, not Joe Conforte.

Had she ever worked at the Montgomery Pass Station brothel, which was another cat house reputedly owned by Conforte?

She admitted to having been employed there for "three or four months starting in March, 1959."

Had she ever been married to the pudgy brothel owner?

"No!"

Had she ever told her mother they were married?

"Yes," she admitted, "right after we got a marriage application," but hurriedly added that even though they received a marriage application, they had never married.

The prosecutor then passed around a two-page document for the jury to study, which was an application for marriage annulment, signed by Elsie Mae, and Conforte.

Bartlett then referred to earlier testimony by Elsie Mae's sister in which she had divulged to the jury that her mother had received a marriage certificate from Mexico.

Bartlett put the question to Elsie Mae.

"Wasn't a marriage certificate issued?"

Continuing to hedge, she answered, "Well, if it was a marriage certificate. I don't know whether it was or not."

The next defense witness was Joseph Campo who testified he'd bought the Montgomery Pass Station brothel from Joe Conforte in March of this year. Campo told the jury he lived at the station with his family, and rented rooms to truck drivers. He also made a point of telling the jury that Jackie Lee had informed him that Raggio was the father of her unborn child.

Attorney, Frank Peterson, in whose office the meeting between Raggio and Conforte took place, was called to the stand and testified that Jackie Lee, had confided to him also, that Raggio was the person responsible for fathering her child.

The trial was then recessed until the next day, Friday, the first of July.

Joe Conforte took the stand Friday morning.

"Had he ever tried to influence Bill Raggio, the Washoe County District Attorney," his lawyer asked.

"I didn't even know what extortion meant, then," he answered. The meeting with Raggio was a "man-to-man talk." Explaining further, he said it was like, "I'm willing to do you a favor. Will you do me one?

"I never had any intention to influence him," Conforte testified. "I had intentions of making peace. I had no intention of wrong doing... I had nothing to hide...in my mind."

Conforte said of Raggio, "We were friends. But after he was elected, "his attitude about me changed completely." Conforte then again faced the jury and said that prior to the election, Bill Raggio had sent an emissary to the brothel owner seeking his support in the election.

Conforte continued to testify in his defense and insisted he had told Raggio he was willing to squash publicity or action of an alleged offense of furnishing liquor to a minor and statutory rape—if the district attorney would dismiss vagrancy charges against him and make a public apology—and also, dismiss a liquor-to-minor charge lodged against Dr. William J. Bryan.

What did Conforte make of the story of Elsie Mae Hitson, the twenty-year old prostitute who said she hid in a room at the Riverside Hotel, while her eighteen-year old sister, had an affair with Bill Raggio?

"It was quite a shock to me. Personally, I don't believe it. It just seems kind of strange," he smiled, looking at the jury.

Again, obviously trying to stroke the jury, he offered an apology in regards to the amount of profanity on the tapes, referring to the incessant swearing by himself, and which the jury had been forced to endure last Wednesday.

Rice, his attorney, cautioned him against addressing the jury in this manner. Conforte disregarded his words, and asked for a short recess so he could review his notes.

After reviewing his notes, Conforte asked his attorney if he could be permitted to talk about the tapes.

"You have been anyway," Rice snapped.

Conforte then expressed an opinion that the tapes had somehow been altered from the original recordings. They have, he said, been "doctored." When asked to explain, he noted that there were moments of silence along with either interference, or the voices had been muddled when things were being said in his favor.

"The district attorney trapped me in the tapes," Conforte insisted, "I felt he was persecuting me for his own political ambitions."

His attorney then brought up the three counts of vagrancy Conforte had been arrested on in Reno. How did the brothel owner know it was Raggio who instituted the charges?

Conforte advised the court that he had friends in the Washoe County Sheriff's Office who leaked the information to him.

During cross examination, Conforte stated boldly, "I have never in my life, run a house of prostitution." When reminded that his record showed two such arrests in Oakland, California, he reconsidered and said, he had been caught in a raid at a cathodes in Oakland, and pleaded guilty only on the advice of his attorney, so that he could get off with a $350 dollar fine.

How well did he know Jackie Lee and Elsie Mae Hitson?

Conforte admitted he once lived in San Francisco with the Hitson sisters, and another hooker, Joan Johnson. He called Jackie Lee a "woman of many faces." He said Jackie Lee moved out of the apartment one day while he was attending a baseball game. Joan Johnson, limping in on crutches, was the next defense witness to take the stand. She testified she had previously worked at the Triangle River Ranch as a prostitute, but was now working as a secretary. She was two months pregnant.

How had she been injured?

Testifying for the brothel owner, she said Jackie Lee had phoned her two days after leaving the apartment and told her that Raggio was the father of her unborn child, and that he had promised to set her up in an apartment, provide a car, and buy her some new clothes. She denied that Conforte had pushed her down a flight of stairs in San Francisco for letting Jackie Lee get away.

At this point the defense rested its case.

First up in the prosecutor's rebuttal, was William Raggio. Had Raggio, indeed, sought the brothel owners endorsement during the election race for district attorney?

"It's an absolute lie! I wouldn't solicit this, nor would I receive it. I'd be ashamed," Raggio shouted, his voice rising in timbre.

On cross examination, Rice asked Raggio if he thought Jackie Lee's participation in the presumed sex-trap was a crime.

"I did not consider it as such...under the circumstances," he replied, "I would say Jackie Hitson's participation was not of a voluntary nature, but resulted from fear of Conforte. She said she was coerced by Conforte." And Raggio was quick to add, "She has been given no promises (by the district attorney's office)."

Jackie Lee recalled to the stand, smiled and stated unequivocally that Raggio, at no time, ever promised her anything. She emphasized that she was also refuting the earlier testimony of Joan Johnson who had said under oath, that Jackie Lee had stated Raggio was going to furnish the younger girl with a car, apartment and clothing. She told the court that was a lie.

Why had Jackie Lee agreed to go along with the sex-trap contrived by Conforte, only to change up and retreat to the side of the prosecution? It was, she said, Conforte's coercion that sent her to Seattle to get pregnant, and then to Raggio's office, to set things in motion. The answer was obvious she said—fear of what Conforte would do if she refused. She brought up the questionable injury Joan Johnson's had incurred in San Francisco when she was living with Conforte. Rumors persisted that the brothel owner had thrown her down a flight of stairs.

Jackie Lee was excused and Harry Spencer, the publicity man who had been with Raggio in the girl's hotel room, was recalled to the stand.

He testified that by prior arrangement he'd made with Raggio on November the eighteenth, he went up to the hotel room first, and Raggio followed about ten minutes later. He testified that Raggio had asked him to search the room for a listening device which he did.

Spencer refuted Elsie Mae's testimony when she said she'd been hiding in a closet. He said under oath, that he'd searched all the rooms including the closet, looking for a bug, and other than a few clothes, found nothing. Elsie Mae was not there in the closet as she'd testified. After having one drink with the girl, Spencer said he and Raggio went back downstairs together.

The jury, weary from the week long trial, and being forced into virtual lockup at the Riverside Hotel, were then informed the trial would continue until finished. He instructed them to return to their quarters. Trial would resume tomorrow, Saturday.

Saturday, the second of July, at 10:30 a.m., closing arguments began. Special prosecutors Taber and Bartlett prepared to close. Taber took the floor.

"The threats of Joe Conforte against the district attorney were cunning, calculated and cagey, and were obviously designed to put the fear of God into Raggio, to get the pending criminal charge of vagrancy dismissed," Taber told the jurors.

Raggio, he said, has been pulled through the "slime of a vicious racket that has flouted under our very noses."

Taber pointed out the conflicting testimony of the two sisters. The testimony of Elsie Hitson, the self admitted twenty-year old prostitute, came under fire.

"Elsie is taking it on the chin for Joe. I have never seen such a pitiful creature on the witness stand," Taber snapped...she has remained, "loyal to her master!"

Pacing in front of the jury box, Taber continued to reinforce his argument.

"Jackie Lee, on the other hand told the truth, "Taber emphasized. "after seeing what Conforte had done to her sister, and not wanting to become involved similarly.

"If Joe Conforte had succeeded (in his extortion scheme) we would have a weak spineless man in the district attorney's office and no law enforcement.

"Bill Raggio did not make a mistake. He had the courage of his convictions. The time has come to clean up this mess and close the file. It is the duty of the district attorney, and we (Bartlett and Taber) stand in his shoes, that justice be done. We urge you to convict this defendant."

Defense counsel then made a stunning announcement.

"On the direction of my client, we waive an argument and allow you to decide it on your own interpretation of evidence," Rice said, directing his words to the surprised jury. He thanked them for the "very difficult, trying task" in determining the weight of evidence presented during the course of the six-day trial.

"You have been forced to be secluded while you heard it," Rice empathized.

This courtroom maneuver automatically precluded the prosecutors from making the state's planned rebuttal to the eight-woman, four-man jury.

At precisely 11:30 a.m., the jury began deliberations. At 1:30 p.m., they broke off deliberations for lunch, and returned at 2:30 p.m.

When the jury filed back in, they informed the judge they wanted to listen to the tapes once again. During the replay, four sections of the recordings were of vital interest to the jury members:

1. Conforte's statement to Raggio that he could squash the threatening scandal of furnishing liquor to a minor and statutory rape, if Raggio in turn would dismiss vagrancy charges and make a public apology to the vice figure.

2. Conforte's statement that "when somebody hurts me for no reason at all, I'm going to hurt back."

3. Conforte's statement to Raggio, "I want to teach you a lesson."

4. Conforte's high-pressuring of the district attorney in saying Harry Spencer would not stand up for the district attorney, but would "save his own skin."

After listening to the tapes, the jury again resumed deliberations.

Shortly after 5:00 p.m., the jurors filed back in and informed Judge Jon Collins, they'd reached a verdict. The twelve jurors were polled individually by Judge Collins. And then the jury foreman stood and announced: "We the jury find the defendant, GUILTY as charged..."

Raggio, now entered the courtroom, along with his wife, Dorothy, who appeared to be near tears. They hugged as Jackie Hitson, obviously emotionally relieved, stood up smiling.

Joe Conforte, looked dejected as Judge Collins informed him he would be detained until sentencing, which was scheduled for July 11.

"Until sentence is passed," the judge said, "the court has no alternative but to order the defendant taken into custody," under the laws of Nevada. He was then lead away by sheriff's deputies.

Gordon Rice, Conforte's unsuccessful attorney, was asked by reporters if he was going to appeal.

"Oh Certainly, certainly," he bellowed.

On July 11, the sentencing date, Conforte was removed from a dank cell at the Washoe County Jail, allowed to shower and shave, and then dressed in a sharp, razor-creased suit, again faced Judge Collins.

Defense Counsel, Rice, started out by making a motion for a mistrial based upon the revelation that during the trial, one juror had been improperly contacted about a possible threat made to her husband, while she was in custody at the Riverside Hotel.

Judge Collins denied the motion, and said it was "beyond the remotest doubt" that the communication with the jury had resulted in "tampering."

When this failed, Rice attempted to engage the two special prosecutors in a debate about whether extortion was a felony, or in actuality, a misdemeanor. Addressing the judge, the attorney said, if it were in fact a misdemeanor, Conforte could be sentenced to no more than one year—in jail—and not state prison.

Special Prosecutor Bartlett, then addressed Judge Collins and described Conforte as a man who aspired to be a "big wheel" in the area, and as a "potentially dangerous criminal."

He said Elsie Mae Hitson, a prostitute who testified for the defense during the week long trial, and who insisted it was she and not Conforte who had tried to frame the district attorney, was "mesmerized on narcotics, or afraid of Conforte" when she testified.

Judge Collins then told the defendant to stand. After hearing the arguments, and in accordance with the state of Nevada laws, "...you are hereby sentenced to a term of from three, to five-years, in the Nevada State Prison, for the crime of extortion."

Defense Counsel, Rice, looked at his swarthy defendant, and assured him he would file an appeal.

This legal process kept Conforte out of prison for a while, however; after all avenues of appeal had played out, the foreign born bordello operator resigned himself to going to the pen and getting it over with. Next stop, the century old Nevada State Prison, in Carson City.

Chapter Two

NEVADA STATE PRISON

Many years before Nevada became a state—while still attached to Utah Territory, an enterprising adventurer named Abram Curry, trekked down the eastern slope of the Sierra Nevada Mountains, pursuing his dream of fame and fortune. Convinced that he could become the area's first Realtor, Curry set up a makeshift shelter among the sagebrush and squaw-tea littered, high desert floor, and weighed his options.

Immediately to the east, he noted a site where children frolicked in steaming water holes that dotted the desert surface, and which he learned, were year-round warm springs apparently being fed from cauldrons deep within the earth's bowels. He also noted, that the area was much traveled by emigrants hurrying to the gold fields of California.

Seizing upon the potential, he contacted the landholder, and was able to bargain away a few dollars and several horses for a generous plot of the spring fed grounds.

The first structure he erected was little more than a ramshackle cabin where a dirt covered traveler could stop and have a drink. Afterwards, the traveler could bask in one of the hot springs and soak off the dirt. Next, a hot meal would be prepared, followed by a bed rental. And here, for a few days the weary gold seeker could lay over until ready to tackle the towering Sierra Nevadas, and the illusory prosperity that lie ahead in California.

In time, the cabin evolved into a prime hotel-spa, and was named the Warm Springs Hotel. Weary travelers trudging across the desert enroute to the California gold fields, began to view the Springs as a welcome oasis. The hotel boasted of serving the finest liquor this side of San Francisco, the choicest meals, high-stakes gambling, and higher-priced women. A livery stable, well stocked with hay, likewise pampered trail weary horses.

When Nevada Territory split from its Utah parent, local law makers relegated Carson City to the stature of territorial capital, and sought funding with which to build a legislative hall. Three-dollar a day legislators, seeking their own stature, spent countless hours a day trying to drum up support and money for their building project.

Abe Curry, shrewdly aware that legislators craved diversion away from their daytime duties, was quick to offer the hotel as a legislative forum, where bills could be argued during the day, and where those in attendance could lose themselves in drink and other pleasures during the evening. To facilitate his offer, Curry hired a band of Chinese laborers to build a rickety railroad line from the Springs to Carson City, a distance of approximately one and one-half miles. When completed, the horse-drawn cars proved to be slow and clumsy. However, the line served its purpose of carrying the legislators back and forth, and was viewed as a sign of progress and development.

Following one day's unusually strong heated debate on the floor of the Springs, angry solons recessed and clustered around the crowded bar, many eyeing each other suspiciously through the expanded mirror in place above the standing whiskey bottles. Most of those present though, ordered drinks, and welcomed a truce. On the other hand, some of the more boisterous among them, rekindled the day's debates and continued arguing.. The drinking and provoking among the most vociferous continued on through the night, until, inevitably the verbal action progressed into pushing and shoving. And then abruptly, the bartender dropped to the floor, as the mounted mirror he had been standing in front of, exploded into a thousand shards, shattered by a heavy whiskey bottle hurled by one of the drunken solons.

This spontaneous happening served as a catalyst among those who were drinking, and within seconds a full-blown destructive riot erupted. Women screamed and dodged for cover. Other customers hid under the tables, as whiskey bottles, spittoons, chairs and assorted debris was propelled through the air with lightning force.

Curry shrieked at the rioters trying to gain control, but until the event played out, could do little except scream profanities and try to protect himself from the sailing projectiles.

As exhaustion overtook the drunken gladiators, they retreated to the glass littered floor licking their nuts and moaning about the events of the day. Curry, though, seeing that it was safe to come out, was furious. "Who's gonna pay for this mess?" He bellowed. "This will cost someone dearly."

This smashing up of his bar, was the first time he'd been exposed to any substantial business losses. He screamed that he would see to it that the local paper smeared all those who had participated.

Dismayed, a few of the more sober solons, knew they were in a jam. A couple of the more ingenious among them quickly discussed their options. They had to come up with something quickly, anything that would salvage their careers. If not, they faced retribution from the locals which could lead to their being run out of office in disgrace. It was essential to placate Curry and smooth things over.

To buy time, they stroked Curry, and suggested they reimburse him for the damages if he would agree to disavow their participation in the fracas. Of course, they rationalized, there are ample funds—taxes collected from local businesses, being held in the legislative strong box which was secured in Carson City, and which now could be used to compensate friend Abe Curry for his unforeseen losses.

Three or four of the revelers then hitched a ride on the makeshift rail-line and rode on in to town. There, it is alleged, they raided the strong box and stuffed their pockets full of tax payers' money. Legend has it that they cleaned out everything, leaving only one dime.

As the early morning sun was breaking the twilight, the sobering solons arrived back at the Springs and pressed the money onto the elated Curry, who promised to hush up the night's adventure.

But by now, other legislators began sobering up and as they did, panic swept through their ranks. How to explain the missing tax payer money? The legislators, themselves, sworn to uphold the law, had now committed a felony (and this during the time horse thieves were hung from the nearest tree). Another plan which would account for the missing funds had to be thought up quickly. Retreating behind closed doors, they again compounded their problems.

The plan would be, they told Curry, to lease the hotel from him, and convert it into a prison. The money they'd given him previously would serve as a down payment—of course, he, Abram Curry, would be appointed warden of the newly founded, territorial prison. The year was 1861.

After all, they explained, the populace was fed up with the lawlessness pervasive in the territory, and with a prison, it was felt, they could lock up many who were rampaging in town, and others, they rationalized, would clear out when it became known the territory had its own working penitentiary.

Curry eyed them suspiciously, and thought about it carefully. The hotel was realizing a profit now, and if he gave it up, what advantage could he gain? The solons explained the benefits in prestige, in self esteem, and a base of operations whereby he could launch his own political careers. In the end, Abe Curry envisioned himself as something of a territorial leader and shook hands vigorously with the law makers. Looking into a mirror, he reflected on the events which had brought him this far.

Wardens of any prison sooner or later build a reputation based upon their relationships with the inmates and officers. Many are thought of as "I-Ls" or "Inmate Lovers,"—soft on inmate discipline.[1] At the other end of the spectrum are the wardens who build a reputation as being brutal toward the inmate population. Within time, Abe Curry, the tenderfoot warden, became regarded as an I-L.

One prisoner, a gambler named Mayfield, had been convicted in the bowie knife stabbing death of a deputy sheriff, and sentenced to hang. The likable Mayfield soon became a favorite of Warden Curry, who was convinced the man had acted in self defense. Curry set about to help the killer escape. He secretly provided Mayfield with the necessary tools he could use to cut himself free of the shackles. Arrangements were also made to have a horse waiting outside the prison and a thousand dollars in cash he could use to find a new home.

Mayfield made good his escape and was next heard from in the Salmon River area of Idaho. Mayfield, apparently attempting to dispel rumors of the warden's complicity in the escape, wrote to the Carson City Daily Appeal newspaper:

"The guard was walking back and forth in the ward room while old man Curry was playing cards with some of the work hands, about ten feet from my cell. I got down on my knees, and watching the old man's eyes, started for the door. As I got to it, I saw the old man raising a 'hand' that had just been dealt to him, and as his eyes were directed towards me, I thought I had better wait until he got a big hand, for being an old gambler myself, I knew it would excite an unsophisticated gambler to have a high hand dealt to him. A few minutes afterwards, a big Irishman who was in the game, got a big hand, queens, and sevens, before the draw. He bet twenty beans. The old man stayed and they took one card each. The old man caught a king, making a king-full. The Irishman drew a queen, making him a queen-full. They bet and bet, until they had about two hundred beans in the pot. All this time I was fixing to go, and I came to the conclusion that if I couldn't go on this hand, I never could, and so I went."

In 1864, Nevada joined the union and became a state. The state then voted to purchase the former territorial prison from Curry, and rename it the Nevada State Prison. The price demanded by Curry, and which the legislature agreed to was $80,000, a tidy profit for the former hotel owner and warden. In addition to the prison site, they also acquired 20 adjoining acres and a stone quarry. Curry was relieved of his post as warden, and the legislators put in their own man, Robert Howland.

Howland was thus the second warden of the Nevada prison, and he soon built a reputation as a no-nonsense person. Unfortunately, no records remain of his tenure. All were destroyed in a fire in 1867. However; an unofficial report given by the Eureka Sentinel, gives some indication of the man's disciplinary measures:

"Bob had then the same reputation for levity that he enjoys, and when he became warden, the prisoners thought they'd have an easy time of it, but were disappointed, as Bob looked well after the discipline, and not a man escaped during his administration.

"Shortly after Bob entered office, George Kirk, a notorious character, was sentenced to imprisonment for highway robbery. The first morning of his stay in prison, Kirk refused to come out of his cell and fall in line with the other prisoners. This is how Howland subdued him:

"The warden quietly ordered Kirk's cell door closed, and the other prisoners were marched out, each man's left hand on the next man's shoulder, to breakfast. Kirk, in the meantime, was raging and cursing, defying the warden or any other blankety blank son, to even try and make him come out until he felt so disposed. The warden went to the blacksmith shop, procured a bar of iron, about twelve feet long, and had it heated, about four feet of one end, to a glow. Then he returned to Kirk's cell, and ordered the recalcitrant to come out and fall in line. The warden was answered with violent abuse, and a refusal. Howland closed the grated door of the cell, and shoved the bar of iron, heated end foremost, into the cell. By this time the rosy heat had dulled, and Kirk grabbed the hot metal with both hands, with a close grip, to wrench it from the warden. With a howl of pain he dropped the iron and retreated, cursing wildly. The warden, without any conversation, swayed the bar back and forth in the narrow confines of the cell, wedging Kirk in a corner, and searing his flesh with every touch. Kirk howled with mingled rage and torture, now bounding over the bar, again dodging under it, and at times striking his head against the ceiling, only to fall back again, on the bar, yelling, screeching, like pandemonium turned loose. At last the outlaw realized the helplessness of his position and begged for mercy."

The newly formed state of Nevada began a series of meetings with its top officials. Prison reform was a heated topic. Laws were enacted under which the governor, secretary of state, and the attorney general were appointed to the Board of Prison Commissioners. The lieutenant governor was named as ex-officio warden, and Robert Howland had to step down. Guidelines were established whereby "barbarous punishment" was prohibited, and one of the warden's responsibilities was to provide each inmate with a bible.

In 1867, inspecting the hotel-prison, officials noted that a section known as the "Old Kitchen," was in terrible repair. Built of rock and makeshift materials; the wind whistled through the open cracks incessantly. Inside, the walls had been patched with tattered pieces of canvas, and where rotted, were augmented by the pasting of yellowing sheets of paper. Looking upward, they could see clouds through the roof where the decaying shingles had opened. They labeled the structure a dangerous tinderbox ready to explode.

What passed as the guard room, was also a dynamite keg, the wooden paneling was tinder dry, cracked and split.. The main structure was not much better; its roof too, permitted light and rain to penetrate below. Plans were made to fund money for repairs, but too late.

On the first day of May, 1867, the whole place erupted into flames. The fire apparently started in the Old Kitchen and quickly spread to the other structures. Surprisingly, the building known as the "Territorial Addition," which housed the inmates, incurred only moderate damage, thanks to the quick response of the Carson City volunteer fire department.

Frontier arson investigators quickly labeled the fire of incendiary origin. Suspects were questioned, but no one was formally charged. The rebuilding process began within a few days, the stones being cut from the quarry and the labor provided by the inmates.

For the next few years, with the newly constructed buildings, things remained relatively quiet until the morning of December 2, 1870, when several inmates armed themselves with knives and bludgeons and attempted to escape. During the ensuing melee, several inmates were shot and a number of guards were seriously stabbed. However, no one made a successful escape.

Less than a year later, another mass escape was attempted, and became known as the "Big Break of September, 1871." During the break, 29 inmates, overpowered the guard staff and fled over the walls. Carson City was thrown into a panic. All able bodied men were pressed into a posse and ordered to shoot on sight any escaping prisoner.

Frank Denver, the Lieutenant Governor, and current warden, was leading the posse, and picked up the escapees running towards the Sierra foothills, where they crossed over into California. Cornered by a large lake, the escaped prisoners, who by now had armed themselves with firearms, made a last-ditch stand. A furious firefight ensued. Warden Denver was seriously injured and one guard and one civilian were killed. Of the 29 escaped prisoners, all were shot down. It is thought that none escaped alive. The lake to this day, is called, "Convict Lake."

Warden Denver, after a long recovery period, assumed his duties at the prison. In the interim, a new Lieutenant Governor had been elected, and he served notice to Denver that he, Lt Governor Bradley, was going to replace Denver as warden. Denver refused to step down, and served notice that the prison was closed to Bradley, as well as other prison board members.

Bradley then ordered the National Guard to assemble a fighting force, complete with riflemen and artillery, with orders to enter the prison and unseat Warden Denver. When confronted with this show of force, Denver issued a statement:

"Under military necessity, and from the fact that you have a superior force in numbers, and if I should stand by my rights by meeting force with force, innocent blood might be shed, and the convicts escape, I surrender to you as the commander of the military force."

So ended the tenure of Warden Frank Denver.

During the early 1920s, funding was acquired for construction of a state-of-the-art, modern cell house. Using inmate labor, stones were cut from the quarry and loaded on horse-drawn wagons which then were brought to the prison site. The four-story cell house, when completed, could house upwards of 400 inmates, behind steel barred cells and dormitories. Cells were racked open or closed by the use of hand-cranked wheels at the end of each tier

In 1925, the federal government was running out of prison space because of prohibition violators. The newly constructed Nevada prison was selected to house many of the federal prisoners at a cost of one dollar and twenty five cents a day per inmate. With this new federal funding, the prison continued to expand and several new buildings were erected, including a license plate factory.

For the hopelessly incorrigible inmate, a cave set into the hard rock facing of the prison yard's west side, was fitted with a strap-iron gate, and was used to hold the most violent and unmanageable inmates. The cave was soon the most feared housing at the prison. Inside there was no lighting, and very little trickled through the iron-webbed front door. The year round temperature, though, averaged a comfortable 72 degrees. However; the absolute isolation forced upon an inmate, took its toll on many prisoners over a number of years.

During this time, one notable inmate was to eventually make the Guinness Book of World Records for being on escape status longer than anyone else before capture..

On May 12, 1920, Leonard Fristoe, #2191, was sent to the prison from White Pine County for the murder of a deputy sheriff and a constable. Fristoe, who had a love of the outdoors, could not adjust to the confines of prison. He felt he had to break out. But he was held in check by the rifle toting guards on the rooftops, who he knew, had orders to shoot to kill anyone attempting an escape.

On December 15, 1923, a cold and windy day that sent most persons indoors, fate intervened. The warden was to drive up and carelessly leave his car unattended while he went inside to warm up. The ever alert Fristoe seized the opportunity and knew inherently, that it was now or never. He quietly got the car running and as a few other inmates in the area stared in disbelief, raced away from the prison grounds amid a hail of gunfire from the rooftops.

A posse was quickly assembled, but their efforts failed. Leonard Fristoe had made good his escape. He made his way to Wyoming where he changed his name to Claude Willis, and became a law abiding rancher. Willis was next known to be in the state of Maine where he ran a service station and a bus station. He had married and had become a father, and again, a law abiding citizen.

On November 20, 1969, nearly forty-six years after fleeing the Nevada State Prison, Willis, who was now living in Compton, California, and who was now partially paralyzed because of a stroke, had become too much of a burden on his son, Claude Willis Jr, and his daughter-in-law. They notified authorites of their father's true identity.

Leonard Fristoe, aka Claude Willis, was returned to the Nevada State Prison, and confined to a maximum security cell in the prison's infirmary. He languished there for only five months.

In April, 1970, the Nevada Pardons Board commuted his sentence to time served. He was sent to live with another son, Leonard Fristoe Jr., in New Mexico. This son was gracious to accept his father, who, he told authorities, had abandoned him not long after he was born.

Leonard Fristoe, prison escapee, died quietly on March 13, 1976. When contacted by the press, the younger Fristoe said he knew he had a father somewhere but he never knew where. And when the two finally met, the son said his father was just an old man and that his mind was gone.

For the next couple of decades, more buildings were added to the prison, again using stones from the quarry and unlimited inmate labor. In 1956, C-Block, a two-story max-lockup unit was attached to the south end of the cell house The cells on the upper tiers were steel-walled, with sliding barred gates, electronically controlled. Though not expansive, they nevertheless provided ample space for a single inmate. At the south end of the tiers, a common, steel-barred bullpen with toilet, provided room for exercise (and additional holding space when needed, where inmates slept on the cold concrete floor).

Below, on the east-facing tier, sixteen, closet-sized darkened cells were used for disciplinary detention. Each steel-walled cell, had a steel bunk attached to the floor, and a *honey bucket* sunk into the concrete floor, used as a toilet. Two doors provided tight security into each cell. On the outside, a solid steel door, with a small observation slot, effectively shut off all light, and lying inside this door, a steel barred sliding cell gate provided additional security.

Whereby the cell house officers had to crank hand-wheels to rack the cells, C-Block cell doors were racked open and closed by officers using state-of-the-art electric switches. Despite the tight security built into the block, it would become one of the most violent units due to the explosive character of the inmates who were housed there.

The officers patrolling the tiers had to be constantly alert to the incessant attempts by the confined inmates to taunt or inflict injury upon them. Body waste, garbage, food trays and other assorted muck could be hurled through the bars at the working officers. And the inmates could be quite ingenious in fashioning prison weapons. Cell extractions too, could become very violent.

Chapter Three
PRISON GAMBLERS

"Any person who shall knowingly permit any gambling game, slot machine or device to be conducted, operated, dealt or carried on in any house or building or other premises owned by him, in whole or in part, except by a person who is licensed...shall be guilty of a gross misdemeanor."

(From the Nevada State law governing the Licensing of Casinos.)

Casino style gambling was legalized in Nevada in 1931. From the above Nevada Revised Statutes, it is clear that any establishment where organized gambling was conducted, required the owners of such establishments to be licensed by the state.

Yet since 1927, open gambling flourished at the Nevada State Prison. Poker, bridge, chuck-a-luck, and other games, were run by the prison inmates who had the means to bankroll the action.

In prison industries, inmate coinage was minted from brass in denominations of five-cents, ten-cents, twenty-five cents, fifty-cents, and one-dollar and five-dollar pieces. Besides the brass coinage, flexible bills were cut from heavy canvas and imprinted in one-dollar denominations. All prison made money—which was the accepted medium of exchange on the yard—was referred to as "brass."[1]

Any inmate who had money in his prison account, merely filled out a *brass slip* for the amount of money he wanted to withdraw, and which was given to him in the form of brass coinage and canvas currency. Thus, possession of brass by inmates was legitimate. As a result, the inmates who had a sizable stash of brass, could buy articles of clothing, toiletries, tobacco, candy and other small luxuries that made doing time a little easier.

Brass could also be used for gambling in the inmate run casino. And too, brass could be used to make illegal purchases on the yard for weapons, bootleg liquor, drugs and other contraband.

During the tenure of Art Bernard, warden of the Nevada State Prison in the latter part of the 1950s, the inmate run casino was housed in its own separate stone building, apart from the cell house, yet still within the confines of the fences and overhead gunposts. The casino was called the "Bull Pen." And when in full operation, the Bull Pen rivaled many of the casinos operating legitimately in town.

Warden Bernard, well known in town, enjoyed the notoriety of condoning an unlicensed inmate run, prison gambling hall. In town, he was always good for a laugh, and at one time, phoned Frank Johnson, a reporter for the Nevada State Journal, and complained that no one was tracking his casino.

"I'm getting lonely," he joked.

"It has been months," he complained, "since the press has been around to expose my gambling den, I'm getting lonely."

In 1960, Warden Bernard, was succeeded by Jack Fogliani, who continued to allow the inmate run casino to operate. Indeed, select persons from the streets were allowed to come in and try their luck in the casino and play against the inmate dealers.

It was considered dashing to be invited inside the prison to gamble. State officials, Kiwanis Club members, and other notables, came in frequently. The chief enforcement gaming control agent, too, made visits inside to squander away small change. George Jolly, the Commissioner of Labor, it was reported by the Journal, was also seen gambling there. He was assured by Warden Fogliani, that the dealers—though not necessarily honest on the street, did not cheat at the prison games.

The gaming control agent took notice that dungaree clad inmates mingled freely next to state officials who were dressed in sharply creased suits and ties, together trying to beat the house. He also took note that licensing certificates were conspicuously absent. Commenting in a tongue-in-cheek tone, he also announced to the warden, that gaming regulations forbid "persons of notorious or unsavory reputation, or who have extensive police records...are unsuitable to work as casino dealers."

Rationalizing humorously, he concluded that the law clearly stated that casino dealers are all "required to have their finger prints on file...and that the gaming is conducted in a location that is easy to police." Done!

By the time Joe Conforte entered the Nevada State Prison, the law-abiding populace knew of, and accepted the goings on inside prison walls. To them, it was just additional Nevada color, no different from the illegal houses of prostitution which dotted the countryside in the cow counties, and which operated openly.

Conforte entered the prison in January, 1962, to begin serving a three-to-five year sentence for trying to extort Bill Raggio, Washoe County D.A.. Having lost all of his endless appeals, the vice lord resigned himself to coming in, doing his time, and getting out. He knew he would be well received by both inmates and staff. He was after all, Joe Conforte, politically connected flesh peddler who was known to be generous with his money. In town, many Nevadans cheered, happy to be rid of him; others, recipients of his generosity, were quietly dispirited.

At the conclusion of the two-week routine intake processing, Conforte was classified to general population, and assigned to the cell house. On his first trek across the yard, other inmates were quick to give him his respect. Did he need help carrying his bedding? Would he like to have his shoes shined? Did he need a haircut? What about his laundry? What cell had he been assigned to? Anything they could do to help?

And not only did the inmates patronize him, the custody staff too, acknowledged his presence.[2] He was, after all, a notorious, local character. Wealthy, and well connected.

It wasn't long before his presence in the casino was felt. He must have been appalled at the low stakes the inmates were playing for. He envisioned expanding the gambling and bringing in more persons from outside. This called for someone with the means to bankroll the action. Could he do it? After running illegal cat houses for years on the outside, why not bank the illegal prison casino? Besides, the wardens had been tolerating it for years. This must have given his ego an exhilarating boost. He was, he knew, destined to take over the gambling concession at the Nevada State Prison. And under his direction, prison gambling flourished. There was betting on all professional and collegiate sporting events; pari-mutual race horse betting; craps; blackjack; high and low-ball poker; panguingui and tonk.

Even in prison, Joe Conforte was still the money man. His

money could buy the good life. Whether passing around currency-wrapped cigars during surreptitious meetings with local authorities in dimly lit alleys, or doing the same thing on a smaller scale inside prison walls, influence could be bought for a price. And along with influence, other benefits not available to the average convict could be had, making life behind bars more tolerable.

In May, 1962, as he was adjusting to prison routine, Conforte got hit with a new rap. A federal grand jury indicted him on four counts of income tax evasion. The stacked charges accused him of evading $28,000 in taxes during the years, 1956, '57 and '58.

Conforte's attorney wasted no time in entering plea negotiations. U.S. Attorney, Tom Wilson, moved to dismiss three counts, predicated upon Conforte pleading guilty to one charge of falsifying an income tax return. Conferring with his attorney and the U.S. Attorney for several months, Conforte agreed to plead guilty to one count, which would be for the year he stated his income had been $37,000, when in fact it had been $97,000, a difference of $60,000. In return for the guilty plea, Conforte was offered a relatively light sentence—specifically, one year.

Conforte was to say later, that the deal had been cast in concrete, however; in 1963, US. District Judge, William Mathes, stated he could not ignore Conforte's past criminal activities, and refused the defense's motion for a one year sentence. Judge Mathes then sentenced Conforte to a three year prison term. Conforte was outraged at Judge Mathes's judicial ruling, and moved to have the judge's decision set aside. He further moved to withdraw his guilty plea, insisting the government had broken its promise to give him only one year. Arguments were scheduled to resolve the matter.

U.S. District Judge, Bruce Thompson, was selected to hear the arguments. This judge, after careful deliberations, ruled that Conforte had sought, but had not been promised, guarantees of a light sentence. He stated further that Conforte had pleaded guilty with full knowledge that he could receive a harsher sentence than expected. And his disappointment that he did not receive the slap-on-the-wrist sentence expected, was tough titties. But it was no grounds for changing his plea. The three year term was to remain in effect.

In 1963, after serving 22 months in the Nevada State Prison, Conforte was released and handed over to the U.S. Marshals to begin his federal prison term. He was transferred to the federal prison at McNeil Island, where he found out the first day, the feds ran a different prison than did Nevada. Rules were rigid. The staff treated him as if he were a street pimp. No frills. No compromising staff. No favors. And specifically, no casino. He lay down and did his time quietly. On October 1, 1965, he was released, and once again, he headed for Reno.[3]

Chapter Four

A LEGAL BORDELLO

Arriving back in the Reno during the fall of 1965, Joe Conforte wasted no time in getting back into flesh peddling. A rundown brothel operating illegally along the Truckee River in Storey County, at the time, named the Mustang Bridge Ranch, was up for sale. Ex-con, Conforte, now 39 years old, looked it over and bought it, paying cash.

Sally Burgess, ten years older than Conforte, and who had owned her own Nevada brothels, competing at times with Joe, hired on as the madam. They agreed that Sally would run things inside the brothel, while Joe's job would be to pack the place with johns. Under Sally's tutelage, business increased dramatically. Also, there was a sort of chemistry between Joe and Sally. They were soon husband and wife.

Sally used to say that she hired on as the madam and ended up marrying the boss. She told friends that she was running the place from the first day she started. Joe's too easy going she would say. If anyone cries, he listens. Of the two, she admitted to being the heavy. And many of the working girls would attest to that. Stories circulated about her willingness to slap them around if she deemed it necessary.

As profits soared in from the cat house (still illegal in Storey County), Conforte systematically set out to reinforce his position. It was said he regularly gave money to Storey County politicians and allegedly contributed $1,000 a month to the county coffers. He set up a series of rental trailers in Lockwood (Storey County), near the Truckee River, offering cheap rent to locals. By so doing he created a voting block of loyal residents. Critics dubbed this the "river vote." And the people living there were expected to vote with Joe on county issues vital to his survival.

During this period of time, there were no more than 450 registered voters in Storey County, and a voting block like the "river vote" could be big enough to sway an election. When the issue of legalizing prostitution became a serious topic in Storey County, in 1970. The elected sheriff, Bob Del Carlo, was proud to say he took the time to speak to all 450 voters to gather their thoughts on legalizing the brothels.

By a large margin, the voters agreed that since Conforte had been running the illegal brothels for the past 15 years, it was time to bring the matter out in the open and legalize prostitution in the tiny county. This, they reasoned, should ease the tax burden on the residents.

Shortly after this in 1971, the Storey County commissioners voted in Ordinance No. 38 legalizing prostitution in that county.[1] Joe Conforte, two time ex-con, was subsequently licensed as the owner of a legal brothel in Storey County. The name was shortened from the Mustang Bridge Ranch, to what it is known as today: The Mustang Ranch.

A year later, Joe, with his arms draped over a few of the girls, was pictured on the cover of Rolling Stone magazine. The caption read, "THE CRUSADING PIMP: Joe Conforte's Fight To Keep Nevada Clean."

Many politicians of the day took freely of his money, as did legitimate charitable organizations. He was quick to call press releases when giving food and clothing to the poor, or when donating money to rebuild historic buildings or sponsoring school sports activities. Many times he took out full page ads in the local papers to ensure his philanthropic contributions did not go unnoticed.

Not only did prominent people receive his gifts, but others, obscure persons of chance encounters, were inadvertent recipients. On a whim, Conforte would offer complimentary brothel tickets to persons at random. He savored the spotlight. He loved the crowds. It was known that he had gold colored "passes" to the Mustang Ranch that he freely handed out to persons of his choice.[2] He was after all, Joe Conforte. And he loved being Joe Conforte. And he was never at a loss for words.

Many times during his career he called the newspapers to air his concerns or to refute stories that he felt had been unfairly printed about him. And the newspapers were happy to oblige. He was good copy.

In the early 1970s, Conforte began to invest heavily in real estate. In 1973, he sold a piece of property located in Sparks, to the convention authority. This large parcel eventually became the Wildcreek Golf Course. Another parcel adjoining the golf course, and which was retained by Conforte, increased in value one million dollars. A tidy sum. The Sparks City Council came under fire.

On July 9, 1975, a Washoe County Grand Jury was impaneled to investigate Sparks city government. Joe Conforte and Hugo D. Vernon, the brother of former Sparks councilman, Jim Vernon, were called as witnesses and questioned as to improprieties by the former councilman, involving the City of Spark's business dealings (the costly grand jury report would not conclude until March, 1976).

Following the preliminary grand jury hearings, on August, 1975, the elected sheriff of Storey County, Bob Del Carlo, announced he was going to go into a joint business venture with Joe and Sally Conforte. The "Cabin In The Sky," an upscale steakhouse in the mountains of Gold Hill, which is part of the Comstock Lode—where hundreds of millions of dollars of gold and silver were mined during the preceding century—was going to be reopened under the managership of ex-con Joe, his wife Sally, and Sheriff Del Carlo.

Many eyebrows were raised in Storey County when this was made public. How could the elected sheriff enter into a business venture with Sally and Joe Conforte—ex-con? Questions of a conflict of interest was obvious.

Del Carlo stated he saw no conflict of interest in the business venture. The arrangement made between the trio would split the profits 50-50, half to go to the Confortes, the other half to the sheriff. Del Carlo said that if a conflict of interest did arise, he had only to give a one-day notice to withdraw from the agreement.

Del Carlo added that the responses he'd received from the Comstock residents were most favorable, but he did acknowledge that there was still a number of Storey County residents who always objected to anything he tried to do in the county. As to his partnership with an ex-con, Del Carlo said that the brothel owner had done his time, and had thereby paid his debt to society. It was time to let him get on with his life.

Del Carlo said the agreement between the Confortes called for them to supply the building and equipment, while the sheriff would manage the place. Under this arrangement, Del Carlo would have to be present much of the time.

After the first few weeks of operation, Conforte and the sheriff both agreed business had increased dramatically since the partnership was effected. Though it was a questionable partnership at best.

In the Reno Evening Gazette newspaper dated August 29, 1975, a blistering editorial called for Sheriff Del Carlo to step down from his elected office. The article pointed out that Del Carlo, being the chief law enforcement officer in Storey County, was quickly drawing the attention of the U.S. Justice Department.

The editorial went on to suggest that Del Carlo, if he continued with the partnership, should turn in his badge. If not, the editorial said, the governor and the attorney general should make an attempt to force him to do so.

In Washington D.C., federal agents took the stand that if Del Carlo continued in his business association with Conforte, the government would deny him access to sensitive U.S. criminal intelligence data.

On September 1, 1975, Sheriff Del Carlo called a news conference to announce he had decided to withdraw from his business association with the Confortes to manage the Cabin in the Sky restaurant. After discussing the affair with his attorney, Del Carlo called a hastily prepared news release. He said, in effect, that in order to better serve the citizens of Storey County, he had terminated his business association with the Confortes. He would no longer be associated with the Cabin in the Sky. He also stated he intended to remain in office as sheriff.

Conforte, in the meantime, had been working on other things. He had already secured a building permit to expand the Mustang Ranch by adding 12 trailers, office space, a dining room and a sauna or swimming pool. Work had progressed well; with about 90% of the construction completed.

At about 3:00 a.m., on the morning of November 20, 1975, one of the buildings under construction, and several nearby trailers erupted into flames. The Truckee Meadows Fire Prevention District sent at least nine units to aid the Nevada Division of Forestry. Additional units were sent from Reno. Unfortunately, the absence of fire hydrants, and the discovery that the two-inch water line supplying the trailers had been severed, sealed the fate of the nearly completed brothel. There was little the fire fighters could do but watch as the Mustang Ranch went up in flames. The fire, of suspicious origin, was placed under investigation. The loss was estimated to be $250,000.

That evening, at about 6:27 p.m., shots rang out from the Mustang Bridge that crossed the Truckee River. Two Nevada Highway Patrol vehicles were dispatched to the scene. The Washoe County Sheriff's Office reported that someone, unidentified, was shooting toward a posted Mustang Ranch security officer, from the bridge.

When Storey County Sheriff, Bob Del Carlo arrived, he was pressed for answers by the media. Was the fire deliberately set? Who was shooting? Was there insurance?

Del Carlo said a two-inch water hose to the building had been cut (indicating arson). He added that they had one suspect.

"Who?" The press wanted to know.

"It's still under investigation," he muttered. "No information will be given out yet."

On Saturday, Del Carlo downplayed the discharge of weapons report and said there had been no shooting. Instead, he explained that the gunshots heard, had only been exploding cartridges from the security officers' rounds that had been lying in the smoldering rubble and had gone off. He now stated that they had no suspects. Conforte could not be reached for comment.

Early in December, Joe Conforte met with Virgil Bucchianeri, Storey County District Attorney, to discuss the fire. After considering all angles, Conforte announced they had reached the conclusion that whoever started the fire, did so as a paid arsonist working for other persons. Conforte was quick to offer the arsonist $5,000 and immunity if he or she would come forward and identify those responsible. Bucchianeri reinforced Conforte's statements, and said that immunity from prosecution was a definite possibility for the arsonist—if he, or she, would give up the conspirators.

In addition, to the cut water hose, reports circulated that three empty gasoline cans had also been retrieved from different areas of the ranch, and had been booked as evidence.

Conforte told investigators that when he'd visited the ranch that morning about 12:30 a.m., he was surprised to learn that the regular guard wasn't on duty. Not thinking much of it, he said he returned home. At about 3:30 a.m., he said he was awakened by phone and advised of the fire.

He said he was fully insured for the loss which he estimated to be in excess of $500,000, not the $250,000 which was the original estimate. He was emphatic when he said since he was the person paying the bills, and not the insurance adjusters, he damn well knew what the place was worth.

How long would it take to rebuild?

Conforte was optimistic when he answered that it should probably take about 90 days.

When asked if he were worried that someone might try to set fire to the planned replacement buildings, he acknowledged that the possibility did exist. However, he assured those present, that he would take extraordinary steps to prevent a repeat of what happened this morning.

Conforte made a point to say the brothel had always been under the surveillance of armed guards and he hinted that he was going to beef up security even more. He refused to offer details, but made a few veiled threats.

"I'm not gonna' stop until I get to the bottom of this. I'm gonna' solve this crime one way or the other," but quickly added, "I plan to do it legally."

A break in the case came on December 10, 1975, when a man was arrested in Las Vegas on a Storey County warrant alleging first degree arson. He was identified as Donald George Baliotis, 39. He was booked into the Las Vegas Metro Jail and held under $400,000 bail.

Baliotis had quite an interesting background. In March, 1969 he pleaded guilty to possession of a bomb making machine inside the city limits, and received four years probation. This was after Conforte had received confidential information his house was going to be blown up. Baliotis acknowledged the bomb was meant for Conforte. He said he made it after some men nearly beat him to death with a rubber hose.

In 1974, he was the key state witness in an unsuccessful Reno prostitution case. He told the Washoe County Grand Jury he was a paid informer on contract with the Nevada Division of Investigation. He also stated he had known Conforte since 1966 and had bought a cat house from him in 1967.

While being held in the Las Vegas Metro Jail on the arson charge, Baliotis's attorney got a court order reducing bail from $400,000 down to $10,000. Baliotis bailed out and vanished.

Storey County officials were livid.

Back in northern Nevada, on December 22, 1975, Baliotis surfaced for his arraignment which was held in the Virginia City Justice of the Peace facility. He entered a plea of innocent to the arson charge. The preliminary hearing was scheduled for January 5, 1976. The District Attorney, Virgil Bucchianeri, pressed for reinstatement of the $400,000 bail. Justice of the Peace, Ed Colletti, upped the bail from $10,000 to $100,000. Baliotis was slammed in the ancient Storey County jail in Virginia City. But not for long.

Baliotis's attorney argued that his client could not be safe locked up in Storey County. There were people who wanted him dead. It was revealed that he was also a paid informer working with the police on organized crime and narcotics in Washoe and Storey counties. It then became necessary to assign two state investigators to guard him while he was being held in Storey County. At this time, the prosecutors and the defense attorneys agreed to move him from Virginia City, down the mountain to Carson City, a distance of less than 20 miles.

Relatively safe in the Carson City jail, Baliotis contacted the departments he insisted he worked undercover for. Following these events, the Storey County D.A., Bucchanieri, made it known that the Nevada Division of Investigations and Narcotics, was squeezing him to lighten up on Baliotis, and to release him.[3]

Storey County officials, pressed by Conforte, fought to keep Baliotis locked up. The Storey County commission reluctantly agreed to fund a special investigator out of San Francisco, and a well known attorney in Carson City, to act as prosecutor. Conforte then put pressure on Bucchianeri to polygraph those persons who he (Conforte) suspected of being part of the conspiracy causing the fire.

Tiring of Conforte's insistence, Nevada State Fire Marshall, Don Quinan, said that lie detector tests had already been administered to a number of persons. Quinan told the press that one person who refused to take the test, was none other than Joe Conforte. Conforte's reluctance to submit to a polygraph had in effect, brought the investigation to a halt, Quinan said. He explained that there was no legal means by which Conforte could be compelled to submit to the test. Yet without Conforte's cooperation, he too became a suspect.

Quinan qualified his statements and did admit that Conforte had stated he would agree to take the test, if the Perri brothers (from whom he leased the Mustang Ranch land), would retake the test. But, as Quinan pointed out, the Perris had already been polygraphed—and this was an expensive procedure. Conforte's continuing refusal to submit himself to the test, cast doubt upon his own credibility.

Quinan said that at one time Conforte indicated a distrust of the tests being administered by the sheriff's department and said that he would submit to such an examination only if he could select a lie detector operator that he could trust.

Quinan, visibly exasperated, said that isn't the way such tests are conducted, "and if Conforte wants to help us he should take the test and clear himself of any complicity in the matter." He finished by advising those present that some insurance companies require that an insured person clear himself before he gets paid, but the company in the present matter, "paid him before the ashes were cold." It was later reported the company settled with Conforte for $327,000.[4]

On March 5, 1976, the Perri brothers, owners of the land occupied by the Mustang Ranch, filed an eviction notice against the ranch and Joe Conforte. The legal document filed in Storey County, demanded that the brothel be removed from its present location.

An attorney for the brothers said the eviction notice stemmed from a number of disagreements which were recently brought to a head by Conforte's demand the Perri brothers take a lie detector test following the Mustang Ranch's arson related fire The brothers passed the test but were furious about Conforte's request.

"And there were a lot of other things," one of the brothers quipped to the press. "They were tired of being the underlings."

When contacted about the eviction notice, Conforte said he knew nothing about it. He also refused to comment on how much land he leased from the pair. But inwardly, he said he had no plans to vacate. In his mind, he envisioned rebuilding the Mustang Ranch on the same grounds, and turning it into the most famous cat house in the world.

On April 14, 1976, Don Baliotis, the prime suspect in the suspicious fire that engulfed the nearly completed Mustang Ranch, last November, appeared for his preliminary hearing at the Storey

County Justice Court. His attorney, Stew Bell, from Las Vegas, emphasized that his client had been in Las Vegas at the time the brothel was torched.

The Storey County District Attorney, Virgil Bucchianeri said he had been holding a series of meetings with Attorney Bell regarding his client's alibi. The two attorneys had reached the conclusion that unless further investigations could be arranged, there was no other course of action except to dismiss charges against Baliotis.

Bucchianeri made it clear that he had only one part-time investigator, and there were other pressing cases. He said he wasn't certain if any of the state agencies were doing their own investigations on the arson.

From all appearances, the dismissal had been prearranged. Baliotis walked. Had the fact that he'd worked as an informant for other agencies influenced the dismissal? What was Conforte's input? Baliotis had after all, been put on probation in 1969, for possession of bomb making materials. And he admitted at the time that he had intended to bomb Conforte's home. Baliotis, a blatant enemy of Joe Conforte, had walked thumbing his nose at the stunned brothel owner. But Conforte had little time to sulk, the Sparks Grand Jury was ready to bring in their report.

Chapter Five

CORRUPTION IN SPARKS

THE GRAND JURY REPORT

On March 15, 1976, the long awaited Washoe County Grand Jury report looking into corruption in Sparks government was made public by Larry Hicks, now the Washoe County District Attorney. The report detailed the million-dollar land deal between Conforte and the Reno-Sparks Convention Authority. Also included were details of Conforte's web of influence spread throughout local politics, with campaign contributions, lucrative real estate deals and offers of prostitutes' favors to catch numerous local officials.

In all, a Reno city councilman, the Reno mayor, a county commissioner, a former state senator, a Sparks municipal judge, and three former Sparks councilmen were implicated. Specifically, the grand jury named two Sparks city councilmen who "were closely involved with Joe Conforte" at the time they were arranging for the purchase of Conforte's 344-acre parcel by the Reno-Sparks Convention Authority in 1973.

The investigation revolved around the land deal engineered by Conforte when he purchased a large parcel of land that the City of Sparks had viewed as a site for a flood control reservoir. Plans for the reservoir were then expanded to include a golf course to be built by the Convention Authority.

During this time of discussions, the two councilmen met frequently with Conforte at his Mustang Ranch brothel, the report stated. According to testimony, the report revealed that city officials visiting with Conforte avoided using the brothel's main entrance. Instead, "they were led to a special area of the brothel where food, drink, and the services of prostitutes were available to them free of charge."

The report did not say whether the councilmen availed themselves of the prostitutes' services or not, but the investigation did reveal that, "Mustang prostitutes attended a party for local public officials held by _____ at his Sparks residence."

In quoting from the grand jury's conclusions regarding Sparks elected officials:

"They did not disclose to the public their relationship with Conforte and proceeded to actively crusade to have public agencies purchase Conforte's property knowing that Conforte would realize huge profits if the sale were consummated.

"In so acting these public officials failed to honor a trust which had been placed in them by the citizens and voters of their respective constituencies."

The report also said a former state senator exercised poor judgment in accepting an $18,000 fee from Conforte for doing little or nothing during the land deal.

"It is not in the public's best interest when any public official receives an extraordinarily large fee for doing little and further attempts to conceal such a fact from the public when the public itself is involved."

The grand jury also noted that a City of Sparks municipal judge was accused of dismissing or reducing traffic charges against certain persons at the request of the two city councilmen. It was also brought out that this same judge's salary was increased after Conforte pressured officials to do so. However, the report did not say that Conforte exercised any direct influence over the judge.

The report noted that Conforte's brothel was probably the largest house of prostitution in the nation. The corrupting influence of the brothel could not be overstated. Located in Storey County, just across the border from Washoe County—where prostitution is illegal— impacted Washoe nevertheless. Cab drivers, bartenders, bell hops and others catering to tourists, were put in a position of solicitation or of pandering, thus breaking the laws of Washoe County.

The report also stated that Conforte had ties to organized crime, but did not list any specifics. When Conforte was called to testify, he at first refused, but later recanted, and was quoted as saying he expected to reap a profit of $1 million dollars from the Sparks land deal since development of the golf course would enhance the value of the land he retained in the Sparks area.

Hicks announced, despite the issuance of the costly 45-page grand jury report implicating local political figures, no criminal indictments would be handed down unless additional information were uncovered.

When pressed for details, Hicks explained that most of the activities reported on were not criminal then, and are not criminal now. But he added, "...the recently passed Nevada Ethics in Government Law, could have made prosecution possible in some cases."

Hicks was asked if he thought the money spent to make the report public—without prosecution, was enough. Hicks, looking weary, tried to explain the difficulty facing the grand jury during the hearings. He said that writing a statute to include every case would be difficult. And so, the matter was dropped.

Reporters tracked Conforte down to ask him his thoughts on the grand jury report. Apparently, he wasn't taking it very seriously. He chuckled that it amounted to little more than harassment.

As to the jury's contention that he had encouraged city officials to vote for the $1 million dollar sale of his land to the Reno-Sparks Convention Authority, he denied it had ever happened. He protested that he had never influenced anybody. And then with a wink in his eye, he told those people who had gathered to hear his thoughts, that he had a right just like anyone else to support the people that were in agreement with his views.

When asked about rumors he kept a "comp list" of men, including elected officials who were granted free services from Mustang Ranch girls, he laughed, but refused to reply.

As regarding the section of the report entitled, "Conforte's Underworld Contacts and Their Effect on Washoe County," Conforte sneered and said that was merely added to reinforce the position of Washoe County Sheriff, Bob Galli's federally funded investigative unit on organized crime.

Conforte also sneered at the suggestion that organized crime had worked its way into Reno politics. Organized crime does not exist here, he told the gathering crowd. And jabbing the air in front of him with a stubby finger, said it never would as long as he is alive. Snickers arose from the crowd. And Joe Conforte grinned, lit a large Cuban cigar, and turned away.

Various political figures were contacted for their opinions on the report. Some issued statements; others deferred. Sam Dibitonto, former Reno mayor, and who had been subpoenaed to appear before the grand jury, was quick to respond. As a member of the Reno-Sparks Convention Authority, and as one who had voted against purchase of the 344-acre parcel, Dibitonto chastised the citizens. He said that until people pay more attention to the character of the persons who run for local office, suspicions of corruption are going to continue surfacing. Nothing in the report was surprising he said.

As a member of the Reno-Sparks Convention Authority, Dibitonto had voted against purchase of the 344 acre-parcel. He also voted against an increase in the room tax from 5% to 6%, a tax Conforte was encouraging.

During his testimony to the grand jury, Dibitonto stated that when he was seeking the mayor's position in Reno in 1973—a position selected by a vote of the councilmen (at that time), he was told by Conforte that the position would be given him, if he promised to make certain committee appointments when put in office.

Dibitonto made no promises to Conforte, and was elected mayor in 1973. After taking over the mayor's role, Dibitonto refused to appoint the selections sought by Conforte. In 1975, he was voted out of office.

The grand jury report served as a wake up call for the former Washoe County District Attorney, Bill Raggio, who was now a state senator.

Raggio had been doggin' Conforte since the mid '50s, and now once again he targeted the brothel owner. Raggio called for legislation to prohibit legalized prostitution within 50 miles of urban areas. If successful, this would force Conforte to move away from any major Nevada city.

He was supported by the Washoe County health officer, Dr. Ed Gallagher, who offered the opinion that many patients currently being treated for venereal disease, had become infected at the Mustang Ranch. Apparently, he and Bill Raggio had spent some time in researching the data, which again put Conforte under fire. But, in truth, their data was open to debate.

Legally, all cases of venereal disease treated by private physicians must be reported to the Health Department, but in actuality, many doctors fail to do this. And for this reason, Dr. Gallagher noted that to accurately obtain a true count of VD infections linked to the Mustang Ranch, could be a very difficult task. And because of this, to accurately gauge the effect of the brothel's impact on the VD rates of Washoe County, would likewise be nearly impossible.

To compound the problem, Dr. Gallagher explained, was that "for many reasons," many cases of VD go unreported and untreated.

"Many people wander out there from California," he noted, and, "what happens to them is never known."

The report also pointed out the time element of the incubation period and other delays in gathering credible data. Even though Conforte has private physicians contracted to keep watch on the girls, there still exists a lengthy incubation period of up to 30 days after the girl has been infected. This means that a busy girl could conceivably infect hundreds of patrons within a 30-day period.

A proposal to come out of the grand jury report also suggested cat houses should be moved at least 50 miles outside of Washoe County which would effectively move them from Storey County, and the close proximity of Lyon County. If this were enacted, Conforte would be out of business. It would be doubtful that he could once again run illegal brothels anywhere near Reno and Sparks.

Realizing that his old nemesis, Bill Raggio was out after him again, Conforte went to the newspapers seeking their support. Though they did not necessarily offer support, most of the local papers were usually accommodating to Joe since he drew local interest.

Several articles appeared in which he tried to defend the integrity of the Mustang Ranch, and the clean health of the girls. What he was fighting for in actuality was the survival of his business. If Bill Raggio could succeed in moving all cat houses far away from major cities, Conforte and the other local brothel owners would be finished.

Conforte pointed out—quite accurately—that if he were moved 50 miles out, the girls would take to the streets as freelance hookers in Washoe county and the adjacent areas.

If this were to happen, they would turn tricks without the

usual physician check ups. And this realistically would lead to an epidemic of venereal diseases.

Conforte pointed out that in Storey County, under supervision, the girls must undergo weekly examinations. He stressed that his brothel had not had a case of VD in the previous six months.

Virgil Bucchianeri, Storey County District Attorney, was quick to come to Conforte's defense and repeated publicly Conforte's contention that moving the brothels out to the desert could be disastrous for the health of the girls and their tricks. The urban areas could be impacted, he stressed. Apparently, he and Joe were reading from the same sheet of music.

He said checks with state health officials, show that examinations of girls working the Storey County brothels, have not turned up any cases of venereal disease.

Addressing the grand jury's actions in implicating local office holders as receiving special favors from Conforte, Bucchianeri questioned whether the grand jury had been improper and whether Nevada law had been violated by the jurors. He said that if a grand jury accuses a public officer of wrongdoing, then they have the responsibility to indict him. If not, then they shouldn't make unfounded accusations.

He also pointed out what he regarded as a flaw in the grand jury report that said there'd been a crime at the Storey County brothel. Had there been a crime in the brothel, in Storey County— Bucchianeri mused, then nobody had informed him.

"And," he said, " as district attorney, I'd have been the first to know."

He finished by saying there were all sorts of unfounded accusations being tossed around, and in his opinion, the persons doing this were merely testing the public's reaction, possibly testing the political air.

It appeared that Joe Conforte had a friend in the Storey County District Attorney's office.

And a friend in need, is a friend indeed.

Chapter Six

THE SICILIAN CONNECTION

1975 marked the tenth year since Conforte had been released from prison. Under Nevada law, an ex-felon who stays clean for ten years can apply to have his civil rights restored. This Conforte did, and boasted of being a shrewd, but ethical, local businessman. Apparently, he and the Perri brothers managed to reach an amicable solution to their previous animosities, because construction on the newly designed Mustang Ranch replacement had gotten underway not long after fire razed the complex..

Weary from all the legal battles, Conforte announced he was going to take an extended vacation. Born in Augustia, Italy on February 6, 1926, Conforte announced he was going to Sicily for a period of well deserved rest and relaxation.. Prior to departing, he took one last shot at the grand jury hearings, and at Washoe County Sheriff, Bob Galli. He repeatedly labeled the grand jury's findings lies including the references to political contributions, and then bid farewell, and caught his flight.

After relaxing for a few days in Sicily, presumably at his brother's house, it appeared not all was going well for Joe Conforte back in Reno. The Nevada State Journal had been working on an investigative story about Conforte's ties to organized crime. The brothel owner had no longer settled in on his vacation, when his associates back home called him with alarming news. The Journal had splashed a denigrating story about him and his mob ties all over the front page of the issue that came out on March 21, 1976.

The article explained their investigative reporters had been working on a story for months, and alleged that in November, 1974, Conforte had met with organized crime figures in Palm Springs to discuss building a hotel-casino on land near the newly proposed Reno-Sparks golf course.

Following this alleged meeting, after Conforte returned to Reno, he was interviewed by the press. Responding vehemently at the time, he denied being anywhere near Palm Springs and offered to bet anyone a substantial amount of money if they could prove otherwise.

Apparently, the investigative reporters did accept his challenge because they continued working on the case until it was ready for publication, which coincided with his arrival in Sicily. The article charged he met with top eastern Mafia figures in a plush Palm Springs hotel.

This plush hotel, one of the most elite in the desert resort at that time, has been the scene of numerous meetings of known crime figures. Confidential intelligence sources have said that during the past decade, many well known organized crime figures have made the country club their winter home.

Now when this story hit the news, Conforte, languishing in Sicily, was caught completely off guard. He was enraged. He screamed obscenities at his callers denying everything. He prepared for a stormy return to Reno to confront the paper's editors.

In view of the fact that the paper was reporting an incident that allegedly occurred two years ago, the question to be answered is why did Joe Conforte panic. Why was this so unsettling? One can only speculate. But for whatever reason, he wanted to distance himself from any alleged crime figures.

It is the author's opinion that these figures felt threatened by the notoriety he had created, and had admonished him to get the heat off them.

And organized crime figures were not the only persons dismayed at the negative publicity that always seemed to track Conforte. Legitimate business interests in Nevada were appalled at the repeated grand jury's reports in which the flamboyant brothel owner was always a central figure. Big money interests felt that the adverse publicity generated by Joe Conforte threatened their positions.

Senator Floyd Lamb, D-Las Vegas, who in 1972, cosponsored anti-prostitution legislation along with Conforte's old adversary, Senator Bill Raggio, suggested a statewide referendum as the best way to settle controversies over legalized prostitution. Lamb was of the opinion that the issue should be put to a vote of the people. If the people felt the need to outlaw Nevada brothels, then

Lamb reasoned, they should be outlawed.

Statewide, other brothel operators were contacted and queried as to their thoughts. Nearly all those contacted, were unanimous in asserting their disdain of Conforte, who, in his position of being the owner of the largest brothel in Nevada, should set a much better example. They were particularly incensed that his behavior had led to a grand jury hearing that included a sharp focus on prostitution, which they feared, could lead to trouble for their livelihoods.

The real fear was that Senator Lamb, and Senator Raggio, would sponsor legislation to bring the matter of legalized prostitution in the State of Nevada, to a statewide vote. If this happened, chances were good that it would be voted out. The state's two large urban counties, Clark, in the south, and Washoe, in the north, had the preponderance of voters, and these two counties had outlawed prostitution. Consequently, legalized prostitution was relegated to the cow counties, which had substantially fewer voters.

A sampling of opinions suggested that a pervasive fear and distrust of Conforte among other brothel owners existed statewide. Brothel owners were polled in all of the cow counties. They were unanimous in showing a disdain for the headline-splashing antics of Joe Conforte. If a vote were put to the people, they agreed, outlawing brothels would become a definite possibility. The two large populous counties, Clark and Washoe, could decide the vote. Whatever their views, most looked upon Conforte as an instigator of problems they didn't need. His enemy list was building.

When he arrived back in Reno, Conforte, accompanied by his attorney, James Brown, stormed into the office of the Nevada State Journal-Reno Evening Gazette, on the afternoon of Thursday, March 25, 1976. Confronting the executive director, he demanded retractions for the two stories printed about him the previous week, alleging ties to organized crime.

The paper's position was that the news stories were fair and unbiased. A retraction would not be made.

As if on a mission to divorce himself entirely from organized crime, Conforte, along with his attorney filed a claim against Washoe County at the close of March, 1976. The legal document directed at the grand jury, petitioned the court to remove his name from any reference to organized criminal activity. Because there were no indictments, "the report makes it clear there was no allegation of criminal conduct."

The claim further alleged that Conforte's constitutional rights were violated when the grand jury issued, without indicting the brothel owner, a 45 page report lamenting Conforte's influence over public officials.

Conforte's attorney cited a Nevada law on grand juries which makes it clear that "no report shall single out an individual with an implied or direct accusation that would be indictable if true, unless the report is accompanied with an indictment.

"By innuendo, imputation, and when read as a whole," the claim alleged, "it accused me of the crime of bribery...without being accompanied by a presentment or indictment."

In addition to the above, the document also alleged that the report subjected Conforte to public ridicule, approbation and scorn. And, it continued, "the district attorney continues to use it for such purposes in the future."

Assistant District Attorney, Cal Dunlap, who answered the complaint, said since the grand jury did not specifically accuse Conforte of criminal conduct, there was no basis for the suit.

Reinforcing Conforte's ire even further, it was also announced that copies of the grand jury report, would be made available to "interested citizens." Subsequently, about 300 of the copies were distributed to locals who showed up at the courthouse.

Twenty-four hours later, Brown filed a second suit, a $2 million law suit against Washoe County. Conforte attempted to explain the claim was not designed to take money from the Washoe County tax payers, but was intended to force the law enforcement agencies to uphold the laws they had created. He also said the feds too, were to be targeted. But this wasn't made clear just how.

During his brief stay in Sicily, there were rumblings on the streets that Conforte had alienated hard-core Mafia members. Did they want his head? The ever zealous Bill Raggio, who could not be bought, was one elected official who mulled this over. He too, would have been happy to see Conforte disappear. And there were other local politicians who despised Conforte's tactics of buying influence.

Other brothel owners regarded the publicity greedy Conforte as a liability; as one whose flamboyance and under the table deals, could bring about a referendum on prostitution in Nevada that would outlaw the profession for a lifetime. If this happened, of course their livelihood would be tossed to the wind, as would the essential tax revenues in the cow-counties.

And from Montana, yet another who'd been associated with Conforte, was trying to answer questions thrown at him from his constituents. William Douglas, a top-notch prosecutor from Libby, Montana, had been named in the grand jury report as another civic official who'd been caught up in the web of Conforte's influence.

The report alleged that Douglas had accepted favors from Conforte, and that the brothel owner was interested in bringing prostitution and casino gambling to Douglas's Big Sky Country. The report said that Conforte and Douglas met on several occasions, both in Reno, and in Lincoln County, Montana, and that Conforte "is hopeful of expanding business operations into that area (Northwest Montana) and that he has established close contacts with the prosecuting attorney of Lincoln County."

When the report reached Lincoln County officials, the elected Sheriff, Mike McMeekin, of Libby, launched an investigation. When the results were made public, Douglas was accused of accepting favors, including free use of Mustang prostitutes, and the failure to take any action to stop or limit illegal gambling in a Libby bar.

The report also noted that if the charges were true, Douglas would have put himself into a position open to blackmail.

"Joe Conforte has a documented history of establishing himself in a county and manipulating politics until he controls the county," the report read.

Lincoln County commissioners, reacting to an inspired citizen's committee, suggested the prosecutor should vacate his office. William Douglas, erstwhile successful prosecutor, was beginning to rue the day he'd become acquainted with Joe Conforte.

The year 1975, and the first quarter of 1976, had been a time of ups and downs for Joe Conforte. He had been pulled up before the Washoe County Grand Jury, had been involved in a questionable business venture with an elected sheriff, and had been accused of bribery and corruption by the newspapers. His association with organized crime figures had been splashed all over the front pages of the Reno newspaper. And he had suffered the loss of his brothel—his livelihood—his identity—at the hands of a criminal arsonist.

Yet, he remained optimistic. The remainder of this year, 1976, he told himself, would bring many new blessings. Construction on the rebuilding of the Mustang Ranch was progressing nicely. Good fortune was portended.

Getting this far, Joe Conforte had passed around a sizable amount of money to a multitude of followers. He bought influence and loyalty. The downside of all this was that he also left in his wake, a multitude of enemies, including a Montana lawman who now faced removal from office because of a brief association with Joe Conforte.

Many questions remain unanswered. Conforte's enemy list had continued to expand. One thing stands out: Some persons would have liked to see Conforte dead. Did they come after him? Allegedly, one did. And when this happened, a world-ranked, heavyweight boxing figure, lay sprawled in a pool of blood, at the doorsteps of the rebuilt Mustang Ranch. Things again, appeared to take a turn for the worse.

Chapter Seven
OSCAR BONAVENA

Argentine Boxers have a reputation of toughness.

Luis Angel Firpo, the Wild Bull of the Pampas, came to this country in 1923, with dreams of becoming the heavyweight champion of the world. To do so, he had to get in the ring with one of the greatest heavyweight fighters of that era, Jack Dempsey, the Manassa Mauler—the champ. The fight was held at the Polo Grounds in New York on September 14, 1923.

Firpo, who stood six-foot-three-inches tall, towered, over his smaller opponent, and at 216.5 pounds outweighed Dempsey by twenty-four pounds. But the ring-smart Dempsey, who possessed a natural killer's instinct, had fought other big guys, and he felt Firpo would cave in like the others had. Firpo would prove him wrong.

As the bell sounded starting round one, Firpo came out of his corner like the mad bull he was, and charged Dempsey who was dancing toward the center of the ring. Startled, Dempsey covered his face with his gloves as a flurry of massive punches rained down upon him from the Argentine's beefy staccato-like fists. In the first few seconds of the fight, the Argentine caught Dempsey with eight smashing overhand rights and hooks that went unanswered, driving his smaller opponent toward the ropes. The eighth right hand smash to Dempsey's jaw caused his head to drop and buckled his knees.

Sensing a quick knockout, Firpo again charged the wobbly Dempsey, and threw another thunderous right hand that caught the champ off guard, that lifted him up and propelled him right off his feet sailing through the ropes and crashing down into the ringside rows below. The entire house erupted in bedlam as their beloved Manassa Mauler crash landed among the newspapermen at ringside.

In disbelief, Dempsey tried to shake the cobwebs from his

head and make sense of what was happening. He sensed instinctively that he was in jeopardy of losing his championship, and he implored the newsmen who were supporting him, to muscle him back into the ring before the count. Firpo, who had gone to a neutral corner, was dancing up and down gleefully, banging his gloves together and waving at a contingency of Spanish speaking countrymen who were coming off their seats spilling beer and cheering madly.

Back in the ring, and dazed from the pounding, Dempsey could only hang on and retreat. Still, he took thirteen more heavy blows without returning one. And then abruptly, out of the blue, and fighting on heart alone, he ripped his own savage blow, a left hook to the giant's head. Firpo had a look of complete surprise etched into his face as he too, crashed to the floor.

The Argentine giant bounced up at the count of three, and Dempsey charged in with another whistling left hook to the head. Again, the startled challenger crashed to the floor, only to bounce right back up again into the line of fire.

Dempsey now moved in with both fists flailing, flashing before the screaming crowd, the patented killer's instinct he was known for. Again, the game Argentine fell to the canvas. Before the gong sounded ending the round, the challenger had been sent to the canvas seven times, five by the champs vicious left hooks, once by a powerful left uppercut, and the other knockdown came from a right swing to the head.

Both fighters slumped wearily in their corners as trainers worked frenziedly over both to revive them for what lie ahead in round-two.

At the start of round-two, Dempsey moved in for the kill, resolved to end the fight as quickly as possible. Bobbing and weaving, he moved in, ripping shots to the body and head, as the Argentine tried frantically to cover up and hold on. Another vicious left hook to the skull sent the challenger to his hands and knees, the position from which he again arose to face his antagonist.

The final blow came midway during the second round when Dempsey again sent the challenger to the canvas with a flurry of lefts and rights to the head and body. Firpo lie sprawled on the deck as the referee started the count. At the count of nine, the game challenger tried desperately to regain his feet. Though his heart was there, his legs were gone. The fight was over. At the count of ten, Jack Dempsey, still the heavyweight champion of the world, moved over toward the prone Argentine, and helped him to his feet and over to his corner. The corner men were gesturing wildly and screaming in Spanish. The crowd went mad.

The next day, both fighters paid tribute to each other.

"I don't want anymore of that fellow, Firpo," Jack Dempsey told the New York Times through swollen lips. "Let somebody else tackle him now and test his wallop."

"He's a tough fellow," Dempsey continued. "I know because I felt the power of his punch. That's why I say I want no more of him for a while. One fight like that is plenty for a few months anyway. I've met a lot of tough fellows in my time, but Firpo's about the toughest of them all. He proved it last night and he'll prove it again if some of the other fellows who are yelling for a crack at the title will chance a bout with him. He's a fighting bull. Make no mistake on that."

Firpo had similar praise for the champion. Though he did question the referee's role in the fight when he failed to send Dempsey to a neutral corner every time he, Firpo, was on the canvas.

"We were told before the bout started," Firpo related through an interpreter, "that the referee would not start a count until the boxer who scored a knockdown went to a corner, and I was surprised when Dempsey several times almost stood directly over me when I was down. But I am satisfied I showed the American people that I deserved a chance at the title, and I am satisfied too that I showed critics their criticism of me was not justified. I demonstrated I had a chance I would like to get another bout with Dempsey. I am sure I could do better next time. I will not say I will win, but I feel I can do better."

The Wild Bull of the Pampas had earned the respect of everyone in attendance that night. When he returned to his homeland, he was met by tens of thousands of admirers cheering amid tons of freshly picked flowers and music. He was a living, national hero.

A half century later, Oscar "Ringo" Bonavena, heavyweight champ of Argentina, arrived on the shores of the United States, carrying the same dreams that propelled the Wild Bull into legendary hero status in his homeland. Ringo too, would be accorded a hero's welcome on his return to Argentina. However, unlike his idol of a half a century earlier, Bonavena was destined to return in a body bag, because of his association with the Mustang Ranch brothel owner, Joe Conforte.

Bonavena, who began his career in 1964, was a southpaw and a devastating body puncher. He was ranked seventh among the world's heavyweight fighters, and like his counterpart, was a crushing aggressor in the ring. His record of 56-9-1, with 43 knockouts, attests to his punching power. It was said he'd do whatever was necessary to win.

Fighting as an amateur in a Pan American games bout, he was paired with an American, Lee Carr. During the fast-paced fight, Bonavena got caught up in the frenzy and clamped down on the American's chest with his teeth, drawing blood. His legend was born.

In the ring, the well muscled, 220 pound puncher, would wade in, willing to take punches in order to dish out his own. And he had been in with the best of the crop. Of his nine losses, most came from the fists of ranked heavyweight fighters.

In 1968, fighting in New York for the state championship, Bonavena lost a close 15 round decision to "Smokin'" Joe Frazier. Frazier had built up an early lead in that fight, but began to tire in the later rounds. The judges gave the final four or five rounds to Oscar. After the decision was announced, it is said Frazier shouted to his manager, "Get me outta' here, I think I'm gonna faint!" Oscar, superbly conditioned, was still dancing around the ring waving and smiling to the crowd..

In December, 1970, he fought Muhammad Ali in Madison Square Garden. From the opening bell, the two fighters went after each other with a vengeance. Ali's boxing savvy was the deciding factor. The grueling fight went into the 15th round, when Oscar was knocked out, the only time he had been stopped in his career. His one great compulsion following this fight, was to get a rematch.

In 1972, Oscar fought a ten rounder with ex-heavywight champion, Floyd Patterson. In that fight, Oscar shattered his left hand in the tenth round. It was necessary to have the hand reconstructed surgically. He returned to Argentina to recuperate and to prepare for a return match with Muhammad Ali.

Returning to the states proved to be more of a problem than imagined. Argentina, at the time, was rife with political machination. He was refused passage out of the country. In 1975, trying to stay in shape in his homeland, he fought 23 exhibitions, mostly with local club fighters. The only serious fight he had that year was a ten-round fight with Raul Gorocito, in Buenos Aires, on the first of November, which he won by decision.

Finally, in January, 1976, Oscar Bonavena, now 33 years old, was granted permission to leave Argentina. On the twenty-second of that month, he departed Buenos Aires, and arrived in New York City by plane that same day. He immediately called his long time friend and advisor, Loren Cassina, in Los Angeles, and advised him he would be arriving in L.A. later on that day.

When Joe Conforte, and long time fight promoter, Bud Traynor, heard that Bonavena was back in the country, they contacted Cassina in Los Angeles, and invited the two to Reno. On February 1, Bonavena and Cassina, arrived in Reno and met with Conforte and Traynor, for a series of discussions..

Cassina had known Oscar since 1968, and remarked, "I guess my thing is the heavyweight title game, and that's why were here. Don King has been running some Ali fights, and we'd like to run some of our own."

It was Cassina's opinion that Oscar was a legitimate contender, right behind Foreman and Ken Norton. Cassina suggested a match up with either Norton or Foreman, with the winner going on to fight Ali. However; it was doubtful that a Foreman-Bonavena match up was going to be inked.

In 1972, and once in 1973, according to Cassina; Foreman and Bonavena had signed a contract which Foreman refused to uphold. "We're still in court with a $100 million dollar suit over that fight (the second contract), scoffed Cassina."

Cassina got right to work lining up fights. By the end of February, 1976, he had lined up three: February 26, a ten-round bout with Billy Joiner, in Reno. Following that fight, Bonavena and Cassina planned on traveling to Albuquerque to fight Roy Rodriguez. Next, they planned to return to Los Angeles where Oscar would prepare for a fight with Ernie Shavers, which, if both parties upheld the contract, would be staged in Cleveland. Three fights within a 32 day period. Bonavena began daily workouts at the Reno YMCA.

The heavily muscled fighter was soon a popular topic among the downtown crowd. He was gruff, but friendly, and always had time for interviews. He said he felt at home here. He commented frequently on the friendliness of the people and the lifestyle of the town.

"I love this town," he would say in broken English. "Town here, like town in Argentina. Good people here. Maybe someday I buy home here and stay. In hotel, the people always say 'Hi Oscar, good to see ya.' I love the good people here."

And the people loved Oscar. He was brash, colorful, and fearless, and always smiling.

Reflecting back on his life in Argentina, he related that everywhere he went, people clustered around him; he was their national hero. He obviously loved being in the limelight. He placed the blame for his not being allowed out of Argentina sooner, on Evita Peron. Peron, he said through an interpreter, may be a good wife, but she knows nothing about being president. Good maybe in kitchen, good maybe at home, but no good to lead Argentina.

He attended local fights, not just to watch the action, but to climb into the ring and be introduced to the crowds. At the University of Nevada, at the Stewart Indian School, at boxing matches held in the local hotel-casinos, he would show up grinning widely, happy to climb in the ring and wave at the crowds.

Boxing fans would always acknowledge his presence. Who would he fight next, they yelled. When would he fight Ali in the rematch?

"Soon, soon," he'd say, waving to the crowd. And then he'd approach the boxers in their corners and wish them the best of luck, feinting a heavy handed fist to their chins. The crowds would roar approval. They loved Oscar.

Some boxing insiders suggested at age 33, his best fights were behind him. Was he now over the hill? He merely played off their remarks.

"It's not young, it's not old," he would say. "It's what you have here," and he'd jab a meaty finger into his chest to make his point.

"It's heart," he would roar. "When the heart is willing, the fighter wins."

Speaking of the current heavyweights, Bonavena offered his opinion.

He jokingly compared George Foreman to a banana eating monkey. Not too bright. Ali, though, he said is much smarter. Pointing to his forehead, he said Ali had much more up here.

The Reno fans who heard these kind of remarks would roar their approval. Oscar Bonavena, indeed, was more than a fighter, he was charismatic, in the same class as Ali. The loved to see him workout, and they loved to listen to his comments. And Oscar loved his fans. So much so, that after his workouts during the day, he could be seen mixing with the late night crowds, and carousing around the casinos and brothels until the wee hours of the morning.

And at the Mustang Ranch brothel, he met Sally Conforte—and a 20-year old prostitute, a tall, attractive blond, a graduate of Sparks High School.

On February 19, Washoe County records show that Deputy Commissioner of Civil Marriages, Darrel Cain, married Oscar Bonavena, and the 20 year old local girl. The ceremony was performed in Spanish for Oscar's benefit, while the girl followed reading from a book printed in English. Sally Conforte stood in as a witness.

Within days, the marriage was annulled when it was learned that Bonavena had a wife in Argentina. Dora Raffade de Bonavena, the boxer's estranged wife, was contacted in Buenos Aires and explained that she and the boxer were still married, but had been living apart for the past four years. She added they were still on friendly terms, and the boxer was the father of her two children, Dora 12, and Natalio 8.

Hype for the Bonavena-Billy Joiner fight scheduled for February 26, 1976, at the Centennial Coliseum, took on a new wrinkle. Many eyes were raised around Reno, when an advertisement promoting the fight, showed Sally Conforte and Oscar Bonavena—Beauty and the Beast, standing together as manager and fighter. Surprisingly, Loren Cassina, Oscar's long time friend, and manager of record had been replaced by Sally Conforte.

Sally, who had become only the second woman in the United States to manage a professional boxer, said her boxer was not only a top-ranked heavyweight fighter, but he was also a gentleman. After we got to know each other, Sally said, the two worked out an agreement whereby she would be his new manager.

She said she enjoyed going to the YMCA and watch "the great white hope work out." She often remarked that many fight managers were uncaring about their fighters; that they were only in it for the money. When the fighter could no longer produce, she would say, these unscrupulous managers would fade out, leaving their fighters to fend for themselves. Not her though. She said she had compassion and respect for Oscar which made for a solid business relationship.

And the rail-birds in town were betting it was more than a business relationship.

Weigh-in for the Joiner fight was at the Mapes Hotel. Bonavena came in at 218 pounds, Joiner at 210.

Thirty-seven year old Billy Joiner, was basically a boxer, not a puncher. His record—9-10-3, though not impressive, was deceptive. Granted, he had lost more fights that he had won, yet his losses, like Bonavena's had come at the hands of world class fighters: Sonny Liston, Zora Folley and Larry Holmes, to name a few.

Bonavena was the odds-on favorite, mainly because of his experience and punching power. Sports writers gave Joiner a sprinter's chance.

"If he can stay away from Oscar's powerful punches and box, he has a chance," was the consensus.

The fight started out as predicted. Bonavena rushed his man in the early rounds, trying to end it early. Joiner, a veteran of 14 years in the ring, using an effective left jab, deftly sidestepped the onrushing puncher. Midway into the third round, Oscar caught Joiner coming in with a smashing left hook to the head which sent the boxer to the canvas.

Joiner, apparently not hurt bounced up and again tried to play his foe like a bullfighter. Bonavena, though, stalking Joiner, repeatedly caught up with him and landed some devastating body shots. In the seventh round, Joiner left himself open, and Oscar caught him with a vicious hook to the body that again sent the boxer sprawling to the canvas.

Joiner, not yet ready to admit defeat, rose to his feet and hung on catching his breath while Mills Lane, the referee, separated them. Then, to the surprise of the active crowd, Joiner smartly sidestepped the Argentinean's rushes, and scored points of his own by using a chattering left jab keeping the puncher off balance. These punches did little damage, but did have the effect of confusing Oscar who was becoming frustrated at not being able to put his opponent away.

Bonavena, fearful that he was being upstaged by the slick

boxer, at times resorted to using his saloon style fighting tactics, slamming with his elbows, shoving, and at times, digging body shots below the belt. Mills Lane, repeatedly warned Bonavena about his rough house tactics.

When the bell ending round eight sounded, Lane tried to separate the two fighters, but Bonavena kept up a flurry of punches, landing four vicious shots before he could be pulled off. Lane pushed him towards the corner and told the corner men he was deducting a point..

The ninth and tenth rounds were carbon copies of the eighth, and as the fight ended, the two were still slugging it out at the bell which had to be rung repeatedly. Mills Lane, his sweat covered pate reflecting the ring lights, had to force himself between the two, warning them to stop. Gasping, Joiner retreated to his corner. Bonavena, loving the spotlight, moved toward his corner and waved to the crowd.

"I hope the people liked it," he gleamed.

The appreciative crowd yelling on their feet, were already showering the ring with money, mainly due to the durable Joiner's stamina. A point deducted from Oscar in the eighth round had little effect on the outcome of the fight. It was a unanimous decision and Mills Lane, raised Oscar's hand in victory.

Joiner, slouched in his corner waiting for his trainer to pull off the sweat clogged gloves, moaned, "I could've won it.

George Gainford, Joiner's manager, and who was the former manager of one-time world boxing champ, Sugar Ray Robinson, agreed.

"Yeah, it's sad, you could've beat him."

The unmarked Bonavena, waving to the crowd paid his respect to the beaten boxer.

"He's very strong, but it's no tough fight." And not quite pleased with having to go the full distance, he added, "The luck wasn't there. I need a little more sparring. The right sparring is necessary."

Sally Conforte smiled approvingly from the corner..

Bonavena, through his new manager, Sally Conforte, announced he was canceling the fight in Albuquerque that had been previously scheduled by Cassina. Oscar responded to questions by reporters and said he had no obligation to Cassina. Sally and Oscar smiled at each other.

As noted earlier, Conforte had gone to Sicily in March of this year for a brief stay before rushing back to Reno to challenge an article in the Reno newspapers linking him to organized crime. While he was gone, Oscar Bonavena and Sally had been seen together with much greater frequency. Now with Joe's return, rumors began circulating of a rift developing between he and his wife. Next the gossips were saying he'd moved out of their Sullivan Lane home into the Mustang bordello. Sally reportedly remained in the home.

On May 15, 1976, the newly constructed Mustang Ranch celebrated its grand opening. It was open house, for both men and women. The public was invited in to see the thick-carpeted lounge and bar area, and be led through guided tours of the offices, the hallways, the kitchen, and the working rooms—the cribs. During the day long gala event, upwards of 5,000 people trekked through the lavishly furnished bordello. Champagne and hors d'oeuvres were in abundance. Pleasant working girls strewn about the lounge area added to the decor. Though they were not working today, they were there to welcome the guests, to answer questions, and generate future business.

Outside, two prison-style gun-towers looked down upon the entire complex which was wrapped securely within a ten-foot high chain-link fence enclosure, and a front facing, iron-barred fence. Entry into the compound was through a reinforced metal gate, controlled by electric circuitry operated from inside.

Following the day long ceremonies, the ranch went into full operation—men only. Visitors desiring entrance, were required to push a buzzer outside the gate, and after being scrutinized by supervisory personnel, were invited in.

Many visitors became regulars, as did Oscar Bonavena, who had since moved into a mobile home adjacent to the compound. At times, it was reported the spotlight-loving boxer became overly boisterous and was causing problems. During his outbursts, it was reported, he bragged about taking over as owner of the place. And he and his manager of the moment, Sally Conforte, who was some twenty years his senior, were being seen together with greater frequency, even though he hadn't fought since the Joiner fight.

On May 18, while he was away with Sally, a break-in occurred at the mobile trailer he had been living in, and an intentional fire broke out which destroyed or damaged many of his personal belongings including his passport. He filed a complaint with the Storey County Sheriff's Office. Willard Ross Brymer, a Conforte bodyguard, was named as a possible suspect.

Bonavena was advised by the sheriff's office that they would launch an investigation. They also advised him that since his passport had been destroyed, he would have to get a replacement. To do so, he would have to visit the Argentine Consulate in San Francisco. Following this sequence of events, he left for San Francisco. His traveling companion was Sally Conforte.

Things were heating up and Joe Conforte was steaming. He called a meeting with his security people and told them that the brothel was no longer open to Oscar Bonavena. He was to be denied entry—period.

Previously, before the newly completed Mustang had been finished, Sally Conforte was named as the owner on the business license. But now, on May 20, when Joe applied for a new license on the rebuilt Mustang, he listed himself as sole proprietor. Sally was not named on the license. Joe had quietly removed her name.

The cost of doing business, was not cheap. The license included fees for prostitution, liquor, merchandise and cabaret services. The Storey County Taxation Department had upped the yearly fees to $30,000, plus $1,250, for licensing the new Mustang.

Joe said he wouldn't protest the raised license fees, but when told his place was also subject to a new county relief tax of one-half percent, snickered, "We don't sell anything, we just rent it."

On Friday, the events of the past week turned ugly. Sally Conforte phoned the Reno Police Department from San Francisco. She sounded scared. Sally spoke to someone in the detective division and said that since arriving in San Francisco to help Bonavena renew his passport, she and the boxer had been receiving death threats over the phone. She said a man, whose voice she didn't recognize, called her and warned her not to return to Reno. She was told that if she did, she'd be killed.

Bonavena too, was sounding the alarm. On that same day, he phoned his estranged wife in Buenos Aires, and told her he had been receiving death threats that week. He also hinted at other problems he was having, but which he refused to go into detail about.

Dora Raffade Bonavena, his estranged wife, said when he

called, he was in a state of anxiety, and asked her to pray for him. She tried to get more out of him, but he said little other than he couldn't flee like a coward.

Prior to departing San Francisco, Sally again called the Reno PD, and expressed her fears. She pleaded with them to meet her at the airport and provide protection. When her plane landed at the airport, a police guard was there to meet her. She had come alone. Apparently, the boxer had remained in the city to drive back to Reno

Sally repeated her fears of coming back to Reno to the police guard, and said there had been many telephoned death threats. She was then escorted back to the Sullivan Lane home, under police escort, without further incident. *And a question as to the validity of the death threats supposedly received by Sally Conforte and Oscar Bonavena, continues to evoke controversy*

Prior to her arrival, other threats had surfaced in the Reno area. Earlier in the day, an excited telephone operator received an urgent call from a man who shrieked a warning that the newly rebuilt Mustang Ranch was going to be blown up. The message was forwarded to the Sparks Police Department, who forwarded it to the Storey County Sheriff's Office.

Sometime during Saturday night, the 22nd of May, Bonavena arrived back in Reno. He was seen playing twenty-one at the Sundowner Hotel and Casino in the wee hours of the morning. He was next seen about 6:00 a.m., when he roared into the parking lot of the Mustang Ranch, braked hard, and jumped out of the car slamming the door behind him and lunged toward the entrance gate.

A heated argument with one of the Mustang's security officers, who was stationed behind the iron barred fence, probably, John Colletti, ensued. What happened next has been a matter of speculation and controversy for many years since.

According to witnesses, the fearless boxer was standing outside the iron-barred fence, loudly demanding to be let in. John Colletti, Joe Conforte's personal bodyguard, on the inside of the fence told him Conforte's orders were to deny the boxer entry.

"You're not coming in here," the guard, warned, and ordered Bonavena to leave the premises.

Sleepy-eyed working girls, many in bed inside their cribs, woke to the loud voices outside, and raised up sluggishly, peeping through the windows, trying to get a glimpse of what the commotion was about. Also, in bed, was Joe Conforte (who later would testify he had slept through the entire episode).

During the 10 minutes or so the argument raged, another security officer, Willard Ross Brymer, came out of the brothel to assess the situation. Sensing a serious problem, he yelled to a 20-year old brothel handyman who was standing nearby, to bring a rifle from one of the gun towers. The youth, whose job it was to chauffeur prostitutes around town, or work the electronic gate, ran to one of the prison-like towers and retrieved a 30.06 hunting rifle.

He handed the rifle to Brymer, and then went back inside.

Suddenly, the early morning, high-desert sunrise, was startled by another shout, a commanding order from inside the fence, "FREEZE!" Followed by an earsplitting blast erupting from the barrel of the 30.06. Two magpies, flapping their wings overhead while looking for road kill, gave a shrill cry, and veered away in panic. In the distance, a dog's barking intensified, signaling its denial of events erupting outside the Mustang Ranch..

Oscar Bonavena, though, was unhearing. The heavy-grain, deer-slaying slug, tore through his chest and exploded from a gaping rupture in his back, trailing blood, bone, and tissue. He was dead before he hit the ground.

Ross Brymer inside the secure fence, hesitated momentarily, and then turned around and carried the rifle back inside the brothel. In the kitchen, he saw the young handyman who had a look of disbelief on his face.

"What happened," the youth stammered.

Brymer looked around the kitchen and poured himself a glass of orange juice. He then told the youth that outside, he had ordered Bonavena to leave the premises. Brymer said his words had no effect on the enraged boxer, who began screaming unintelligibly in Spanish, and then abruptly lurched forward toward the gate..

"I shouted at him to freeze," Brymer said, "but instead he grabbed for his boot."

"When he did that," Brymer told the youth, "I feared he was going for a gun, so I raised the rifle in my hand and fired one shot through the bars."

In another part of the bordello, someone was waking Joe Conforte.

Lloyd "Mac" McNulty, the Chief of Security, went out past

the front gate to where Bonavena lie in a pool of blood. McNulty bent over the body, and as he did, he slid a small calibre pistol under the body. Not bothering to throw a blanket over the fallen boxer, he went back inside.

When Brymer heard Conforte's voice, he arose from the table and went to meet him. Brymer informed the brothel owner of the shooting, and asked, "Joe, what shall I do?"

Conforte told his bodyguard to pull himself together, and said he would notify the Storey County Sheriff and the coroner.

"When they get here," Conforte said, "you will have to give yourself up, but it's obviously a case of self defense."

Another member of Conforte's security team had already telephoned Sgt. Bill Tilton, a Storey County deputy who lived not far from the bordello (and who was also the deputy coroner), and told him, "We've got a dead man here."

Within minutes, Tilton was on the scene, and was quickly joined by the Storey County Sheriff, Bob Del Carlo, his undersheriff, Jim Miller, and the Storey County District Attorney, Virgil Bucchianeri. Storey County was well represented.

In the meantime, the Washoe County Sheriff's Office had picked up news of the shooting on their scanners, and dispatched a SWAT team to the area where they took up positions on the Washoe County-Storey County border adjacent to the Mustang Ranch.

After Sheriff Del Carlo arrived on scene of the shooting, he did a cursory examination of the body, and then approached Conforte who was standing inside the fence. Conforte told the sheriff that Brymer had shot the Argentine boxer in self defense.

Del Carlo demanded to know why Brymer was still employed at the brothel.[1] Conforte said nothing.

Shortly after 6:30 a.m., a team of officers from Washoe County's SWAT team that had been observing events from across the county line, poured into the parking lot. When Conforte looked out and saw them, he blew up.

Conforte stormed out to the parking lot screaming at them and calling them "dogs." He continued to berate the team and spelled out to them that they had no jurisdiction in Storey County, and ordered them back across the county line, a distance of maybe a quarter of a mile.

Conforte then pointed to the corpse and told them, "It's just a dead man. You can't do anything about it now. So we got a dead man here. So what?"

He was joined by Storey County Sergeant, Bill Tilton, who advised them it would be in everybody's best interest if they would comply. The team reluctantly pulled back across the county line.

Brymer was still inside the brothel making small chatter with a few prostitutes and customers. Because he still had the 30.06 rifle with him, the Washoe County SWAT team members formed a line along the county border, and kept their rifles and shotguns at the ready position.

It took about an hour for Brymer to come out of the brothel and surrender. When he did, he spoke quietly to Sgt. Tilton for a few minutes, and then stood motionless while the sergeant frisked him and secured his wrists with handcuffs. He was then put in a Storey County sheriff's patrol car and whisked away to the county jail in Virginia City and booked for investigation of homicide.

The boxer's body lie in place for a couple of more hours, and then was removed to the Washoe Medical Center pending an autopsy. The Storey County homicide team remained to gather evidence, and interview witnesses.

News photographers had descended on the parking lot eager to take photos of the crime scene. When Conforte saw this he charged out of the ranch screaming at his security officers to stop them. Two of the burly guards were seen confronting the cameramen, and then were seen going back into the ranch carrying rolls of film.

In Buenos Aires, Dora Raffade Bonavena, the boxer's estranged wife, was bombarded by newspaper reporters trying to get to her. She told the Argentine news reporting agency, Telam, that she and the prizefighter had been separated for the past four years, but that they remained on friendly terms. She told how he had called her the day before his death asking her to pray for him.

"I am the only one who knows the names of those who caused him all his problems over there," she said, "and one day I will say who they are." She then asked to be left alone with her grief.

Muhammed Ali, when he heard of the fighter's death said he was shocked and dismayed to learn of the tragedy.

"He was a good fighter and I respected him," Ali said. "He

was a big guy and I needed everything I knew to put him away. I am sorry he had to die like that."

Ali's manager, Angelo Dundee, said Bonavena was a great fighter who had fought fighters in many other parts of the world, and who always gave a good account of himself.

After being booked in the century old Virginia City jail, Ross Brymer was moved to the Nevada State Prison—Max, as an SK.[2]

On Monday, the 24th, Storey County Sheriff, Bob Del Carlo answered questions for the media. He told the news people that Bonavena had $6,161 dollars in his pocket when he died. And he said, his office had recovered the murder weapon, a 30.06 hunting rifle which was being held as evidence. No motive had as yet been established for the shooting, he said, but he added that he expected to recommend a murder charge be filed against Brymer. Brymer, he said, has yet to say anything about the shooting.

Del Carlo said they had detained a witness to the shooting, but declined to give out the person's identity.

"It will take us several days to piece this together," Del Carlo told the press.

Making no mention of the pistol that had been slipped under the boxer's body, Del Carlo informed the news reporters that a .38 caliber pistol had been found in a holster inside the boxer's boot. The gun, he said, had not been fired.

When asked to explain more about the boot pistol, Del Carlo said he had no idea where the boxer got it, nor who owned it. He also informed those in attendance, that Bonavena, being an alien, could not legally carry a firearm.

He said the possibility of a link between Bonavena's slaying, the previous fire at his trailer home, and the threats allegedly made to Sally Conforte while they were in San Francisco, had to be considered.

Was the Mafia involved? The press wanted to know.

The sheriff was emphatic when he said the reports circulating about a Mafia connection to the shooting was unsubstantiated.

"If the Mafia were going to do this, they surely wouldn't do it in that particular light, in front of the world."

An autopsy was performed on Sunday, but a formal report was delayed pending completion of toxicological results. When contacted, Sheriff Del Carlo said it could take another week or so to get the results. The pathology reportedly includes several chemical tests which must be completed in laboratories out of state. And tissue samples have been sent to the medical examiner in Los Angeles, County, where electronic equipment available could identify a particular gun used which inflicted the wound.

Del Carlo also said that the Storey County Sheriff's Office did not have the man power to conduct an in-depth investigation, and indicated it may be necessary to call in a state agency. He concluded by saying they were looking into reports the shooting was linked to a marital dispute between the brothel owner, and his wife Sally, who had recently separated.

On the same day that Del Carlo was giving the interview, Vincente Bonavena, the late boxer's brother, arrived in Reno to claim the remains. Vincente, a professional soccer team manager in Buenos Aires, was met at the airport by Sgt. Bill Tilton.

Oscar Bonavena's body, peaceful in death, lie in an open casket in the funeral home. The Argentine ambassador from Washington DC, had sent an elaborate floral arrangement which draped over the casket. Other freshly cut bouquets sent by the Argentine counsel in San Francisco, and scores of mourners, lined the viewing area.

Vincente said since arriving in the United States, he'd learned little of the details surrounding his brother's death, and stressed that he had no accusations to make toward anyone. He told the media that the just wanted to retrieve his brother's body and return to Argentina as soon as possible.

He gave thanks to the Storey County officials for their "courteous and considerate treatment," and the Argentine Embassy in Washington, and the Counsel General, in San Francisco for their assistance.

"Particularly," he said, he "wanted to thank very much the American Ambassador in Argentina, who has helped us greatly."

On Tuesday evening, Sally Conforte sat quietly in the Reno airport terminal, as the casket holding the Argentine boxer, was prepared for flight—not to Argentina—but to Los Angeles. The body had been consigned to the Los Angeles County, coroner's officer, for "further investigation." Accompanying the flight, was the late boxer's brother, Vincente, and an agent of the Nevada Division of Investigation and Narcotics.

Dr. Thomas Noguchi, renowned pathologist at the Los Angeles County Coroner's Office, conducted a second autopsy on the boxer's body and issued his findings. Noguchi said the 30.06 rifle was probably the murder weapon, but because the bullet that pierced Bonavena's heart fragmented in the body, it would be of interest to match the fragments with the expended cartridge shell and other rounds found during the search of the premises.

After the required stopover in Los Angeles, Vincente Bonavena again renewed efforts to continue on to Buenos Aires, accompanying the coffin holding his deceased brother. Arriving in Buenos Aires, the body lie in state for 26 hours at the Luna Park Stadium, where the boxing ring normally rests, and where the popular fighter had scored many impressive victories.

Upwards of 150,000 persons filed past the flower bedecked coffin throughout the day to pay their last respects. Light heavyweight champion, Victor Galindez, middleweight champion, Carlos Monzon, and former Argentine President, Alejandro Lanusse, were among the notable.

Addressing the crowd, Lanusse said, "Bonavena had the wisdom of the sincere man, he was extremely unaffected. That is why I want and can consider myself his friend."

On Sunday morning, a funeral procession of nearly 40 vehicles, led by the solemn black hearse, left Luna Park, for the slow drive to Chacarita cemetery, where the national hero was laid to rest.

Chants of, "Ringo lives!" "Ringo is all heart," and "Argentina...Argentina," rose from the throngs, many of whom tossed flowers into the procession..

Covering the national event, the press reported that not since the burial of famed tango singer, Carlos Gardel, in 1935, had so many countrymen turned out to mourn one of their own. Like Bonavena, Gardel too, had been laid to rest in Chacarita cemetery.

Meanwhile, on Tuesday, Ross Brymer was officially arraigned in Storey County on a charge of open murder in the death of boxer Bonavena, and returned to the Nevada State Prison, on a no-bail hold. The preliminary hearing was scheduled for June 8.

After the brief court appearance, Sheriff Del Carlo seated at his desk in the Storey County Sheriff's Office, in Virginia City, fended off questions from the media.

"Joe Conforte is getting out on thin ice," he said. ""I'm wondering if the people of Virginia City are going to put up with this."

Reporters questioned him about his specific role in the investigation. He admitted that he was not a seasoned homicide investigator, but he said, the people who were handling the investigation were. The case was in their hands, he said, and he didn't know exactly how far they had progressed. The conversation moved toward Conforte's practice of hiring ex-felons. Del Carlo told the crowd that he told Conforte on Thursday, two days before the shooting, to get rid of Brymer. Brymer, being an ex-con, should not have been a hired gun for Conforte, Del Carlo said. Though Del Carlo did concede that he knew another ex-con working there as a bartender. He said he couldn't hold that against the bartender, because he certainly had a right to earn a living. But, Del Carlo said, this man works the bar, and is not a hired gun for Joe Conforte.

On Thursday, John Colletti, another Conforte bodyguard, was picked up in Martinez, California, on a warrant and returned to Nevada as a material witness. The warrant named him as one of Conforte's personal bodyguards, who was on duty the morning Bonavena was gunned down. Officials said Colletti was being held in lieu of $400,000 bail, set to ensure his appearance in court when needed.

The next day though, Virgil Bucchianeri, Storey County D.A., dropped both the warrant and the high bail, and then Colletti was immediately served with a federal subpoena to appear before a U.S. Grand Jury, in Reno the coming month, on another matter.

Colletti now became the object of threats. A caller phoned the Mustang Ranch and said, "If John Colletti doesn't get lost back in California, something real bad's gonna happen to him."

Nevertheless, Colletti was released on his own recognizance and ordered to appear at the Storey County Court, June 2, for a hearing scheduled to determine the possibility of bail for Ross Brymer.

Investigators concerned about the new round of threats, wanted to again question Conforte, but now were unable to locate him. Calls made to the Mustang Ranch were played off by Sally Conforte. No, she didn't know where he was. No, she could not contact him. No, he wasn't in town. Yes, he was probably out of the state.

When would he return?

She didn't know.

Stan Brown, Conforte's Reno lawyer, was contacted by a reporter, and queried as to Conforte's whereabouts. Brown replied that Conforte was in California, but would be coming back to Reno in a few days.

While he was gone though, Sally left no doubt as to who was running affairs at the Mustang. She disarmed the security forces first, by terminating employment of the four armed guards. She then hired four replacements. The newly hired guards were forbidden to carry firearms.

On June 2, Ross Brymer, under prison escort, and in chains, along with his attorney, Jerry Polaha, arrived at the Storey County Court house to argue the possibility of bail. Also in attendance, were Virgil Bucchianeri, Joe Conforte and John Colletti.

District Judge, Frank Gregory[3] listened as Polaha, cited a 1974 Nevada Supreme Court decision , the Louis St. Pierre case, that made bail possible on all murder charges except capital murder.

Bucchianeri, pointing to the state's possible witness, John Colletti, informed the judge that his witness's life could possibly be jeopardized if Ross Brymer were granted bail.

"The bail should be so high that it should minimize any threats to our witness."

Judge Gregory listened intently, and after the arguments, informed the court that "Brymer was an ex-felon, had illegally possessed a weapon, and that the court had to take into consideration possible jeopardy to an alleged eyewitness to the killing."

Judge Gregory then set bail in the amount of $250,000.

Outside of the courtroom, reporters pushed Conforte for answers. He was quick to say the slaying had been an act of self-defense on Brymer's part. Stan Brown, Conforte's attorney interrupted and cautioned his client not to say anything.. He warned him that the judge had placed a gag order on the witnesses and the district attorney involved in the case. To continue spouting off to the reporters, Brown told him was to invite a contempt of court charge.

As Conforte continued his verbal defense in front of the quizzing reporters, Brown grabbed his arm and hustled him away. Glancing over his shoulder, Brown pleaded with the reporters to withhold printing anything Conforte had said.

On Sunday the 30th, the same day that Bonavena was buried, the Los Angeles Coroners Office issued a press release relating to the Bonavena autopsy, and confirmed the 30.06 rifle used in the shooting, was indeed the murder weapon.

"The bullet fragments recovered from Oscar Bonavena's body have been analyzed by Dr. Noguchi at the Los Angeles Coroner's Office," began the report.

"Through use of scanning electron-microscope and X-ray analysis, Dr. Noguchi finds the metal elements and proportions to be consistent with the ammunition used in the suspect murder weapon, a 30.06 caliber rifle."

The release went on to say that the trajectory of the bullet and the characteristics of the entrance and exit wounds, indicated the boxer had been in a slightly crouched position when hit, and had died instantly.

As if driven by notoriety, and against the advice of his attorney, just two weeks after the slaying, Conforte sat for an interview by a reporter of the monthly Comstock newspaper, the Gold Hill News. A featured article appeared in the June issue:

"As far as I'm concerned, this man that died, it's nothing but justifiable homicide. If he hadn't been killed, he was headed for my room here to kill me.

"Now this Ross Brymer, he could be the worst man in the world. But he saved my life. And this will be brought out at the trial. If this man (Bonavena) hadn't died, I would be dead right now.

"He came here to kill me, is what he came here for. With a loaded gun in his boot. It was found in his boot. He came here to kill me.

"I was sleeping and the guard outside there begged the man to leave this place. He begged him for 10 minutes, because I had given orders not to let this man in here. I had given orders to everybody not to let this man in here.

"Because I knew if he'd have got in here somebody would have got shot. The guard that first confronted him at the gate begged him for 10 minutes to leave the place and son of a bitch wouldn't leave. Well, don't call him a son of a bitch because he's dead, that's the only reason. But he wouldn't leave. He wanted trouble.

"He wanted to shoot somebody. He was telling everybody for weeks that he was the new owner of this place. And he was telling them, see, 'You work for me pretty soon. I kill Joe, you work for me pretty soon'

"Then, when he insisted on coming in—and he reached for his revolver—is when they let him have it. That's exactly what happened. Now this man Brymer, after he shot Bonavena, he came up—by that time I was awake; after the man was dead, they woke me up.

"And by the way, I'm glad they woke me up after he was dead. Because if he hadn't been dead, I would have been dead. In other words, I would have had to confront him if they'd woke me up before.

"So after he shot him, by that time I was up, a few minutes later and he came to me and he says, 'Joe, what should I do?'

"I says, 'There's only one thing to do. Just wait here and I'm going to call the district attorney and the sheriff and the coroner and as soon as they get down here, you give yourself up.' And that's exactly what this man did. Nothing else. I made the call myself for the sheriff and the district attorney to get here.

"We asked for the state to come in on the investigation because then they can't say it was a whitewash if the guy does get exonerated. We wanted the state to come in. I asked for the state to come in. I don't mean that they're going to do what I say, but I did ask for them to come in.

"And I was the one who asked for Brymer to be put in the Nevada State Prison, so they don't think we're going to give him special treatment or something. And I could bail Brymer out right now if I wanted to.

"You know any judge is going to give him bail on an incident like that. But no, we prefer that he stays in there so he don't get in any more trouble. Now you know that this offense is bailable. It's not a capital offense. It's not premeditated murder. Anybody can see that it's not premeditated murder. He didn't ask for it, the other guy came here. I could bail him out in two minutes. But I want the truth to come out and I want to see that there's no special treatment in this case.

"Nobody's denying that there was bad blood between that guy and I. But nobody asked him to come here and shoot me! He came here to shoot me! Instead, he got shot. I never hurt anybody in my life. You prove that I ever hurt something in my life and I'll give you this place."

Tiring of defending himself, and Brymer, he now attacked the Reno newspapers.

"The Reno papers are after me because I'm the only man that ever stood up to them. That's why. Everybody else is afraid of them.

Everybody else shakes when they mention their names. I don't shake. Joe Conforte don't shake. The Reno newspapers as far as I'm concerned are nothing but garbage and you can quote me on that."

He also had something to say about television and other newspapers.

"The televisions have been beautiful with me, perfect. They have been very, very fair. Every other newspaper has been very fair to me."

(Reprinted through the courtesy of the Gold Hill News, Virginia City, Nevada)

Reading Conforte's account in the Gold Hill News, one had to wonder.

Was it truly self defense?

A eight-foot high iron-barbed fence stood between Oscar Bonavena and the Mustang security officers.

Was it premeditated?

Had other sinister forces sent the boxer on a mission to whack Joe Conforte?

If Bonavena had been admitted past the fence, would he have gunned down the sleeping brothel owner?

Did Bonavena truly desire Sally Conforte, a woman old enough to be his mother?

Who was the true owner of the pistol found in Bonavena's boot?

And lastly, was the Sicilian Mafia involved?

One man knew the answers to all these questions. And he wasn't talking. He was being held in isolation in a cramped cell in C-Block, Nevada State Prison: Williard Ross Brymer.

Chapter Eight
WILLARD ROSS BRYMER

Willard Ross Brymer, was born in Houston, Texas, on April 7, 1945. While still a child, his family moved to Reno. During his formative years, he attended Reno schools, dropping out of high school in the tenth grade.

Standing in a crowd, it would be difficult not to see him. He stood out. The barrel-chested, iron worker towered over others and weighed in around 260 pounds. His jet black hair hugged his neck and ears. One of the most striking features other than his imposing stature, was a right eye which roamed by itself, and which had limited vision.

At thirty-one years old, three-time loser, Brymer had seen the seedier side of life, and had done time in the Nevada State Prison, on marijuana and assault charges. He had a difficult time staying out of trouble. Merely a week prior to the Oscar Bonavena slaying, he had been arrested by the Washoe County Sheriff's Office, just across the Storey County line, on a charge of brandishing a weapon, and two counts of battery.

The first day of the preliminary hearing for Ross Brymer, was held on Tuesday, June 9, in the Storey County courthouse. Brymer, under escort by several officers, was dressed in a dark suit and an open collar white shirt. His wrists were secured tightly by a chain restraint locked around his waist. A similar chain was attached to his ankles.

Thirty curious spectators crowded into the aged Storey County Justice Court chambers, to listen to the first witness called, Sgt. Bill Tilton, Storey County Deputy, and deputy coroner. Tilton had been the first law officer to arrive at the scene of the Mustang Ranch shooting that early Saturday morning..

As proceedings began, Tilton was asked to recreate the events that transpired after he arrived at the Mustang Ranch. He began by saying, that as soon as he arrived at the ranch, he secured the scene, allowing nobody to enter or leave. While awaiting the arrival of the sheriff and undersheriff, Tilton testified, he was approached by Lloyd "Mac" McNulty, chief of security at the ranch. McNulty advised him that the boxer was dead, and that he, McNulty, had planted a gun under the dead boxer's body.

What happened next?

About this time, Undersheriff, Jim Miller, and Sheriff Bob Del Carlo, pulled into the parking lot. After getting out of their vehicle, the two walked over to where the dead boxer lie. Bonavena was lying on his back, staring upward with lifeless eyes. Miller began a routine check of the boxer's body, and let out a low whistle when he found, concealed in the left boot, a holstered .38 caliber snub-nose pistol.

Surprised at the concealed pistol in the boot, Tilton told the undersheriff that they'd probably find a second gun under the body. Miller looked at him quizzically.

"McNulty told me he'd put a gun under the body," the sergeant explained.

Continuing his testimony, Tilton said, at that point, Sheriff Del Carlo, raised his eyes and asked his sergeant, "Did he?"

"I don't know," Tilton replied, "I haven't touched him."

Del Carlo inquired of Tilton why McNulty would have planted a gun under Bonavena's body.

"I don't know," the sergeant said, but "I told him he made only one mistake, telling it to an honest cop."

Tilton then gazed out at the crowded courtroom, and related how Miller had rolled the body over on its left side, and found another handgun, right where McNulty said they would. Had McNulty been charged with planting a throw-away gun under Bonavena's body? Judge Gregory wanted to know.

"I'm not going around charging people," Bucchianeri explained, "and have 50 million lawyers on my back. We have plenty of time to charge people. Besides he (McNulty) is a crucial witness."

Two Mustang employees were then sworn in, and in turn, testified that after the shooting,

Brymer admitted to them both that he had shot the boxer.

They also testified that on the morning of the shooting, they'd been outside and heard Bonavena threaten to kill Joe Conforte.

John Colletti, the Conforte bodyguard who'd been brought back from Martinez, California, to testify, took the stand next. Colletti testified that on the morning of the killing, he had been arguing with Bonavena who was outside the fence, and wanted in. Colletti said they'd been arguing for about 10 minutes, and since Bonavena was outside the controlled gate, he (Colletti) turned to walk back inside. Suddenly, he said, he heard a shout, "FREEZE!" Followed by the sharp report of a high powered rifle cracking through the early morning dawn. He turned sharply to his right, and saw Brymer who was standing near the fence, holding a 30.06 hunting rifle.

Colletti, at that time turned back toward the brothel and ran inside. He was joined soon after by Brymer, who was coming in and was still holding the deer rifle. Colletti asked him if he'd shot Bonavena, and Brymer answered, "Yeah...Yeah...Yeah."

Listening intently to Colletti's testimony, were two of the deceased boxer's brothers, Vicente and Juan, who had flown in to watch the proceedings. Sitting with them, was Sally Conforte.

At 10:40 a.m., Sally appeared ill and was helped out of the courtroom by another woman. Vicente Bonavena followed her out. They did not return that day.

The next day, Wednesday, Undersheriff, Jim Miller was put on the stand. He testified he'd found a small pistol on the pavement, under the left side of the boxer's body. He described it as a loaded, blue-steel, .38 caliber revolver with a three-inch barrel.

Quoting Lloyd "Mac" McNulty, the Undersheriff told the courtroom that McNulty had claimed to be the owner of the gun (which proved to be untrue) found under Bonavena's body. When asked how it ended up where it did, under the boxer's bloody body, McNulty said when he bent over the body to take a pulse, the gun fell out of his waist band and onto the pavement. He then testified that when that happened, he slid it under the body.

When asked to explain why he slid it under the body, McNulty replied he was fearful that other persons in the vicinity who were watching, and who didn't see the gun drop, might think he was taking the gun from the body, so instead, he acted as he did.

Had the weapons been traced? Miller said both of the pistols found on the deceased, were traced to Sally Conforte. Bonavena had no license to carry a concealed weapon. Bonavena's car, which was parked in the parking lot, was searched, Miller said. Inside, a white envelope, with the name "Sally" written on the front, was retrieved from under the seat. Inside the envelope, several .38 caliber bullets were found.

Miller told the court that the 30.06 rifle used to kill Bonavena, turned out to be owned by John Colletti.

Dan Nucholls, an agent with the state Identification and Communications Division, testified that the weapons were all clean of fingerprints. The only print he'd recovered was a palm print taken from the boot weapon. But he had no way to compare it with the boxer's because during the autopsy, only fingerprints were taken—no palm prints had been done.

Brymer's attorney, Jerry Polaha, declined to put his client on the witness stand, or to offer any evidence to refute the earlier testimony.

As the prelim concluded, Willard Ross Brymer was ordered to stand trial in Storey County District Court, on an open murder charge in the slaying of Argentine heavyweight boxer, Oscar Bonavena. Visiting Carson City Judge, Frank Gregory, was named to handle all future court matters. The arraignment date was set for July 16.

On June 2, Ross Brymer, under prison escort, and in chains, along with his attorney, Jerry Polaha, arrived at the Storey County Courthouse to argue the possibility of bail. Also in attendance, were Virgil Bucchianeri, Joe Conforte and John Colletti.

District Judge, Frank Gregory, listened as Polaha, cited a 1974 Nevada Supreme Court decision , the Louis St. Pierre case, that made bail possible on all murder charges except capital murder. Bail was then set in the amount of $250,000.

Brymer was ordered to remain in custody until such time as bail could be posted. As he was led out of the courtroom by the officer escorts, the reporters asked him what he thought of the hearing. He tried waving a hand which was held in place by the waist restraints, and told them he was innocent and would be acquitted.

On Wednesday, June 23, 1976, Joe Conforte put up his Cabin In The Sky restaurant, as collateral for the $250,000 bail required to free Brymer until trial. After being released from the Nevada State Prison, Brymer and Conforte met briefly and spoke in hushed tones. The two longtime associates, then got in a limousine and sped away.

On July 16, Brymer, accompanied by his attorney, Jerry Polaha, appeared for the arraignment before Judge Frank Gregory in the Storey County District Court. Polaha argued that the judge should issue a writ of habeas corpus to dismiss charges against his client. In his arguments, Polaha contended that Brymer should not have been bound over from Justice Court to stand trial because there was insufficient evidence.

Judge Gregory ruled against this, but did grant a continuance and set a new date for the arraignment, August 20.

On that date, Brymer and Polaha again stood before Judge Gregory. Brymer entered a plea of innocent. Polaha filed for a writ of habeas corpus to free his client, again citing insufficient evidence. There was nothing to tie him to the shooting, Polaha told the court. Nothing that was brought out in the lower court could show that Brymer had fired the weapon that killed Bonavena, he argued. Nor was it shown that the rifle seen in Brymer's hands, was actually the murder weapon. And lastly, no one had actually seen Brymer fire the weapon.

Polaha brought with him to court, a medical skeleton with which he hoped to demonstrate the angle of the bullet that struck the boxer. He wanted to point out that the bullet which killed Bonavena, entered the chest near the third rib and exited at the tenth rib. Polaha told the judge that according to statements made by witnesses, Brymer was standing 25-30 yards away, holding a rifle at his hip. If so, he argued, there was no way the bullet could have taken the downward angle that it did.

District Attorney, Virgil Bucchianeri testified that evidence brought out at the preliminary hearing showed Brymer allegedly admitted the killing to at least one witness. And at least one witness testified that Brymer had been handed the rifle by one of the Mustang handymen. Further, he had been seen holding the weapon immediately after Bonavena was shot.

"Not all killings are punishable as crimes," Polaha countered.

In conclusion, Judge Gregory said there was ample testimony indicating Brymer was in possession of a high powered rifle on the morning of the shooting, and that the defendant had made a statement that he'd shot the boxer. He then denied the motion to dismiss the murder charge against Brymer, and set May 2, 1977, as the date for the trial, which would be nearly a year from the date of the shooting.

But May 2, did not happen for Brymer. On that day, Judge Frank Gregory was starting a court hearing being held for two prison inmates, accused in the murder of two others in the maximum security prison's culinary. The Brymer trial was put off until October 3, 1977.

On October 3, the long awaited trial finally got underway. And right from the start, Brymer's attorney, Jerry Polaha, challenged the jury selection. Polaha said the panel subpoenaed for the trial excluded residents of the Mustang Ranch-Lockwood area. He reinforced his argument by saying that prospective jurors from the nearby Truckee River voting area, adjacent to Lockwood, included only 13 of the 40 who were eligible to serve. The majority of jurors, he told Judge Gregory, came from the Virginia City area (where the trial was to take place), a community not quite friendly to Joe Conforte.

What did he mean by this?

Polaha explained to the judge that he'd previously taken a pretrial survey of residents living in Virginia City. The survey showed a majority of eligible voters living there would be more likely to harbor anti-Conforte sentiments, than those of the Lockwood area who live next door to the brothel.

Judge Gregory asked Virgil Bucchianeri, the prosecuting district attorney, to respond to the allegations. Bucchianeri explained that it would be too expensive to bring up a mass of voters from the Truckee River region. The river area contains a "large transient population," he told the judge, including a multitude of ranch prostitutes, which presents a difficult problem when trying to sequester a jury. He told the judge he feels prostitutes have every right to vote like any other citizen, but when paneling a jury, "it is entirely too difficult and too expensive to try and track these people down."

He was interrupted by Judge Gregory who admonished him that it made no difference how difficult it was to subpoena jurors from that part of the county, if "it appears some favoritism or partiality were shown." Because, he reminded Bucchianeri, this could confirm Polaha's challenge. The judge then recessed the matter until that afternoon.

Polaha's next challenge was directed against the Nevada Division of Investigation and Narcotics—DIN (who had been called in by Sheriff Del Carlo, to assist in the investigation). He told the judge that DIN had not filed all the names and addresses and potential testimony of witnesses the state agency had spoken to.

Just the night before, Polaha explained to the judge, he had learned of a witness who told him agents of DIN had talked to him and instructed him not to speak to anyone on the Brymer defense team. Polaha went on to tell the judge that during the prelim which was held on June 6, 1976, he had been supplied with—what he thought—was a complete list of potential witnesses, but now he learned there may be additional witnesses who had remained unnamed until now.

For this reason, he told the judge, he now was seeking a postponement of the trial until these allegations could be either confirmed or refuted.

Bucchianeri stood up to tell the judge that he had no intention of calling any witnesses the defense hadn't been advised of.

"I intend to proceed with the witnesses I have," Bucchianeri told the judge in measured tones. "I don't know—never heard of these witnesses, can't know what they intend to say. For that reason, I don't intend to use them."

The district attorney though, quickly qualified his statements, and said he reserved the option of calling rebuttal witnesses at the last minute, if he deemed it necessary.

In his ruling, Judge Gregory denied the motion for postponement, but he did order agents from DIN, to "make full disclosure to the defense under oath, of names and addresses of all witnesses interviewed by them in this matter with a brief summary of their testimony." This was to be completed, the judge warned them, within 24 hours.

Court was recessed until the following morning.

On Tuesday, the slow process of selecting the jury continued. Throughout the day, throngs of prospective jurors had been interviewed; and at least 25 had been excused and only three seated. Curiously, the three who were seated all came from the Truckee River area, near where the brothel was located.

Sharply dressed in a western style blue suit, defendant Brymer sat calmly throughout the proceedings occasionally taking notes, and frequently directing his attention toward the prospective jurors who were being questioned in turn. He was permitted to move about freely in the high-ceilinged court room, but limited his conversation to his attorney.

The next day, Wednesday, the continuation of the jury selection was delayed for an hour because Brymer failed to show up in the morning at the appointed hour of 10:00 a.m. He strolled into the courtroom an hour late explaining to the judge that his alarm clock had failed to go off.

Unruffled, Judge Gregory announced to the court that the defendant's tardiness could be overlooked. The jury selection for the third day, then began with the prosecutor and defense attorneys questioning prospective jurors.

Each side was limited to eight preemptory challenges. Curiously, the prosecuting district attorney never used his challenges when several Lockwood area jurors were questioned and seated. Three of those, admitted during questioning that they had known the defendant when they all lived in the Lockwood trailer court, owned by Joe Conforte.

In response to Polaha's questioning, those jurors seated so far, said neither Conforte's involvement, nor Brymer's association with the brothel, would influence their reaching a verdict.

After the tedious process of seating the first seven jurors, the selection began taking on the appearance of a *stacked jury*. Six of the seven were from the Lockwood trailer court area. To add to this, a former state senator, James Slattery, admitted that during his 18 year tenure in the senate, he had received campaign "help" from Joe Conforte. He was seated as juror number-eight.

What were Polaha's thoughts as to how the jury was stacking up?

"I'm pleased with it," he said, "I couldn't say otherwise."

At one point during the questioning, one prospective juror told the judge that Conforte's close association with the defendant, would affect his ability to work toward an objective verdict.

"Are you aware the brothel is legally licensed under an ordinance of Storey County?" The steely-eyed judge inquired. "And are you aware also that Joe Conforte is not on trial here?"

The juror was excused.

Another Virginia City resident said he had bad feelings about Jim Miller, the undersheriff, who would be a star witness.

"I don't trust him and I don't want to have anything to do with him," he stated flatly.

For the first time in the jury selection, Bucchianeri used a challenge "with cause" (which did not count as a preemptory challenge) and dismissed the man.

After court was adjourned for the day, Bucchianeri was asked why he hadn't challenged any of the Lockwood jurors. He answered their questions by saying none had indicated any impartiality when questioned. But, he told the crowd, he may use some of the preemptory challenges Thursday, to unseat some of them.

On Thursday morning, the jury selection was in its fourth day of arduous screening, and it appeared the jury would be seated today. Early in the afternoon, a youthful construction worker from Virginia City was questioned. During routine questioning, he was asked if he were related to anyone in law enforcement. He replied in the affirmative and said Jerry Wilke, a Sparks Police Captain, was his brother-in-law.

He was asked by Polaha if Conforte's role in the case would prejudice him against Brymer.

"If Mr. Conforte is going to be a witness in this trial and he's shaking hands and putting his arms around jurors, I'm going to have to take it into consideration, " he blurted out. "How is it he's allowed to be amongst us potential jurors?"

Obviously taken aback by this juror's revelation, the judge asked, "Did you see this behavior on the part of Mr. Conforte with people in the jury box?"

The youth cleared his throat and said, well, yes, he had seen Conforte socializing with a woman juror, but he'd only seen it one time. He did not identify the woman.

Judge Gregory then looked squarely at the jurors seated in the box, and asked each one if they were aware of the youth's incrimination.

One lady rose to her feet and identified herself as a co-manager of Joe Conforte's Lockwood trailer court.

"I spoke to Mr. Conforte before I was seated on the jury," she offered.

Conforte was then asked if this were true. He told the judge he'd only patted her on the arm (he later denied this)

The judge now directed his remarks back to the lady who was still standing.

"I would think that's only natural. You are the manager of his trailer court."

Now the other Lockwood jurors entered the fray. Another trailer court resident volunteered that he'd said hello to the brothel owner when they were in the hallway.

This prompted another juror, a woman, who arose and said, "I stood and talked to him at lunchtime...but only in passing."

A man then stood up and said to the judge, "I waved hi," to him this morning outside the court.

Exasperated, the judge then called a hasty conference of the attorneys in his chambers. When they emerged, the judge again took his seat and scowled at the courtroom. He informed the court that the incident was "inadvertent, not willful, and not intentional.

"Nevertheless," he said, "it creates an atmosphere that could conceivably raise the question of the jury's ability to be impartial."

As if apologizing for the turn of events, he said, "I find no fault with any of us; it's simply one of those things that happens that forces the court to do that which is most distasteful to us. In this case, I must declare a mistrial."

With that, he dismissed the jury panel. Bond for Brymer was to remain at $250,000 he told the court. He thanked everyone for their participation and patience, and then retreated to his chambers.

In explaining the reasons for the mistrial, the judge said he didn't regard Conforte's actions as jury tampering (which is a felony), but because Conforte did create an "inference of jury-tampering," there was no other alternative but to declare a mistrial.

"And because of this," the judge explained, "...we've got to be as circumspect as possible that the defendant gets a fair trial and that the state also gets a fair trial."

Reporters then converged on the youthful juror whose testimony prompted the mistrial. Responding to their questions, he told them how he played basketball and socialized with many of the Sparks policemen. He told them flatly he felt no pressure from his role in ending the trial, but emphasized that because of the events inside the courtroom, he felt he had no choice but to bring it out in the open.

Ross Brymer, who had been waiting 18 months for the trial to begin, was obviously dejected. He huddled out of earshot with his attorney, Jerry Polaha, for several minutes, and then began to walk away.

Polaha took a few moments to tell the reporters he was not happy with the mistrial, in view of the fact he and his client had been waiting a year and a half for the trial to begin. The district attorney, Bucchianeri, who had been listening quietly, offered his feelings and said he felt let down. But, he said, it would not have been in the best interest of Storey County to go to trial with a cloud of jury tampering hanging overhead.

Conforte, who had been pacing up and down in front of the courthouse was loudly proclaiming any idea of impropriety. He barked at the reporters saying many members of the jury were friends of his, people he was acquainted with—tenants of his trailer parks. What was he supposed to do?

"They said hello to me first," he bellowed. "That's as far as it went."

The spectators who had gathered outside the courtroom seemed to support Conforte's actions. A few of them, mostly white-haired locals, approached him shaking hands and patting his back. Conforte grinned widely and continued chatting with the reporters.

Maria Laura Avignolo, of the Argentine paper, "Gente," had been covering the Brymer murder trial in the Virginia City courthouse. Following the mistrial, on Friday, Ms. Avignolo said she expected to see the Argentines were going to be upset to learn of the mistrial in the death of their national hero. She said mistrials do not exist in the Argentine legal system, and some of her countrymen may regard the Virginia City mistrial an improper delay of justice.

Ms. Avignolo revealed to the local press that her paper had known back in May or June that Sally Conforte had visited Bonavena's family in Buenos Aires, ostensibly trying to negotiate a settlement following a $7.1 million dollar civil suit they'd filed against Joe and Sally Conforte, and Ross Brymer for the wrongful death.

When Joe Conforte was told of the Argentine paper's assertion of a Sally Conforte payoff, he became outraged and said there was no truth to it. He said it was obviously a cheap trick of the paper to sell more issues.

Chapter Nine

THE LONG ARM OF THE LAW

Prior to the aborted October 3rd trial in Virginia City, Joe and Sally Conforte had been pulled up in front of U.S. District Judge, Bruce Thompson, on an income tax evasion charge. The feds had been tracking their payroll reports and concluded the Conforte's had been evading withholding and Social Security taxes on maids, security guards, and other non-prostitute brothel workers. Both Confortes had been free on $40,000 bail each.

The matter was heard on September 16, 1977, before Judge Bruce R. Thompson, in U.S. District Court in Reno. Joe and Sally claimed in their defense, that the wages paid to the workers actually came from the prostitutes, therefore, the ranch workers did not work for the Confortes; they worked for the prostitutes.

The judge, after deliberation, dismissed six counts of the ten-count indictment, however; he found the two defendants guilty of four counts of evading employee wage taxes on the workers in question. Judge Thompson said the evidence was overwhelming that the Confortes destroyed financial records at the brothel, which he described as "a big tax rip-off."

On October 28, three weeks after the aborted Virginia City trial, Joe Conforte and Sally arrived at the U.S. District Court for sentencing. Joe was dressed in a stylish dark suit and tie. Sally, appearing overweight and feeble, wore a long fur coat open in front. Nearing her sixties, the career brothel madam walked unsteady into the courthouse. A cane held in her right hand helped to maintain her balance.

Joe was the first to address the judge. Conforte told the court that the name of Bruce R. Thompson, was renowned in Nevada for fairness. In baseball terms, he said, the judge had a fairness batting average of 1000. And facing the judge squarely, he intoned, "And

I hope it continues to be 1000 after these proceedings."

Judge Thompson now stared hard at the nattily dressed defendant.

"That isn't going to do you any good," he cautioned, "and you may not think so when this is over."

Conforte tried to continue the baseball analogy but the judge motioned for him to get on with his other statements..

The defendant then switched lanes and conferred with his tax attorney, Bruce Hockman. Joe told the judge that he'd received a letter back in 1972 from the Internal Revenue Service, in which they advised him to start withholding taxes on the non-prostitute brothel workers. He told the judge that he put the letter in the hands of his tax attorney at the time, Clyde Maxwell. Maxwell never advised him to start the withholding process until June of last year, he said

Now, Conforte assumed the role of a philanthropist explaining to the judge that he was an "easy touch" for money. He has, he told the judge, probably given away a million dollars to charities, and needy causes, not to mention others who had the courage to ask him for money. That is not the act of a man who cheats the government out of a few dollars in taxes so he can give away that much more, he added.

Judge Thompson was not swayed.

"I think all of us would be more generous and philanthropic if we didn't have to pay our taxes," he smiled. "At least we would be able to be."

Las Vegas Attorney, Harry Claiborne, then addressed the judge in Sally's defense, and told him that the evidence of Mrs. Conforte's complicity, "was very very thin," and she was convicted solely on the basis of being Joe Conforte's wife.

Without excess oration, Judge Thompson then faced the two standing defendants. He explained to them and the attorneys that the sentences he was about to hand down were structured in such a way that they would be subject to modification by a higher court, contingent upon the higher court's finding that the defendants did indeed have a right to withhold details of the brothel's cash flow.

The significant question that had to be answered, the judge said, was whether any taxpayer involved in a cash business such as a brothel can file tax returns stating an arbitrary amount of taxes and then refuse to supply documentation.

The judge then sentenced Joe Conforte to five years on each count, to run consecutively, a total of 20 years in federal prison and a $10,000 fine on each count totaling, $40,000.

Sally got off lighter. She too, was fined a total of $40,000, but was given a four year sentence on each count. However, her sentences were to run concurrently, which meant a maximum of four years in prison. The judge then advised her was taking into account her lack of a serious criminal record, and her failing health. He then withdrew the prison time and placed her on probation. Terms of the probation were that she file complete tax returns for the brothel or any other business that she may acquire.

Judge Thompson noted that with this conviction, Joe Conforte was now a three-time loser in Nevada. However; this fact was not significant in his handing down a 20 year sentence, he insisted, since the current felony would have had to been filed under the federal habitual criminal statutes.

Also, Judge Thompson postponed the sentences until such time as a higher court could review the case. He allowed the Confortes to remain free on bail of $40,000 each, which coincidentally was the amount of the fines he'd imposed. Bail was arranged so it would revert back to the court to satisfy the fines, and not be returned to the Confortes.

The well paid attorneys for both Confortes immediately notified the court of their intentions to file appeals right on up to the Supreme Court if necessary. This could be a lengthy process and they were determined to keep Joe out of prison for as long as possible. Joe and Sally walked on out past a plethora of news reporters and said nothing.

As the Confortes were being dressed down by the federal judicial system, a federal grand jury meeting in Reno, in 1977, had been looking hard at Ross Brymer, who was still awaiting trial on the Bonavena slaying.

The grand jury had been delving into events following a robbery of the First National Bank branch, at Second and Virginia Streets in Reno, on June 14, 1976,[1] by a convicted bank robber, Robert E. Mitchell.

A federal indictment accused Brymer of warning Mitchell that he should flee the area because he was being sought by federal agents, and with providing Mitchell with phony identification.

In addition to this, the indictment also accused Brymer of

"offering, from November the 9th, through the 22nd, 1976, to hide Mitchell, to provide Mitchell with a map showing a hideout in Mina, Nevada, and providing Mitchell with another map, showing a potential hideout in the Nevada ghost town of Marietta."

In December, 1976, Mitchell was arrested by the FBI, in Marietta, charged with conspiring to rob and aiding and abetting in the robbery of the Reno bank. Four months later he was tried and found guilty, along with two other defendants, Benjamin Pavane, then one of the FBI's 10 most wanted men, and a Cincinnati lawyer, Arthur Clark. Mitchell and Pavane were subsequently convicted of other bank robberies in the San Francisco bay area.

Ross Brymer was named as an accessory to the bank robbery and was ordered to stand trial. If found guilty, he could be imprisoned for up to ten years. On November 3, 1977, U.S. District Judge, Bruce Thompson, issued a bench warrant for Brymer's arrest, and the U.S. Marshalls were told to bring him in.

The next day, Friday, Ross Brymer was brought in and appeared before a federal magistrate, to be served with an indictment charging him with being an accessory to the Reno bank robbery.

Magistrate Harold O. Taber, set Brymer's bail at $10,000 and ordered him arraigned before Judge Bruce Thompson, on November 11.

The trial on the accessory to bank robbery charge for Brymer got under way on Wednesday, January 4, 1978, in U.S. District Court in Reno, presided over by Judge Bruce Thompson. Jury selection progressed smoothly and by 10:20 a.m., the jury had been seated.

In his opening statement, U.S. Attorney, Raymond Pike said he would prove that Brymer sided with and abetted in the robbery of the First National Bank of Nevada, at Virginia and Second Street in Reno. He said he would also prove that Brymer aided suspect Robert E. Mitchell, in eluding federal authorities.

Quoting Brymer, Pike told the court that Brymer had said to Mitchell, "The feds are in the area. I decked a policeman who was asking questions; you've got to get out of here."

On the second day of the trial, Brymer, wearing a checkered sport coat, and tie, and with his dark wavy hair combed neatly in place, was accompanied by his long time attorney, Jerry Polaha.

Polaha addressed the jury and told them the feds were after Brymer, only because he was Ross Brymer, not because he'd helped a fugitive.

"This is not a fair prosecution," he said in his opening statement.

Polaha said he would offer evidence that Brymer intended to help Mitchell secure employment—and not to hide from federal agents, as the prosecutor claimed.

The first witness the prosecutors put on the stand, was none other than Robert E. Mitchell, the convicted bank robber, who had made a deal with the feds to become a government witness and testify against Brymer.

Mitchell testified that while he was still hiding out, he returned to Reno in October, 1976, and phoned Brymer who was staying in Mina. He told the court he pleaded with Brymer for help saying he was hot and he needed a place to hide out. After speaking to Brymer, he said, he caught a bus to Mina and met Brymer there.

In Mina, for a while, he stayed at Brymer's house. Then, Brymer drove him to Marietta, a desolate ghost town, where there was an old miner's trailer and which he used as a hideout.

Mitchell's testimony, appeared very damaging.

The defense's first witness was a Mustang Ranch employee, Debbie Sterling.

Ms. Sterling testified that sometime in November, 1976, Brymer and Mitchell were visiting her in her Reno apartment. She said that during the visit with the two men, which lasted about one or two hours, she never once heard Mitchell say "I am hot," nor did she hear anything that would indicate to her that Mitchell was in trouble with the law.

The witness continued her testimony and stressed that all Mitchell's talk that day centered upon his marital troubles, and his need to find work. She said Brymer was able to hook him up with a construction job site in Mina, and then she and Brymer took him to the bus depot, where he boarded a bus for that tiny town.

In his opening arguments, Polaha told the court when Brymer found out Mitchell was wanted, he went to Marietta and confronted the bank robber.

"I think you're lying to us," Polaha quoted Brymer accusing Mitchell, "and you're not going to get me in trouble."

Mitchell was recalled to the stand, and during questioning, he said he'd never explained to Brymer, exactly why he was hot. When the prosecutor pressed him for details, Mitchell said he and Brymer had served time together, and in the joint the prisoner's code is not to discuss your crime with others. This unwritten code is also respected on the streets, Mitchell said.

Mitchell, under cross examination by Polaha, testified he thought Brymer had been the person who'd turned him in. Polaha used this admission to suggest to the jury that this was the reason Mitchell had turned state's witness trying to convict Brymer. Further, Mitchell revealed that he felt there was a contract on his life in the state prison.

Mitchell also said that while in prison, he worked as a "jail house lawyer," but on the outside, he said he was a bank robber.

"It pays more, " he grinned.

Another government witness Betty Kidwell, of Reno, said she'd known Brymer for 25 years. She told the court she'd called Brymer to alert him about "Mitch," and told him not to harbor him because the FBI was looking for him for a bank robbery.

On Thursday, Brymer was put on the stand and admitted helping the fugitive, but insisted that Mitchell had never mentioned being "hot." Brymer said all he had done was try to help an ex-con with family problems.

Refuting the testimony of Betty Kidwell, who'd testified she had tried to warn Brymer of Mitchell's status, Brymer said the only reason she'd called him was to report Mitchell had stolen her television set. The FBI, he said, was only mentioned in passing. And actually, Brymer said, when the lady had called, Mitchell was already housed in Marietta.

On Friday, Polaha opened his closing arguments by saying the government indicted Brymer only because they felt he would never be tried on the Bonavena slaying charge. He made a point that Brymer had only been indicted on the robbery accessory charge, after the Bonavena case had been declared a mistrial in Virginia City, last October. The government, said Polaha, had all its evidence as far back as December, 1976, but did nothing with it until the mistrial. The government targeted the man by trying to get something on him, and the flimsy Mitchell case was all they could come up with.

The real question, the lawyer said, was whether the Kidwell

phone call in which she mentioned the FBI, was in reality, ample reason for Brymer to notify the FBI about a fugitive from justice. The law, he argued, is clear on the point that a defendant must have positive knowledge that a subject he tries to help, has actually committed a crime.

In Brymer's case, he continued, the government tried to bend the law by saying the defendant need only have knowledge of a "high probability" of a crime having been committed.

The prosecutor, Ray Pike, then addressed the jury and tried to clarify the government's position. Pike told the jurors that they could convict the defendant if they concluded from Mitchell's or Betty Kidwell's testimonies, that Brymer had made a conscious effort to avoid learning the true status of Mitchell. Such an effort, Pike said, amounts to the same thing as aiding a fugitive.

The case was then sent to the jury.

Usually, a quick verdict works in the defendant's favor. And this one today was no exception. After deliberating for less than two hours, the jury brought in a verdict of "not guilty."

Brymer thanked his attorney and walked out of the courtroom a free man. Free, at least, until he got over the hurdle of the Bonavena slaying.

On Brymer's mind, was a letter that Virgil Bucchianeri had made public two years earlier. A letter written by Oscar Bonavena that the district attorney said he would use as evidence to convict Brymer when the case was finally tried.

The boxer had written the letter two days before his death, and had given it to the Argentine embassy while he and Sally were in San Francisco. In it, the letter outlined Bonavena's fears of being killed. He said in the letter, that if anything happened to him, Joe Conforte should be held responsible, because the brothel owner had once threatened his life. Bucchianeri refused to release further details, but indicated they would be presented to the jury during the retrial which was scheduled for March 6, 1978. This never ocurred.

On the morning of February 17, 1978, Ross Brymer appeared at the Storey County courthouse where he entered a surprise pleas of "no contest" to a reduced charge of voluntary manslaughter in the death of Argentine heavyweight boxing figure, Oscar Bonavena.

This surprise move, in front of Judge Frank Gregory, was the result of plea negotiations carried out by Brymer's attorney, Jerry Polaha and Virgil Bucchianeri, district attorney of Storey County.

Bucchianeri told the judge that he doubted he could have won a murder verdict during a lengthy trial. Bonavena had been armed when shot, the district attorney said, making it difficult to prove first degree murder. He also advised the judge there could be problems sequestering a jury, as there had been in the first scheduled trial. With the plea negotiations, he explained to the judge, a costly trial could be avoided.

Judge Gregory, listened as both sides appeared to be in accord. The judge then set the date of March 10, for an evidentiary hearing prior to sentencing the brothel guard.

Brymer was asked what he thought of the no contest plea to the voluntary manslaughter charge.

"It doesn't rest easy with me," he answered. However, he also said he was glad to see the case coming to a close, and without the necessity of going through a trial on a murder charge.

On March 10, all parties again faced Judge Gregory. Polaha pointed out that Brymer was partially blind in his right eye, and had little experience with firearms.

"The gun went off in my hands," Brymer testified. "Oscar Bonavena looked at me. To my satisfaction the gun went off over his head. He looked at me. I looked at him. I wasn't aware he was shot until he grabbed his chest."

Brymer insisted he was under no orders to shoot the boxer.

"I did not at any time have the death of the man in my heart," he said. "The only reason I had a gun was because I knew that Oscar Bonavena was armed."

Other testimony confirmed that Bonavena was carrying the small revolver in his boot, and that Brymer thought the boxer was going for it when he bent down just before being shot..

The day long evidentiary hearing included ample testimony from the brothel owner. Joe Conforte testified that only this week did his wife Sally, tell him she knew the boxer was out to kill him. Quoting her, he said Bonavena called her two hours before his death and roared, "I'm going down there [to the brothel] and I'm going to shoot Joe and anyone else in sight." Conforte said his wife told him that she knew then the boxer had one of her guns.

Conforte told the judge he pleaded with his wife to come

with him to court today and testify. He said she refused.

"She still feels emotionally involved with Oscar and she still hates Ross Brymer. In her mind, Ross Brymer killed her lover, and that's why she is not here today."

In the week before his death, Conforte said he was so upset with the love affair between his wife and the boxer, that he considered taking the brothel out of her name (which he did).

"As soon as he moved into my home," Conforte told the judge, "he got chummy with Sally. He got her mesmerized. Anything he would say, she would go for it. One of the biggest mistakes I made was when he came to live in my house instead of a hotel."

Sally was taking money from the brothel and giving it to Oscar, Conforte told the judge. She would give the fighter "$300, $400, $500, a day."

At one time, Conforte said, the fighter asked him for $3,000 to send to his wife and children in Buenos Aires. Conforte said he later found out that Oscar had lost the money gambling.

When the new Mustang was opened in May, 1976, things really got scary. Conforte said on one occasion, he glimpsed Bonavena smoking one of his cigars, and watched as the boxer tested the loyalty of some of the brothel employees.

"How do you like my new joint?" The boxer was smiling as he quizzed some of the workers.

Conforte said he interpreted this to mean, "I've got Sally now, all I need to do is get rid of Joe."

Conforte said some of his friends, and some of the brothel workers started coming to him telling him that Bonavena was bragging about taking over ownership of the ranch.

"This thing was building up like a storm," Conforte said, "and I was waiting for it to go away. In my mind he wanted to legally or illegally, eliminate me and end up with the ranch. In my mind, in some months he'd hurt Sally too."

Several days before the shooting, Conforte told the judge, he offered Bonavena $10,000—$2,500 in cash, and a check for $7,500, to get out of Nevada. The boxer agreed to do so, Conforte said, but instead he took Sally and went to San Francisco.

"And," said Conforte, "in San Francisco, he went to the Argentine consulate and filed a report saying I had threatened to kill him."

When I heard he had returned to Reno, and was armed, I was "scared to death for the for the first time in my life," Conforte said.

A Mustang brothel guard was put on the stand and testified that at one time he had seen Bonavena point a shotgun at Conforte's back and pull the trigger. Apparently there were no shells in the chamber, because the gun failed to go off, the guard said.

After listening to testimony throughout the day, Judge Gregory remarked, "The case seems to be somewhere between voluntary and involuntary manslaughter."

"I think that what happened," the judge said, "was in the heat of the moment, Mr. Brymer overreacted. He had no business with a rifle, but he didn't know what he was doing."

The judge said he was satisfied that with Brymer's blind right eye, and lack of shooting experience, he could not have accurately fired a 30.06 rifle at Bonavena through an iron-barred fence at 30 feet. The angle, he said, would have provided a "bulls eye" no larger than four inches.

With that assessment, Judge Gregory sentenced Ross Brymer to two years in the Nevada State Prison. With good behavior, the judge noted, Brymer could be out in as little as 11 months.

Chapter Ten

QUESTIONS LINGER

Sally Conforte was a shrewd business woman. She had been the driving force behind the Mustang Ranch's success. While Joe was out grabbing headlines and doing the town with scantily clad working girls, Sally was back at the ranch tending to business. And under her tutelage, the ranch had become a very lucrative business. She was a no nonsense manager, one who'd heard all the scams. Her close friends were all in agreement: Sally was the one person who made it go. Joe was around to accept the recognition.

Why then, did she go head over heels for Oscar Bonavena, and jeopardize all she and Joe had worked for? Testimony was brought out in the evidentiary hearing that she and the boxer had a torrid affair going. Other testimony brought out the fact that the boxer had been carrying at least one of her pistols, and that he told her he was going to kill her husband.

Did she think he really meant to do it?

Yes.

Is it possible she encouraged him?

It is possible.

Conforte testified that when the boxer moved into their home, Sally became "mesmerized." She would do anything the boxer asked. She began taking hundreds of dollars a day from the till to give to Bonavena which he used to gamble and otherwise squander away around the Reno clubs.

At the time of the boxer's death, Sally, was 59 years old and in failing health. The 33 year Argentine boxer, was 26 years her junior. Had Oscar too, fallen madly in love with the aging brothel manager?

Doubtful.

A few months earlier, Bonavena had married—if only briefly, a twenty-year old blond Mustang prostitute, which attests to his preference for young women. Was he playing Sally?

Probably.

Did he have her pistol in his boot that May morning with the intention of killing Joe Conforte?

Certainly.

Did he really believe that once Joe was out of the way, he'd take over the Mustang Ranch along with Sally?

The ranch, yes. Sally, no. Sally wasn't really in his plans.

The question that must be answered is: Who put him up to do it? Sally?

Sally was probably a contributing factor, however, it is doubtful that she was the primary factor. Who else then lead him to believe he'd take over the ranch once Joe was dead?

Enter the Sicilian Mafia.

Despite the emergence of new crime groups like the Chinese Triads, the Colombian cartels, The Russian/Armenian crime families, Jamaican posses, and others, La Cosa Nostra continues to be the most powerful criminal organization in America today. They keep their ranks under control. They have a saying, "You live by the gun and knife, and you die by the gun and knife."

How does one become a "made Mafioso?"

It usually starts in childhood. The child looks up to and is awed by the presence of "wise guys." These wise guy demand and get respect, recognition, money, political influence, and stature among their own. This may leave an indelible impression upon a youngster.

Being initiated into a Mafia family, and thereby being "made," usually takes several years. The prospect, usually someone the godfather, or one of the "capos" has known for many years, or is related to (which rules out infiltrators), is brought along slowly. He starts out on the payroll doing tasks for the family. This may be collecting taxes from street level crooks, collecting loan shark debts, delivering payoffs to political figures, breaking bones, or other sundry tasks.

He is watched closely by his superiors who make regular progress reports and send these on up the chain of command. The ability to follow orders without question is of primary significance. When he has met all criteria, the day comes when he is initiated into one of La Cosa Nostra's crime families

The initiation is a somber ceremony, usually held in a darkened room, lit by candles. The family's top echelon are there to conduct the rites. Blood oaths are taken by the initiate, who swears to uphold the vows of:

- Omerta, the vow of silence..
- The willingness to endure physical pain.
- The willingness to serve this generation of Mafioso's.

To seal the oaths, the initiate's finger is pricked drawing blood. Drops of blood are then collected on a photo of a Catholic Saint. The blood stained photo is then set afire by passing it over the flame of a candle. The initiate then must hold the burning photo in his hands until it is reduced to ashes. During this part of the rite, he repeats, "If I betray the family, my flesh will burn like the photo."

Was Joe Conforte a made Mafioso?

Doubtful.

Was he friendly to them?

Certainly. The Palm Springs, California Police Department, documented his meeting with known Mafia crime figures in that desert city, in 1974.

La Cosa Nostra strives to be a secret society. As pointed out earlier, any Mafioso, or associate who violates the vow of Omerta, will have a contract put out on him. $100,000 may be paid to the shooter who successfully completes the hit against a traitor. Also, made Mafioso's avoid undue publicity. Keeping their business out of the newspapers or other media publications, is enforced. They demand from their members, strict silence. They say, "Don't publicize our business."

A few Mafioso's have violated this code of silence. The ones who have, and who have testified against the LCN crime families have had to spend their remaining years in the federal Witness Protection Program.

Did Joe Conforte avoid unnecessary publicity?

Quite the opposite. He was always in the papers. Many times he called the papers to air his views. Following the mistrial of the Brymer case in Virginia City, he initiated an interview with the Gold Hill News, against the advice of his lawyers. He craved publicity.

During his vacation in Sicily, in 1976, when the Reno newspapers broke the story of his involvement with Mafia crime figures in Palm Springs, he canceled the vacation and stormed back to Reno attacking the newspapers. He was loudly unsettled. He appeared to be under unusual pressure.

Had he drawn the ire of organized crime because of his flamboyance?

Very possible.

Had he failed to pay the required taxes to the LCN?

Probably not, however, this remains a possibility.

Had the LCN put out the green light on Joe Conforte?

This too remains a direct possibility.

Suppose, for instance, that the LCN had decided Joe Conforte was dragging their name into prominence and they had voted to whack him. How best to do it? Use one of their torpedoes?

Maybe.

How about using a fall guy; a patsy? But who? Who could get that close to him?

Answer: Oscar Bonavena.

Oscar was already hooked up with Joe's wife, and he was spending a lot of time at the Mustang Ranch. Could Oscar be compelled to do it?

If he thought by whacking Conforte, he'd take over the Mustang Ranch, possibly he would. He loved the lifestyle of a bordello big shot. Nobody doubted his courage. Sally let him have at least one of her pistols, which he carried in his boot, even though he had no permit to carry a concealed weapon.

After the slaying, rumors began circulating on the streets that the East Coast Mafia was behind the plot. These rumors persist until this day.

Organized crime in the Reno area does not exist. Prevailing street gangs, predominately, Hispanic, are more or less limited to car stripping and fighting among themselves and getting high. African American and Native Americans operate similarly. A few whites engage in hate crimes.

The Reno area crime scene consists of countless disorganized killers, bank robbers, stickup thugs, drug dealers, car thieves, burglars, meth cookers, purse snatchers and other assorted small time crooks, on down the line to the bottom of the barrel, slimy rapos (rapists) and cho-moes (child molesters).

Most of these fringe element thugs have few assets; many

latch onto the welfare rolls. What money they do score, usually goes to feed the monkey on their back. Not exactly high class crime figures.

Disorganized as they are, they nevertheless maintain communication among their own peers. Hispanics keep informed of things within their own community: which gang member got shot or got sent to la pinta; which clica got crossed out; who fled back across the border, where best to score mota, etc. The African American criminal element in the area, as well as the Natives and whites do the same.

Many of the Caucasian thugs live around the Sun Valley area. They're acquainted in the sense that they know the others by association or reputation. They know their peculiarities, their criminal expertise. If they've done time, and most have, they have this common bond. When a major crime is committed in the area, they usually know who should get the recognition.

They like to hang out together in the local honky tonks, the casinos and the brothels. Most of them, at one time or another, had a passing acquaintance with Ross Brymer.

After the Bonavena slaying, the talk on the street was that the Mafia had ordered the hit. Sources indicated that because of Conforte's flamboyance, the LCN wanted him silenced. But who could do the hit?

Allegedly, the Mafia viewed Bonavena as a patsy. Someone not too bright. But a person who could be induced to whack Conforte, especially with the promise of taking over the Mustang Ranch. And with Bonavena's alien status, coupled with Conforte's negative notoriety, there was a remote chance that had Bonavena successfully whacked Joe Conforte, he may have been able to escape prison time by merely being deported back to Argentina.

Is this a viable explanation?

Possibly. But there is no proof. The best that I can say, is that at the time, this was the talk on the street and in the prison system.

Brymer entered the Nevada State prison system for the third time, in March, 1978, nearly two years after the slaying. The yard was abuzz with his presence. He stood head and shoulders above the others, both in physical stature and background. Ross was no ordinary junkie. He'd been Conforte's muscle, his right hand man for years. He drew the respect of the other inmates, merely by his presence. He did not have to make up stories like the others.

Did he reveal anything?

No. He never discussed the shooting, other than to say it was self defense.

Brymer, a career criminal, got out on an early release on the Bonavena slaying, after serving 15 months. It wasn't long before he came right back in through the revolving door like so many other recidivists. . .

From January, 1978, until December, 1997, when the author retired as a correctional sergeant at the Nevada State Prison, he worked face-to-face with many of the characters described in this work, including Ross Brymer.

One, a murderer who was doing a life-without-parole sentence, was seriously stabbed by another inmate inside the cell house during the early 1980s. During a prolonged recovery in the infirmary, officers were assigned to monitor his progress and to prevent a recurrence of the attack. This inmate liked to talk. He once told the attending officer that he too, had worked for Conforte. Indeed, he said, he'd been there the morning Bonavena was shot. This inmate then confided to the officer at his bedside, that prior to Bonavena's arrival at the Mustang Ranch, Joe Conforte ordered the killing. The inmate said he, and Ross Brymer, flipped a coin to determine who should do it. Ross won—or lost—the toss, depending upon how you look at it.

Can this inmate be believed?

Maybe.

Do inmates tell lies?

Frequently.

Do they tell the truth?

Sometimes.

Do they exaggerate?

Always.

Is there anyway to confirm or refute this inmate's revelation?

Polygraph.

Would the inmate consent?

Doubtful, however if he dreamed it would buy him a pardon, he may.

What would be the outcome?

If he passed, and if he agreed to testify, Joe Conforte would be indicted for conspiracy to commit murder. There is no statute of limitations on murder.

Would this inmate have to testify?
Certainly.
Would he be *put in the box*?
No doubt.
Would he be safe in prison?
Contract hits are carried out in the nation's prisons. Some of the well known prison gangs engage in the lucrative murder-for-hire business. Even in protective custody, there are no guarantees a target will not be hit.

Over the years, the author has seen other inmates turn against former criminal associates, and testify against them, in the hope the authorities would do something to lighten up their own heavy sentences.

Does it work?

Sometimes,[1] but usually not.

In a book by Ovid Demaris, "The Last Mafioso," Demaris alleges that "Jimmy The Weasel" Fratiano, who had close contact with mob connected gaming figures in Nevada, revealed additional details about the Bonavena-Sally Conforte relationship. According to the book, Fratiano said that he was acquainted with a San Francisco mobster who'd met Bonavena and Sally Conforte on one of their trips to the City By The Bay. During the meeting, the mobster quoted Bonavena as saying, "How much it cost to get Joe Conforte killed dead?"

Taken aback by the abrupt query, the mobster replied he would "check around."

Again, quoting from the book, Fratiano said a few days later he received an urgent call from Joe Conforte asking him to come to Reno.

When the two met at the Mustang Ranch, Conforte asked, "How's your nerve?"

"What are you talking about?'

"How do you feel about icing a woman? Have you ever iced one before?"

"Joe, don't come up with those questions Are you a prosecutor?"

"Let's say it's Sally. Now I'm not saying it is, you understand. I'm just trying to get a ballpark figure. Would $10,000 do?"

"Let's lay it out in the open. If it's Sally, it's gonna' be one hundred grand. Think it over and let me know, and I'll let you know."

"I'd like to have it done in South America. She's going on a trip with Bonavena."

Two weeks later, Bonavena was shot dead. To this day, many questions linger. Answers vary, depending upon who does the answering.

Joe Conforte knows the truth.

Sally Conforte knew.

Dora Raffade Bonavena, Oscar's estranged wife, learned much from her husband prior to his death. She has never made this public.

Willard Ross Brymer knew the truth. He never revealed any of this publicly. And death sealed his lips forever.

Ross Brymer's son, Ross Jr., may know. The author knew him also in prison. After RossJr. was released in December, 2000, the author interviewed him several times in Reno. Ross Jr., well muscled and street smart, learned much from his father. But other than what is already known, would say little more.

Chapter Eleven
THE FISH TANK

In every prison there are inmates, and there are convicts. The term inmate describes a run-of-the-mill prisoner. The inmate may irritate others, he may be a cell thief, he may be a trouble maker, he may be a predator, he may be a snitch, he may be a punk, or he may not be any of these things. But what separates him from a convict, is that he really has few qualities that set him apart from the others. He *blends in.*

A convict on the other hand, does his own time. He knows how to keep out of trouble. If however, trouble comes to him, he handles it himself. He will not go to the man for help. He'll have a shank stashed within easy reach, and if necessary, will use it to ensure his presence on the yard or housing, is not jeopardized. He will adhere to the unwritten prison code of ethics, and will not snitch or *check in* (go to protective custody). By the way he carries himself, and by his reputation, the convict will glean the respect of other inmates, and many times, also the custody staff. If the officers have to bust him for any violation, the convict will usually not turn on the officers. He'll accept the results of his actions and move to isolation with few problems. He won't whine or blame others. He is a *stand-up convict.*

Ross Brymer was this type of convict. He entered prison on March, 1978, for the slaying of boxer Oscar Bonavena, carrying a two-year stretch for voluntary manslaughter. Many of his old friends in prison had been following the events and were happy to know they'd get a chance to see him again. The talk on the yard was that Brymer's relatively light sentence had been worked out between Joe Conforte and the Storey County officials. The fix was in. Brymer indeed, was well connected.

The intake center—the *fish tank,* was located at the Northern Nevada Correctional Center—NNCC, a medium security facility located five miles south of NSP—Max. The fish tank actually was confined to one wing of Unit-5, a multi-use housing unit, isolated from the main yard by razor wire topped chain-link fences. Entry into and out of the area, was through a vehicle gate and a pedestrian gate, both controlled by an overlooking gun-tower.

New commitments were called *fish*. Returning prisoners, such as Ross Brymer, were referred to as *retreads*. For the most part, the fish were scared, unsure of what lie ahead, and as a result, looked to the retreads for advice, and in some cases, especially among the weaker inmates, protection. The danger here for the fish, was that once they showed weakness, they could become easy prey for the hard-core predators.

Unit-5 had three wings (also called streets), extending out from a central rotunda, at an equal distance from each other. Looking down at the unit from above, M-wing, faced south from the rotunda at a 4:00 o'clock position; N-wing, faced north at 8:00 o'clock and O-wing faced east from 12:00 o'clock. Each wing held thirty cells, fifteen on either side of the tier. Doors were solid steel with a small observation window at eye level. Originally, each cell was equipped to house just one inmate. This idea was soon discarded, and two-tiered bunks replaced the single ones. When stretched to the limits, the cells could house three prisoners, two on the bunks, and one sleeping on the concrete floor.

The rotunda housed the ID office where a central file—a C-file, was started on all new commitments. Each new commitment was assigned a *back number*—a number he carried as long as he was in prison. When Ross Brymer came in, on this, his third fall, the sequential numbers had reached 30,000 (today they are fast approaching 70,000).

Other offices in the rotunda supplied work space for counselors, the psychiatrist and psychologist, and other staff members. There was also a laundry room, a property room, linen room and storage rooms.

In the center of the rotunda stood the *bubble*, a floor to ceiling control room. Inside the bubble, the officers, who could see down each street, directed traffic. Electronic switches and indicator lights controlled all cell doors. Sealing off each wing from the rotunda, was a ceiling high, sliding barred gate, also controlled by the bubble. An iron escape ladder inside the bubble offered access to the roof in the event the officers had to flee the unit. On the roof they would be covered by the gun towers.

The fish tank was restricted to all the cells on N-wing. No other inmates were housed on that street. All new commitments were assigned close custody, which meant they were confined to their cells except when they were brought out for intake processing. The intake process usually took about three weeks to complete. There was routine medical and psychological testing, interviews with the counselors, gang officers, chaplain, and related staff members. When out of their cells, they were tracked closely by the officers. They were not allowed to converse with inmates who were housed on the other wings.

The officers usually selected one person from the group to act as tier runner. Runners were selected on the basis of their willingness to work, their demeanor, and the ability to get along with the officers as well as other inmates. In the eyes of the locked-up fish, the tier runner had an enviable position. He was not confined to a cell like they were; he could move up and down the tier talking to others in their cells, and he occasionally had access to a telephone in the rotunda. During feeding, the officers gave him an extra food tray.

But he had to earn these benefits. He was required to mop the floor after every meal, clean the walls as necessary, and in general help the officers keep the tier clean and quiet. Other chores put on the runner were passing out toilet paper, soap and writing utensils and related items to the fish. On laundry day, he had to gather up each person's dirty clothing and bed sheets, and bring them to the rotunda to be laundered.. When finished, the clean laundry was returned to the inmates. All fish wore white coveralls, with the initials, NNCC, stenciled on the back.

Moving up and down the tier all day enabled the runner to keep in touch with the others, and to pass messages or tobacco, from cell to cell. Although, against the rules, the officers normally looked the other way if the runner was otherwise doing a good job. And the fish were appreciative of the runner's help, and if able to, slipped him a little tobacco, candy, or maybe a postage stamp.

All food trays were prepared in the main culinary on the yard, and wheeled over to the unit in a hand-pushed cart. Inside the unit, the job of feeding the inmates fell on the officers. This was a not a suitable job[1] for the tier runner, who like the others, was locked-up during feeding and routine counts.[2]

Following the meal, the tier runner was again brought out to go up and down the tier picking up the dirty food trays and other garbage. (Because the cell doors did not have food slots, the officers usually opened the cell door to feed the inmates. However, when the inmate finished his tray, there was ample space under the cell door to slide it out onto the tier floor.)

Occasionally, a troublesome inmate would refuse to give up his food tray. When this happened, all movement on the wing ceased. The lieutenant in charge of the unit had a zero tolerance for any disruptive act. An officer extraction team would be quickly assembled and prepared to use whatever level of force was necessary to retrieve the food tray, and gain compliance. Nothing was negotiable. The officers were running the unit, not the inmates. When the lieutenant ordered a cell extraction, he normally authorized the use of a stun gun.[3]

In front of the cell door, the lieutenant would order the inmate to lie face down on the floor and interlock his hands and fingers behind his head. This order was not repeated. If he failed to comply at this point, the door was opened and the offender was slammed with the bean bag. The officers then rushed in to overpower the offender. Next the offender would be stripped down to his shorts, and everything in his cell that wasn't bolted to the floor was thrown out onto the tier. The inmate then would be left to ponder his actions. And other inmates peering out through their cell door windows, quickly got the message: Behave yourself in the fish tank.

If there were two inmates in that cell, the trouble maker would be moved to a single, stripped cell. In the rare event that both inmates chose to confront the officers, the same procedures applied. It made little difference to the unit lieutenant. The officers would win the battle. The medical department was routinely notified of possible injuries, and responded within a reasonable amount of time.

These types of incidents left a lasting impression on the fish. They were quick to learn that it didn't pay to cause problems for the staff. They were especially awed by the leadership and swift counteraction of the lieutenant in charge, Henry Sharpe.

Sharpe, 55, a retired naval petty officer and Vietnam veteran, shunned an administrative post. Standing no more than five-feet, six-inches, tall, and at 210 pounds, Sharpe was built like a fireplug. He had short muscular arms, and short stubby fingers, not exactly suitable for punching a typewriter. His expertise was doing what he did best: run a tight unit, and he backed his officers to the hilt. And when he ordered a cell extraction, he lead the charge. A quality that had earned him the respect and admiration of all the officers under his supervision.

He came close to being injured seriously one day, when he was walking on the yard. A deceptively violent prisoner,[4] who had an intense dislike for the lieutenant, ambushed him lashing out with a prison made shank. Sharpe was able to sidestep the attack, and wrestle the knife away. He then applied a carotid restraint hold on the inmate which he held with sufficient force until the attacker dropped unconscious. After cuffing the proned inmate, he casually called for backup.

THE NUT WING

O-Wing housed the psychiatric patients. Dr. Freestone, a psychiatrist, was in charge of the wing. In addition to supervising the psyches here at NNCC, he also had to cover the mental health unit at max, which was a series of dungy lockup cells at the maximum security prison, five miles north.. He preferred to work with his O-wing patients, and spent as little time as possible at max. However, he was successful in bringing over from max, violent heavyweight psyche patients which he placed on O-wing, much to the consternation of Lt. Sharpe and his custody staff..

The officers knew that Dr. Freestone had no interest in security, and the max inmates he had brought over, they felt, were manipulating the psychiatrist solely for the purpose of being moved here to a medium security facility, which would give them easier access to drugs, and more importantly, a facility which was regarded as being easier to escape from. Lt. Sharpe's protests to the administration usually fell on deaf ears. Programs,[5] not custody, was running the psyche unit at NNCC.

The differences between NNCC and max were striking. Max housed the most violent and assaultive inmates. At max, they were under much closer security than at NNCC, yet despite the tighter security, max inmates were responsible for a much higher incident of rapes, assaults, stabbings, murders and gang fights than occurred at NNCC. Max inmates were clad in prison dungarees; inmates at

NNCC—against sound correctional procedures, were allowed to wear civilian clothing on the yard. The administration rationalized this questionable practice by boasting of a monetary savings in prison issue clothing.

Visiting at max was closely supervised. Inmates and visitors sat across from each other on hard chairs set up on either side of a long wooden table. Contact was nearly non-exisent. At inmate friendly NNCC, visiting was in a large room plentiful with sofas and easy chairs where the inmates and their visitors could engage in contact, many times leading to heavy petting and exchange of drugs.

Because of the vast differences between the two institutions, max inmates were constantly scheming to transfer over. Many played the psyche game on Dr. Freestone, who too often, arranged transfers for some of the worst. Lt. Sharpe and his line officers were always at odds with Dr. Freestone on most of these transfers.

At NNCC, the warden, who was amiable enough—had never worn a custody uniform. He had promoted through the ranks of Programs, specifically, the educational department.

The inmates on the yard referred to him as, "Promisin' John," a nickname he earned because of a habit of always responding to a request by saying, "Yes...yes, I promise you I'll do it, etc. etc." Rarely did he come through.

Under his guidance, as stated earlier, NNCC prisoners were allowed to dress in civilian clothing. Other problems overlooked, but somehow rationalized by the administration, continued to eat away at the fragile security in place at NNCC. A questionable service—a proprietary plasma center—was allowed to operate on prison grounds. Prisoners were encouraged to *bleed* on a regular basis.

Donating (selling) plasma is not the same as donating blood. To begin with, the plasma donor lies on a stationary gurney set up in the plasma facility, and one unit of blood is drawn from an arm vein, which takes maybe 15 minutes. Next, this whole blood is centrifuged until the plasma and blood cells separate. The plasma is then siphoned off, bottled and placed in a cooler. Next, the compacted blood cells are diluted with sterile saline and infused back into the donor's circulatory system through the line into the arm vein

The reader can then see that what the subject has lost has

been only the plasma, which is naturally replaced by the body within 24-36 hours. An inmate then, was able to bleed as often as twice a week. The problem this created was that the administration allowed the center to pay the inmates for each bleed, $5.00 in quarters. An inmate bleeding twice a week was earning $10.00 in quarters which he could take back out to the yard. Simple arithmetic will show that if as few as two-hundred and fifty inmates bled twice weekly, $2,500 cash would flow out onto the yard each week. On the yard, quarters could easily be traded for *green* (U.S. currency, which was not authorized, but which was easier to conceal or pass through visiting, than a sack of quarters).

This type of cash flow will corrupt any prison. Open gambling, prostitution, drugs, weapons, extortion, protection, thievery and all the other lucrative prison rackets flourish in any prison where this is allowed. Attempts to escape also rise.[6]

What did the plasma center do with the plasma it collected?

Plasma is processed commercially in the cosmetic industry and is used in pharmaceutical applications. It is a lucrative business. Profits rise substantially where there are continuous donors.

Did any of the administrative staff receive kickbacks from the plasma center?

It has never been proven. However; it is certain the plasma people paid rent to prison officials to operate their facility on prison grounds where there were no lack of donors.

Who did the administration select to do the pre-bleed physicals?

Dr. Freestone.

Dr. Freestone related well with the inmates. He too, had done time. Back in the Midwest, he was convicted of armed robbery and sent to state prison. After several years, he was released and came to Nevada. Here, he was granted a limited license. The license authorized him to practice psychiatry and dispense medicine, within the confines of a state institution only.

For him it was a good deal. He was an ex-con from the Midwest, but in Nevada, a salaried state psychiatrist. And in 1979, Prison Director, Charles Wolff Jr., named Dr. Freestone medical director of the prisons. Everything he needed was furnished for him: his office space, a medical lab, x-ray, psyche technicians, and other elements that doctors on the outside had to provide for themselves.

The uniformed custody staff referred to all psychiatric patients as "nuts." Dr. Freestone and the psychologists were referred to as "nut doctors."

Dr. Freestone, mindful of his own felony background, was disdainful of the uniformed custody officers. On O-wing, surrounded by the nuts, he felt at home. He referred to the custody officers as the "Gestapo." When he needed muscle, he preferred to let his inmate psychiatric attendants—IPAs, provide it for him.

If a violent inmate needed to be restrained so the doctor could force medicate him, the job of subduing the subject fell on the IPAs. Two or three of them would go into the cell and slap the inmate around as much as necessary to get his attention. The good doctor then provided the injection. If, as happened all too often, one of the nuts smeared his cell with his own excrement, the IPAs, and not the uniformed custody staff had to clean it up.

This procedure was gratefully accepted by Lt. Sharpe mainly because it kept his own men out of a hands-on incident, and the unenviable job of cleaning up a loathsome cell. It also reduced the amount of paper work required when custody was involved in any kind of fracas.

The drug of choice for violent inmates was Prolixyn. One injection of this long acting psychotropic drug would slow down a violent inmate for as long as two weeks. It wasn't a drug liked by those who received it. There were serious side effects,[7] most notably, confusion and lack of control of voluntary muscles, and excessive salivary and lacrimal secretions. To the officers, it had the desired effect of creating zombies out of otherwise unmanageable violent inmates. To watch a violent nut reduced to a shuffling, drooling passive zombie, pleased the custody staff; for as long as the inmate was medicated, he could cause few problems. And while in this state, the incidents of injury were greatly minimized, to both the staff and other inmates.

Most of the psychiatrist's IPAs, themselves, had mental health histories, and many had been sent to prison for the most heinous crimes:

"Randy," a mild mannered, bespectacled, balding inmate, had been sent to prison from Las Vegas, doing three consecutive life sentences. In Vegas, Randy had worked at one of the clubs writing keno tickets. He lived in a small single wide trailer set up in a low rent court in Vegas. One night while at home drinking and brooding, Randy was beset with agonizing thoughts of self doubt and uncertainty. Inside his head, compelling voices seemed to be urging him to take out his anguish on other people.

A woman and her three children, who lived in a nearby trailer, were inadvertently thrust into the role of becoming victims of Randy's emotional distress. The young girls were playing and chattering as children will, in the confines of their trailer, and the shrillness of their voices wafted over to where Randy was struggling with his demented thoughts. In the deep recesses of his mind, he had no space for the intrusive chattering of the little girls. He exploded with hatred and rage.

In a stupor, he stumbled into his kitchen knocking items from the shelves and bumping into the walls. Groping aimlessly through the drawers, he clutched the handle of a large carving knife, and bolted outside charging toward the direction of his torment.

Like a monster groping out of a horror movie, Randy crashed through the front door of the woman's trailer, screaming unintelligibly and slicing the air in front of him with the knife. Shrieks of disbelief and terror from the girls and their mother filled the trailer and escaped into the night air, alerting others of the carnage taking place inside. Sirens wailed in the distance.

When the police arrived, one little girl, covered with blood and tears—and who was the lone survivor—stood quivering in the doorway holding a baby blanket.

"Why did he kill us, mommy?" She whimpered, "Why mommy...why?"

"Robbie," was an equally nice guy. As a child, he loved to torture small animals and he derived a perverted sense of pleasure from inflicting pain on others. These proclivities followed him into his teenage years. His classmates had by then made him a target of their jokes, and in school he was held up to ridicule. Slightly built, standing five-feet-five, and weighing no more than 130 pounds, Robbie could do little more than retreat inside his own dream world, thinking bad thoughts .

In his early twenties, he was earning a modest living in a variety of mundane jobs. He lived alone in a one bedroom apartment in Las Vegas, where he pretty much kept to himself. One afternoon, a girl scout innocently rang his door bell, and asked if he'd like to buy some cookies. Leering down at the little girl, an evil grin crossed his face. He invited her inside, and when she hesitated, he grabbed her by the arm and pulled her in. She began to cry that he was hurting her. and begged him to let her go. Instead, he stuffed a gag in her mouth and shoved her inside a closet. There he began to play out his fantasies.

When found, she'd been slashed more than 50 times with a razor sharp knife. But what brought the hardened detectives to tears, was knowing that most of the razor cuts had been solely for the purpose of torture. Few could have brought on her death. In fact, at autopsy, the cause of death was determined to have been traumatic shock brought on by loss of blood.

"Parnell," a hulking black killer, had robbed a Las Vegas dry cleaners of their day's receipts, and after getting the money, forced four employees to kneel on the floor and face the wall. He then bound each one's hands behind their backs. As they pleaded for mercy, he ruthlessly shot each in the back of the head. After executing three of the four, he had to stop and reload, while the fourth begged him to spare her life. After reloading, he finished her off like the others.

Next he doused the floor and equipment with flammable cleaning fluid and tossed a match. The place erupted in flames as he ran off. Emergency personnel were on the scene within minutes and were quick to realize they had a multiple homicide. Sifting through the rubble for clues, it wasn't long before they named Parnell as the prime suspect. He was subsequently arrested and indicted on four counts of murder, arson, and armed robbery. Found guilty, he was sent to max carrying four life terms *running wild* (consecutively).

Because his four victims were white, prison authorities felt Nevada's Aryan Warriors may try to kill him when he arrived at max. Classification decided to send him out of state for his own protection. He was moved to the California Department of Corrections under the interstate compact, a procedure used by many western states to swap inmates. While imprisoned in California, the Aryan Brotherhood, who had been alerted of his arrival, made an effort to light him up as he had done his victims. He was quickly returned to Nevada, where Dr. Freestone took a liking to him right away. He became one of the good doctor's IPAs.

Another IPA, was a hulking psychotic killer, "Lester." Lester was usually somewhere out in La La Land on Prolixyn. On the drug, he was mild mannered and easy to supervise. We could always tell when his medication had to be renewed, when we would glimpse small pockets of table salt spilled around the corners on the floor.

Lester, a paranoid schizoid, believed that sprinkling salt around like he did, would keep the communists out of the unit. And he was right! As long as I worked that unit, I never once saw a communist.

After the Alan Taylor negotiated plea agreement that severely limited Dr. Freestone's use of Prolixyn on psyche patients, Lester began going without his. One day while brooding in his cell and in a deep depression, he slashed the brachial artery inside the bend of his elbow. When found by the officers, he had bleed to death.

These four IPAs were a sampling of Dr. Freestones's attendants. In all, he had five of six regulars always on duty, and the same number classified as trainees. Randy, the lead IPA, received top pay, $50.00 a month; the others got $30.00. Trainees were required to work for nothing for the first month, and after that, the pay was $5.00 for the second month, graduating on up to $30.00 after six months.

The reader should be reminded that NNCC was (and still is) a medium security facility, certainly not a suitable prison to house violent inmates like the above examples. Yet, Dr. Freestone usually got his way with the administration—a weak administration, where sensible correctional procedures, many times were ignored.

Count time in the nut wing could be tricky. It was the job of the IPAs to ensure the nuts were locked in their cells before the wing gate was racked open. When the gate was opened, three officers entered the wing, the only wing in the unit that could never quite erase the murky stench of urine, Pine Sol disinfectant, and tobacco smoke that at times could cause the eyes to water. One officer remained at the open wing gate to serve as backup in case of trouble, and the other two moved down either side of the tier counting flesh through the observation cell windows. At the end of the tier, they turned, passed each other and then retraced the other's steps moving back up toward the wing gate continuing to count. Back near the rotunda, they compared their count totals, which had to match. They then exited the wing and racked shut the gate.

This was sound correctional procedure. However; when the

unit was operating with reduced staff, only one officer went down the wing to count. The officers complained to admin about the lack of adequate staff repeatedly, but were usually told the budget wouldn't allow too much overtime. They'd have to do the best they could.

The author was working at this institution one night when an officer we called "Radar," went down the wing to count. As he passed the open walled shower room, a violent inmate, Frank DePalma, jumped out of the shadows clutching a prison made shank in one hand, and attacked the officer from the behind. The inmate was able to get an arm-bar choke hold on the officer, and with his other hand, began stabbing the officer in the chest.

This incident, which very easily could have resulted in an officer fatality, was minimized when the shank, which had been fashioned from a metal spoon, bent after several thrusts, and failed to reach the heart or other vital organs. Hearing the commotion, a couple of IPAs came out of their cells (which were usually not locked during count time), and helped to subdue inmate, DePalma. Radar was taken to the hospital where his injuries were determined to be non life threatening. The IPAs came under fire from custody who wanted to know why DePalma was allowed to hide in the shower instead of being locked up. They all denied knowledge of his actions. But none of the custody staff would ever believe that the IPAs had not allowed the attack to happen.

The third wing of the unit, M-wing, was sort of a Motel-6 wing. There were cells used for temporary housing of inmates who were in transit from court. Unit workers were also housed there as were several protective custody inmates. Also, the wing housed a dozen or so SKEs—"safe keeper evaluations." When the wing was overcrowded, it was these SKE cells that housed three prisoners, two on the double bunks and one on the floor.

SKEs were for the most part, youngsters who had been sent to prison by the judges on a 120 day evaluation program. The youngsters received, were being given a last chance to avoid lengthy prison terms. Because of their ages, and the beneficence of certain judges, the youngsters were being given an introduction into the realities of life behind bars. And hopefully, they would be scared away, would change their ways, and would not return.

Upon completion of the 120 day program, they were sent back to court to again face the judge. Their future was wrapped up in the evaluation that was sent back with them. If they had programmed well, this was reflected in their evaluation, and increased their chance of being granted probation.. If not, there was a good chance the judge would deny probation, and sentence them to hard time. They all knew this, and most of them made every effort possible to take an acceptable evaluation back with them when they faced the judge.

The SKEs were the drones of the unit. To them, was assigned most of the clean up and upkeep of the unit. They worked eight hours a day sweeping, mopping, cleaning windows, waxing and buffing the floors. They also had to do all the dirty laundry, shine the officer's shoes, polish the bars of the wing gates, keep the food cart spotlessly clean and thoroughly scrub all empty cells. Vinyl covered mattresses had to be wiped clean with harsh disinfectants. Picking up trash outside the unit was also thrust upon them.

They lived with daily anxiety and uncertainty and were harassed and intimidated constantly. Not so much by the staff, but by the other inmates, especially the hard-time inmates who looked upon them as objects of derision or in some cases, objects of sexual pleasure. It seems somebody was always playing them for something.

To keep them working at designated chores, an inmate known as "Slick," was assigned to oversee their work. It was Slick's job to get the unit work assignments each day from Officer J.C. Taitano, the lead officer, and then assign the various chores to the SKEs. If, for any reason, the work was not completed, Taitano pulled up Slick and held him responsible. Slick, therefore felt free to bully his crew when necessary. He liked his position and wanted to keep it.

Slick had come over from max as one of Dr. Freestone's nuts and for a while was housed on O-wing. After a few months, the good doctor said that his patient had progressed so well, that he could be taken off the nut wing and placed on M-wing. This infuriated Lt. Sharpe, mainly because he felt all along that Slick had been playing the doctor, first to get over here from max, and now to be taken off O-wing and placed among the workers and the SKEs..

To compound matters, Dr. Freestone had convinced Programs that Slick should remain at NNCC and be given a prison job. This, Dr. Freestone said, would help to continue the inmate's progress. It would also help, he said, if Slick were paid a small monthly fee. Programs went along with his wishes, and assigned Slick the position of supervising the SKEs in their unit work. They also allotted a $10.00 a month pay number to the position.

Slick, lean and wiry, stood six-feet tall. His face had the blackness of coal, and was matched by the Vaseline coated jheri curls of his hair. A bushy Fu Manchu mustache framed strong white teeth which he flashed continually, and which tended to disarm others. However, looking into the deep-set blackness of his eyes, the con-wise custody officers could see the reflection of evil, a trait apparently unobservable to the nut doctors.

Lt. Sharpe impressed upon his officers that Slick did not belong at NNCC. In the first place, he had only eight years in, on a ninety-year sentence for kidnapping and aggravated sexual assault. And while at max, he'd been targeted for murder by the Aryan Warriors because of his endless self-serving efforts trying to turn out young white inmates.

Lt. Sharpe spoke to his officers and advised them to watch him closely and if at all possible, get enough on him to override Dr. Freestone's efforts to keep him here. The goal, he emphasized, was to get him shipped back to max where he belonged. But they knew that Slick was con-wise and nobody's fool. If they were going to be successful in shipping him back, they would have to give him enough slack to where he felt comfortable. And then, they reasoned, sooner or later he would get caught *slippin.'* Officer Taitano, quietly spoke to one of his select informants and asked him to track Slick daily, and report back whenever he noticed the inmate violating any of the house rules. Taitano, a tournament class judoka, was well liked and respected by the inmates housed in the unit. Many of them would approach him daily to offer bits of information on what was happening.

Slick was constantly watching his back; he inherently sensed the uneasiness of the custody officers. In his favor though, he did a credible job of supervising the SKEs, and the unit was looking cleaner than it ever had. When he was told by Officer Taitano that a specific clean up job had to be done, he immediately put the SKEs on it, and tracked them conscientiously through completion. Slick did not want to go back to max; he liked it here, and he was feeling more secure in his position. He also was beginning to spend more time in some of the youngster's cells.

After his blood cleared,[8] Ross Brymer was picked to be the fish-tank tier-runner. He was pulled up by Officer Taitano, who outlined his duties. Brymer explained that he'd do whatever was necessary on the wing, and the only thing he'd ask for, would be a few phone calls. This was agreeable, Taitano said. And then Brymer explained his position further.

"This is my third stretch," he smiled, "and I've never been a bitch or a snitch, and I'm not going to start now. If you expect me to snitch anybody off, you'll be disappointed. That's not my style."

Taitano looked at him squarely and grinned. The two immediately felt a mutual respect for each other. Brymer, drawing on his background and past prison incarcerations, was quick to read people. He sensed that Taitano was a no nonsense officer, but one who never *changed up*. He was, thought Brymer, the same person every day, and his word was his bond. If he made a decision, or if he made a statement, Brymer knew it was not negotiable. It would stand.

In explaining the tier runner's duties to Ross Brymer, Taitano told him he'd have to come off the tier throughout the day, picking up laundry or supplies, or at times to carry messages back to the fish from the counselor's or nut doctors, or occasionally the chaplain. And Brymer knew that the fish would be writing *kites* constantly asking for something: requests to see the shrink or medical doctors, more food, clothing, reading materials, postage stamps, and phone calls.

New commitments were not allowed to make personal phone calls out. They were though, allowed to make legal calls to their attorney or other defense advisors. They first had to fill out a kite listing the attorney's name and phone number, and give this to one of the officers. After the name and number was verified, the inmate was brought off the tier and escorted to one of the counselor's offices and allowed to make a collect call out. All attorney calls were confidential and were not supposed to be monitored by custody, however....

As he settled in, Brymer appreciated the time out of his cell. He got along well with the officers, who appreciated his help on the wing. They usually let him make phone calls out without restriction. The other inmates on the wing knew this and were always driving on him to make calls for them, by offering him tobacco or maybe postage stamps. He had to walk a thin line in doing this. He wanted to help those on the wing who were his friends, but he also knew that too many calls out would tie up the phone and draw a response from the officers.

One morning, after getting off the phone, he started back to the wing, when he heard a voice from across the rotunda.

"Bates, get to movin' faster. We gotta get this floor done!"

The voice, he knew, came from an African American inmate he had no use for, an inmate he'd had trouble with a few years ago at max: Slick. He looked over toward the O-wing gate and saw five or six SKEs working on the rotunda floor. Slick was moving around the group barking out orders. Brymer continued his gaze and as Slick looked up, their eyes locked. They both looked very surprised. For a moment, neither said anything.

Slick was the first to break the silence.

"Hey, Ross, what it is? I heard you were comin' back." And he flashed that patented smile from across forty feet of floor space. "Fact is, everybody here been waitin.'"

"Yeh, well all I got is a deuce," Ross shouted back. "I'll be back out before your laundry's dry."

"Sho yo right, big man."

"Hey, Ross! Remember me?" One of the group of SKEs cut into the chatter. A sorry looking youngster, in his late teens, named Bates, but who the others called, "Master Bates," was trying to get Brymer's attention.

"Hey, Ross, it's me Charlie Bates, remember?"

"Sure, I remember you, Charlie. What're you doing here?"

"A hundred and twenty days eval. Judge Agosti, in Reno sent me here; been here for almost a month."

Brymer had known about Bates casually when they both lived in Sun Valley. The kid was always getting into trouble as a juvenile. Auto burglaries, break-ins, ten-cent stupid crimes. He was, thought Brymer, a candidate for doing life on the installment plan. And it would be difficult for him. The kid stood only about five-feet eight inches, and weighed no more than 140 pounds, and couldn't fight a lick. He always wore a quizzical expression on his face, as if he were continually trying to find an answer to something. When he raised his eyes, which was often, his forehead creased with deep furrows, much too pronounced for a kid his age. His face had the color of a wet sheet and chronic facial acne contributed to his sorrowful expression.. His unruly black hair was rarely combed..

"Well, Bates, take a look at me. This is my third fall, and unless you wanna spend the rest of your life locked up, ya damn well better learn from this now, and make some sensible changes in your life. Get outta here, and stay the hell out!"

The shouting across the rotunda had drawn the attention of Lt. Sharpe, who came out of the bubble and walked over towards Brymer. Placing a pinch of snuff under his lip, he faced Brymer and advised him to get back on N-street. Sucking on the tobacco, he moved over to where Slick and the SKEs were gathered.

"Get 'em back to work, Slick," Sharpe barked. "Too much bullshit goin' on. I want the floor waxed and buffed before we leave shift today, so get the kids on it."

Slick advised him that the buffer, which had not been working for over a week, had not yet been fixed. Officer Taitano walked over and said that maintenance had the buffer and had promised to get it back by tomorrow.

"No matter," Taitano said, "We got plenty of rags. The kids can apply the wax using rags, and when the floor dries, they can buff it the same way. Get 'em to work!" That said, Taitano walked back to the bubble.

Slick smiled widely, and looked at the kids and barked, "Okay, ya'll heard what he said, get on it. Get on your hands and knees—you know the position—and spread on a thin coat of wax. Not too heavy. We want it to dry." Amid subdued grumbling, and giggling, they slowly hunched down and began applying the wax.

Lt. Sharpe came over to speak to Slick and glanced at the kids spreading the wax.

"Ya got a bunch of lazybone kids, Slick. Bet they'll all come back with hard time. I sure as hell hope so. It's job security," he scoffed. And as he did, he cleared his lungs and ejected a frothy glob of phlegm and tobacco juice toward a can placed on the floor for the occasion. The missile missed by inches and landed squarely on the floor splattering Bates.

"Oh sorry," he guffawed, "I meant to hit the can." Looking down at Bates, he smirked, "Clean it up, Bates, less ya want me to write some shit about ya." And he sauntered on back to the bubble, chuckling as he did..

Slick bent down to speak to Bates.

"Try not to feel too bad, kid," he said, "Lt. Sharpe's not a bad cop, even though he's a cracker."

Slick bent down and placed his arm across Bates's shoulders and moved closer to whisper into his ear.

"After we finish working this afternoon, you can visit me in my house before lockup. I got some cookies, and we can smoke a little *bud;* I scored yesterday." He winked and slowly rose to his feet, looking down eagerly at the youngster on the floor.

Bates looked up quizzically, his forehead furrowed as if searching for an answer.

When the wax had dried, pieces of a blanket were laid out on the floor and served as buffing rags. The SKEs, joking and chuckling, were able to stand on these rags, and by shuffling their feet and swiveling their hips, were bringing out a high luster on the waxed floor. Watching their merriment and shuffling on the rags, Slick stroked his Fu Manchu and grinned.

After the evening meal had been served, and the clean up completed, the SKEs were allowed to shower, two at a time, in the open shower at the end of the tier. After they had all showered, they were told by the third watch lead officer, that because of the hard work they did today in polishing the floor, they would be allowed to remain outside their cells until the 8:00 p.m. count.

Slick, who was pacing up and down the tier, wearing only shorts and shower clogs, spotted Bates and motioned for him to come into his cell. Inside the cell, Slick sat down on the lower bunk and reached underneath stretching his arm for something. He grinned widely at Bates, who was still standing, as he brought out a full box of chocolate cookies and a plastic bag of hard candies, both items purchased from the prison canteen.

"Hey, that was cool of the cops to let you dudes stay out until count." Slick smiled. "Sit down kid; here's a couple of cookies."

"Thanks man, it ain't often we get this kind of a treat. Ya got any cigs?"

Again slick explored the underside of his bunk, and this time came up with a half filled can of Bugler tobacco. Deftly, with the expertise gained from years of being locked up, Slick rolled a near perfect cigarette and handed it to Bates. He motioned for the youngster to sit down next to him, and when he did, he lit the hand rolled cigarette. Bates drew deeply filling his lungs with the harsh tobacco.

"You think the judge will cut you loose when you go back?"

Slick asked.

"God I hope so. I don't think I could stand to do time like you're doing. How'd you adjust?"

"Drivin' iron, joggin', conditioning. And ya gotta have a connection, a candy source."

"Candy? What'ya mean candy?"

Slick laughed. "Candy; the kind ya smoke."

"Oh, I get it, ya mean the green leafy."

"Sho yo right."

"Ya got some now?"

Slick's eyes narrowed, and when he answered the kid, the flashy smile was not there. "You ever tell the cops, and I'll slice you up like a cucumber."

"Hey-now-now, Slick, I-I ain't no snitch. No-no siree, I ain't," he stammered.

"Okay, cool it kid. We don't want the cops to hear. Relax." Slick started rolling a Bugler smoke for himself.

"You thought much about how you'll survive if the judge sends you back in here?" Slick flashed that toothy grin.

"I-I'll...I don't know." Bates had that quizzical expression when he turned to face Slick.

"I- jus-just might have to commit sideways. I don-don't know."

"You come back in here, you're gonna need a friend, someone to look out for you."

Bates suddenly felt uneasy. He avoided looking into the inmate's eyes, but looking down at the white shorts Slick was wearing, and the black spider-like legs protruding, caused him to shudder. "Whada'ya mean a friend?"

"Look kid, you're frail and scared. If you come back in here and go to the yard, you'll be punked the first night out. Ya damn well better have someone, someone who's tough, to keep these jockers off ya."

"What, what if I go PC?"

"You think you'll be safe in protective custody? Bool-chit! There's more chicken hawks in PC than ya'll find in the cellhouse at max."

"Well...what if I go to max? Will the Aryan Warriors protect me?"

Another brilliant smile, "You'll be their kid," he guffawed

loudly. "They'll pimp you all night and all day. You'll have to turn tricks for them till you're dead. All you'll be to them is a piece of meat and a money makin' ho.'"

"The AWs pimp their kids to the blacks?"

"Shit yes," Slick chuckled. "You'll be on the radiator hose most of the time. Blacks pay more for kids like you. You think they like black-ass niggers all the time?"

Bates pinched the butt of the cigarette which was about to burn his fingers. He drew heavily and tossed the hot butt into the steel toilet. "I-I ain't gonna do it. I'll carry a shank. I-I'll."

Slick interrupted the kid. "Like I said, if you come back in here, yo damn well better have someone to protect you."

Slick stood up and walked over to the corner of the cell. On the floor was an open box of Tide detergent, another prison canteen item. He poked around inside fishing with a pencil. Abruptly, he came up with a small plastic baggy which he held up to the light. Bates looked up from the bunk with raised eyebrows. Inside, he could see five, maybe six *pin rolls*.[9] Slick slipped two out of the baggy, and went to the door to see if any cops were around.

Not seeing any, he lit one for Bates, and one for himself. Sitting back down on the bunk next to the kid, Slick, the experienced smoker, filled his lungs and motioned for Bates to do the same. The sweet smell of reefer soon filled the small cell, causing other inmates out on the tier, to peer in. Slick gestured for them to get away, and to keep quiet He reached again under his bunk and came up with a small cone of culinary cinnamon he'd got from the food cart pusher. Lighting this helped to quaff the odor of pot.Slick gazed into Bate's reddening eyes.

"You like word games?"

The kids' forehead had lost its furrows. "Wha? What's a word game?"

"You don't know what a word game is?" Laughter split the cell. "I give you a word and you have to use it in a sentence."

Bates again pulled smoke into his lungs, "Okay, go ahead, Slick."

"Aw—right, use the word fascinate in a sentence."

"Super easy," Bates said, "I am fascinated by these pin rolls." He grinned.

"No! Not fascinated. Fascin...ate!"

"Okay, Slick, you try it then."

Slick grabbed the kid's shoulders and gazed into the redness of his eyes.

"I got a new pair of 501 jeans that's got ten buttons on the fly," Slick grinned. "Sometimes, when I feel like I do now, I can only fasten eight." Again his laughter rocked the small cell.

And again that quizzical look spread across the kid's face.

"I ain't gonna ask why," Bates faltered.

"Okay, here's another. If Anita Bryant married Moby Dick, what would her name be?"

Bates was eyeing the hard-time convict through eyes that were rapidly glazing over, as was his mind.

"Anita Dick?" He mumbled.

"So do I." Slick again grabbed the kid's shoulders and moved closer to his face chuckling like a circus clown. He put his hand on the kid's thigh.

"Hey man, hey!" Bates was resisting. "What're ya a homosexual?"

"Hell no, I ain't no homosexual. Why'd ya say that? "I may pitch, but I sure as hell don't catch."

"What's the diff? You mess with another man, that's being a homo."

Slick tried to rationalize.

"I ain't no homosexual kid, but I can pitch without catchin'. But there's a lot of 'em in here and at max too. You come back in here and they gonna punk you. But not me, I ain't gonna."

Bates appeared somewhat relieved, and drew in another deep smoke.

"What if I come back in here and get a celly whose been down a long time How can I tell if he's aw-right?"

"You'll know kid, by the next morning..." and Slick's voice trailed off.

Bates again had that bewildered look on his face. "I-I don't feel too good."

"Relax kid, I got something for that too." Again Slick went fishing under the bottom bunk, and this time came up with a widemouth plastic jar that carried a label indicating protein powder, another prison canteen item. He removed the wide screw cap, and held the jar under the kid's nose. An odor akin to rotting garbage rose from inside.

"Pruno?[10] Damn, you take chances. How long this been

cookin'"

"Long enough for us to drink it. It's good shit too. I used some raisins the con on the food cart slipped me. A couple'a shots o' this and you ain't gonna have a care."

It wasn't long before the ceiling over Bates's head was spinning.

"I don't feel too good," Bates whined, I'm going back to my house."

"Whoa, not so fast. We still got another hour before count. You feel shitty, go ahead and lie down here for a while."

Bates rose on unsteady feet and staggered toward the door.

"I-I don't think so, Sllick," he murmured, "I gotta get back and take a shit."

Slick got to his feet and moved toward the steel door and closed it quietly. Covering the observation window with a piece of cardboard,[11] he steered Bates back toward the bunk.

"Hey now," Bates protested, "I wanna get up outta here."

Slick shoved him back down on the bunk, and again reached underneath his bunk, this time coming up with a toothbrush shank.[12] This he held against the kid's neck in the area of the jugular vein. Forcing the kid into a prone position on the bunk, he whispered, "You make a sound you pizza-faced bitch, and I'll kill ya."

The next morning, Ross Brymer was leaving the counselor's office after making his morning phone call. He started back to N-wing when he noticed Bates carrying a bundle of sheets into the laundry room. Something was wrong, he thought. Bates's hair, never combed properly, was now a tangled mass of weeds; his facial acne seemed more noticeable, and Brymer was sure, he saw tears in the SKEs eyes. He asked permission from one of the unit officers to check on some laundry.

Inside the laundry room, Brymer moved past the large noisy commercial washers which were rumbling under their heavy loads. Initially, he could not see the youngster, but as he moved around, he pulled up quickly when he saw Bates cowering on the floor near one of the large dryers.

"Hey, something wrong kid?" He moved over to the hunched up youngster and put a meaty hand on the kid's shoulder.

The kid looked up and peered into Brymer's face.

"I-I gotta get a shank Ross," he stammered. "I gotta kill

some no good son-of-a-bitch."

Slick's name popped into Brymer's head immediately.

"It's that no good toad, ain't it?"

"How...how'd you know?" Bates, looked up and Brymer could see the anguish in the kids tearful eyes.

"Cause that's what the son-of-a-bitch was always pullin' at max. The AWs would have killed him if that dumb nut doctor hadn't moved him over here to kiddy land. Bad mistake."

"Well, Ross, ya gotta help me get a shank...or a club...or somthin'"

"Kid, you don't have enough mustard. He'd take it from you before you made a move. Look's like I'll have ta' take care of Slick. He punk ya?"

Bates stared at the floor. "Well...he didn't screw me, but he...he *slick-legged* me last night."

"WHAT? He did what? He slick-legged you? What the hell does that mean?"

Bates told the con how Slick had plied him with weed and pruno and how he'd been held down by the larger inmate, and sexually assaulted.

"Yeh, okay, but what the hell is slick-leg?"

"He...he told me if I didn't scream, he...he wouldn't put it in." Bates was speaking hesitantly in obvious shame and grief.

"Go on."

"He made me lie on my stomach and he pulled down my pants."

"What about your shorts?"

"No. He didn't make me take them off. He greased his dick with Vaseline, and told me he'd only put it between my legs. He said that was slick-leggin'"

"So he didn't actually go up your ass?"

"No, but he said he was gonna keep doing this until I got to likin' it. After that, he said, he'd start going up me."

"You ain't gonna do shit for that rotten bastard. I'll take care of Slick"

"You...you better be careful Ross. He's got a shank."

"His shit don't worry me a damn bit." Brymer tried to instill a bit of courage into the scared youngster. "Listen kid, a can of chili in a laundry bag is ten times better'n a shank."

Slick leg, eh, mused Brymer, guess that's why they call him

Slick.

"You get back to work Bates." Brymer stormed back to the N-wing gate, all the while cursing under his breath. He detested jockers who did things like this to weak youngsters like Bates. After he was back on the wing, the gate was racked closed. He positioned himself where he could keep an eye on the rotunda. He was looking for, and patiently waiting for Slick to appear.

It didn't take long. Just before 10:00 a.m., Brymer caught a glimpse of Slick walking in the rotunda. Brymer needed to get past the gate, and he caught the attention of one of the bubble officers. Motioning with his hands, he was able to convince the officer he needed to get out and bring some dirty sheets into the laundry room. Casually swinging a laundry bag, he entered the rotunda.

Once in the rotunda, he moved over to where Slick was talking to a couple of SKEs, and pulled up in front of him..

"I found a really cool bong made out of a large bone which was thrown in with these dirty sheets," he goaded Slick. Wanna' look at it?"

"Sho...sho do," Slick grinned.

"Follow me." They both entered the laundry room which was filled with steamy heat, and fortunately for Brymer, the noisy clamoring of the machines.

Inside, Brymer turned savage and slammed the surprised black into the wall like a linebacker.

"You rotten sonofabitch," Brymer snarled, pinning Slick against the wall. "You rotton no good sonofabitch!"

A look of terror shown in Slick's eyes.

"Wha...what up, Ross?" Slick coughed. "What'd I do?"

"Punkin' these Caspers again, you bastard. Ya could've picked on one of those punk-ass pieces of coal down the wing," Brymer growled slamming his shoulder into Slick's midsection. "Well, you ain't gonna do it here no more."

"Hey... now... Ross ...hey man," Slick winced. "Ross...Ross, lighten up. Ya..ya mean that Bates kid? Hey it ain't no thang."

"Yeh, it's a THANG, you chicken hawk bastard," and Brymer started flailing with the weighted laundry bag.

A few officers outside in the rotunda, paid scant attention to the muffled sounds bouncing around inside the laundry room. The machines were always making noise.

Abruptly, Brymer emerged from the room, wiping the sweat

from his brow, casually swinging the laundry bag as if he didn't have a care. He was let back into the wing, and as he walked back to his house, stopped to holler a few words to a couple of friends through the cell doors.

Inside his cell, he began going through his personal items. Toiletries, candies, tobacco and matches, and a few extra socks and underwear he'd lifted from the laundry room, and a few pieces of fruit he'd been given. These little luxuries that make life behind bars a little more bearable, would soon be taken from him if he retained them. He moved up and down the tier, sliding these items under the cell doors where a few of his friends were housed. He knew he'd soon be going to the hole.

When the officers found Slick, he was lying on the laundry room floor, dazed, bleeding from several lacerations of the head and face, and breathing heavily. A toothbrush shank was lying on the floor a few feet away. C/O Taitano placed the shank in an evidence bag and covered Slick with a blanket and told him to lie quietly until medical staff arrived. Slick nodded in obvious anguish.

When the medical team arrived, they bandaged his wounds and lifted him onto a gurney and moved him to the infirmary. To his credit, he didn't rat off Brymer, but this was not because he was a standup convict. Quite the contrary. He felt that he and Brymer, both, would be going to max, and he didn't want to give Brymer any more reason to repeat what had just happened.

When the investigators arrived in the unit, the officers reported they had seen Slick and Brymer going into the laundry room together. Brymer, they said, was the only one they'd seen come back out. Where was Brymer now? The investigators were told he'd gone back to his cell.

In N-wing, the investigator's strip-searched Brymer, looking for weapons and injuries. None were found. The suspect was placed in handcuffs and leg irons and moved to administrative segregation pending investigation of battery by a prisoner. Did Brymer have anything to say to them?

"Nothing."

After depositing Brymer in the hole, the investigators went back to the fish-tank and tore Brymer's house apart looking for anything that would tie him to the attack. They noted a laundry bag soaking in the toilet, but other than that, nothing that could tie him to the assault was uncovered. They did note however, that there was an unopened can of chili beans under his bed; an item usually not available to fish-tank inmates. Routine photos were taken. They spent the next several hours interviewing officers and inmates, looking for someone who had witnessed the assault.

Bates was pulled up and interviewed in one of the counselor's offices.

"Look, kid," one officer (Good Guy), began, "you're only an SKE; you'll be goin' back home soon. Slick's gonna be here until every hair on his head is white. What'a ya got to tell us?"

"I didn' see, or hear nothin'"

The other investigator (Bad Guy), broke in.

"Okay, smart ass, you damn well better remember seeing something, or so help me God, I'll see to it that you get sent back in here with more time than that asshole has."

Bates was foolish, but not foolish enough to go for this time worn Frick-Frack routine. "I'm tellin' both of ya, I was in the storage room scrubbin' walls. I didn't hear or see shit."

"How old are you Bates?" It was Good Guy's turn. "I'll bet you're about my kids age. You and him would get along great. He's a good kid too."

"You got a son my age?'

"Sure do."

"Black or white?"

"Okay you smart-ass punk," Bad Guy jumped up knocking his chair backwards, "get the hell back to your cage. You've just bought a one way ticket back into this armpit."

"Now hang on, Spence." It was Good Guy's turn. "I've heard that Slick was punkin' some of you kids. Now if that's true, I guess whatever he got, he had comin.' I couldn't care less who thumped him."

Bates looked at Good Guy with that quizzical expression.

"You heard straight shit. It's too damn bad he wasn't kilt. Should'a been"

"Was he takin' booty?" Bad Guy had decided to try again.

"Like I said, he's a no good sonofabitch. Should' had his dick cut off."

The two investigators told Bates to leave the room, but instructed him to hang loose outside the door in case they had more questions. When they emerged a few minutes later, they told him to go back to his wing.

"Without a credible witness," one of them muttered, we got nothin' on Brymer."

After a few days, Ross Brymer was removed from the ad-seg cell and returned to N-wing to finish the fish-tank processing. He had lost his job as tier runner. Three weeks later, Ross Brymer along with the other the fish-tank inmates were escorted across the yard to the visiting area. There they would appear before the initial classification committee, a routine procedure in all prisons.

The classification committee consisted of facility wardens, high echelon uniformed staff, counselors, the psychiatrist, the chaplain, and related personnel. Decisions made here assign a custody level to each inmate (minimum, medium, maximum or max lockup) depending upon the person's sentence structure, escape potential, behavior, past incarcerations and other significant data.

Ross Brymer, doing two years, had a relatively light sentence, however; because of the nature of the offense, his past incarcerations, and because he was suspected of being responsible for the assault on Slick, he was classified to housing at the maximum security prison. He was transferred that afternoon, along with several other hard-core prisoners.

At max, he settled in comfortably; he'd been there before for two previous stretches, and now enjoyed kickin' it with some of his old friends. The current topic of the day was one notorious character, Jesse Bishop, who'd arrived there at about the same time Brymer had. Though Bishop was housed on death row, the two inmates struck up a friendship by passing kites and verbal messages which were relayed by law clerks, culinary workers and at times through prison staff members (against the rules).[13]

The months rolled by, and Brymer remained relatively trouble free. During the Christmas, season, he and some other inmates managed to score some fruit and jelly from the culinary which they mashed together along with bread (for yeast) and brewed some pruno. The cellhouse rocked that Christmas night but the prison staff—if they caught on—let it slide. No write-ups were issued.

Early in June, 1979, Prison Superintendent Robert Lippold agreed to let a news reporter in to interview Ross Brymer.

Lippold said Brymer had been a quiet, trouble free inmate and was scheduled to be released on June 29, this year. He kept to himself, bothered no one, and did his own time, Lippold said.

Brymer was asked if this were the case, and he agreed that he just tried to do his time quietly without getting into any trouble.

"I just found a cubby hole and stayed out of people's way. There's no such thing as the toughest guy in the joint. No matter how tough you are, you have to go to sleep."

Brymer was asked about the Bonavena slaying, and how he felt about it now. He offered little more than what had been brought out during the court appearances.

He spoke about his early childhood growing up in Texas, which he said was a fight for survival. Fighting was a way of life.

Brymer told the reporter that when he got out he wanted to avoid trouble if possible and go back to his first love which was country music. A guitarist and singer, he said he once played with Willie Nelson, and he wanted to continue doing gigs around the Reno clubs.

He said he feared getting another felony case because he knew under Nevada law, it could mean a life sentence if he were adjudged a habitual criminal.

How did he feel about Bonavena now? What about the rumors circulating on the street that some of the late boxer's friends were going to avenge hs death.

Brymer said he held no grudges against Bonavena's family, however, "... if anyone comes after me, they're gonna get hurt," he said.

Brymer said he could have applied for a parole last December, but decided against it, not wanting *a tail* after he got out. He said too many ex-cons who accept a parole come right back into prison on a parole violation, the result of over zealous parole officers barging into houses day and night, looking for drugs and weapons. He told the reporter that he feared getting another felony case because he knew, under Nevada law, it could mean a life sentence if he were adjudged a habitual criminal.

Asked if he were still on friendly terms with Joe Conforte, Brymer acknowledged nothing between them had changed. After all, it was Joe who had put up the Cabin In The Sky restaurant as collateral for the $250,000 bail money which kept Brymer out of jail while awaiting trial.

On June 29, 1979, Willard Ross Brymer, self admitted slayer of Argentine boxer, Oscar Bonavena, was released from prison. He'd served 15 months of a two-year sentence. His last night at

NSP brought little sleep. He'd been awake most of the night thinking about this day, and visualizing the things he was going to do.

Before being escorted out past the front gate he had time to give away a few of the personal items he'd collected, and to crack a few jokes with the other cons. They wished him well. As he paused to say goodbye, the uniformed officer at his side told him to knock it off.

"Ya wanna' stay here for another stretch," he chided. "You'll have enough time to bullshit tonight."

Brymer grinned and the two started walking down past the lower yard under the watchful eye of the rooftop mounted gun posts. Moving past the block holding the CMU inmates, Brymer turned his head and shouted, "Take care, Jesse; don't let 'em get you!" Yet he knew his words were futile. Jesse Bishop was destined to be the last person put to death by lethal gas in Nevada.

As they ambled past the culinary, he couldn't help but whiff the familiar odor of greasy hash browns and scrambled eggs cooking on the grill.

"God, I'm glad I don't have to eat that shit any more," he quipped to the officer.

"Sure, Ross, you hate it here. It's a cold world out there where you're goin' now. After you've been living under the bridge for a month or so, you'll be knockin' on the gate to get back in here."

The last gate holding the convict a prisoner was suddenly opened and Ross Brymer found himself standing on the black-topped surface of the parking lot, a thousand miles away from prison walls. Ignoring the shotgun toting officer at the top of One-Tower, he gazed skyward at the blue Nevada sky and smiled broadly.

Exalted to be free again, yet saddened to think of leaving his friend Jesse Bishop behind, who was scheduled to be executed later this year, Ross drew in a deep breath of fresh air filling his lungs, and faced back toward the cellhouse, "So long, Jesse!"

"Your ride's over there." It was the officer at the top of the tower pointing to a chauffeur driven limousine parked nearby. Another deep breath of fresh air, and a final glance at the cellhouse, Brymer turned back and then scurried over to the limo where the driver was standing at attention by the open rear door. Next stop: Joe Conforte's Mustang Ranch where a warm welcome awaited him.

EPILOGUE

Slick, instead of being sent back to max, was transferred to a different prison in another western state. He continued preying on young white inmates. One evening, two whites, members of a prison wrecking crew, rolled in on him as he was lying on his bunk. Armed with pipes, the two beat him to death.

On January 23, 1984, Dr. Freestone's contract with the Department of Prisons, to serve as medical director and psychiatrist was revoked under a "no fault, no cause" provision. He was replaced by a matronly female psychiatrist. Dr. Freestone announced he would file suit.

After serving 120 days evaluation, Bates was returned to court where he was granted probation. After several months of freedom, he was picked up on a burglary charge. This time the judge slapped him with a five-year sentence.

Chapter Twelve
GEE JON AND LETHAL GAS

Jesse Bishop, self admitted contract killer, knew his friend Ross Brymer, at this very moment, was speeding toward the Mustang Ranch. Lucky guy, thought Bishop.

Bishop would never see Ross again, nor would he ever see the streets again, nor the Nevada brothels. He would never again taste whiskey, smoke a joint, nor fix heroin. Bishop was destined to be the last person put to death by lethal gas in the state of Nevada. Cigars were his only solace.

He lie on the steel bunk in the Condemned Men's Unit, chewing on the end of the soggy tobacco while staring at the ceiling. He reflected on the thirty-one other Nevada inmates who had been dispatched by lethal gas.

Who had been the first?

Who cares?

Though, somewhere in the back recesses of his mind, he seemed to recall that an itinerant Chinaman, again a Nevada killer, had been the first in the nation to be put to death in this manner.

He had no way of knowing how it all came about, nor why.

Nor did he give a shit.

Who was the Chinaman?

Who cares?

Gazing up through swirls of harsh cigar smoke, he snickered. Chinamen were opium freaks. Himself? He preferred the more refined end product: heroin. Although, he had to admit, there were times he had to settle for paregoric, or sometimes cough mixtures containing codeine. All were products of the beautiful poppy, and in varying degrees, similarly affected the user.

Chinamen and me, he snickered. Worlds apart. Yet so much in common.

As his eyelids began to droop, he tossed the still smoldering cigar butt on the concrete floor. Thoughts passed lazily. And then, a face slowly materialized. A gaunt face. A sad face. A balding Chinaman.

Who the hell was he? Was he real?

And then as if from a deep tunnel, came a muffled whisper: Gee Jon.

Who the hell was Gee Jon?

On August 27, 1921, Gee Jon, a 28 year-old reputed hitman for the San Francisco based, Hop Sing Tong, traveled to the tiny northern Nevada mining town, of Mina, on a mission. His target, Tom Quong Kee, a 74-year old member of the Bing Kung Tong, who was living in a small cabin in what was then, Mina's, Chinatown. A 19 year old youth living in Mina, Hughie Sing, and who was a Hop Sing sympathizer, had previously agreed to guide Jon to Kee's cabin.

Just before dawn, the two crept up to the front door of the cabin and knocked softly. Inside, Kee, slow to arise, was unsure of who could be calling this early. Rubbing the sleep from his eyes, Kee stumbled out of bed and lit a candle and then proceeded to the front door. As the door swung open, Kee had only a millisecond to ponder his mistake. The .38 caliber revolver held in Jon's hand exploded in fire and lead and Kee was hurled backwards by the impact, dead before he dropped to the floor.

This killing was one of many that year among rival tongs, in what was rapidly becoming an escalating tong war. Kee had been targeted because someone from his tong had reportedly been responsible for kidnapping a slave girl who belonged to the Hop Sing Tong.

The sound of the gunfire alarmed other Chinatown residents who clamored out of bed intent on securing their meager belongings from what they guessed was to be another impending raid by the white citizenry bent on driving the yellow devils out.. Anti-Chinese sentiment was at an all time high, and the migrant Chinese feared more what the white citizens would do than what the tong messengers would. Many times in the past, the whites had barged in on them in force to wreak havoc on their settlement. The whites, persistently violent in their disdain for the Chinese, had voted in an 1880 referendum, 17,259, to 183, to restrict further Chinese immigration.

Partly because of the fear of the whites, the Chinese were quick to give up the identity of the two Hop Sing Tong suspects. Jon and the boy, Hughie Sing, were summarily arrested and thrown into jail to await trial. Despite the pervasive anti-Chinese sentiment, they were apparently given a fair trial. The two were found guilty and sentenced to death. Gee Jon, was to make history as being the first prison inmate to be put to death by lethal gas in the United States, if not in the entire world.

Prior to Jon's execution, hanging was the usual method of capital punishment in Nevada. Most hangings were carried out in the county where the crime was committed. Others were done at the state prison. Occasionally mishaps occurred.

A malfunction on the gallows could be inordinately distressing. There were instances when the body weight and the drop distance had not been calculated properly. These mishaps resulted in the condemned person being decapitated, or, if the fall failed to break the condemned's neck, strangled. Many of the spectators had to turn their heads as the condemned person's gurgled screams filled the air while struggling with flailing arms and legs trying to stay alive.

Some of the other states were using the electric chair, but death by electrocution too, could also be unnerving to those in attendance. People often spoke of the instances when the first jolts failed to dispatch the subject, who then had to endure succeeding jolts.

Back in 1911, the Nevada legislature had passed a law giving the condemned a choice of execution: hanging, or death by firing squad. For whatever strange reason, most of the condemned preferred hanging. The law abiding citizens though, made it known they would like to witness a death by firing squad for a change.

In order to tone down the circus-like atmosphere of a firing squad, an elaborate "killing machine" was constructed on prison grounds. Three rifles were mounted inside an enclosed wooden shack, whose barrels poked out of three port holes. The condemned would be strapped to a high-back chair a short distance away, and a red, heart-shaped paper pinned to his chest. Inside the shack, the rifles were mounted on sturdy supports, aimed and then locked in place by viselike iron jaws. Next, the rifles would be loaded, two with live rounds, and one with a blank. Strings were attached to the triggers leading back to three guard volunteers who were out of sight. When the warden gave the signal, the rifles would be fired by the men pulling on the strings. If everything went right, the two live slugs finished off the condemned, and the men pulling on the strings never knew which firearms had the live rounds.

The first and only man to be executed by this method in Nevada, occurred on May 14, 1913. Andriza Mircovich, a Montenegrin, was shot in accordance with the law for the stabbing death of a fellow countryman in Tonopah. The execution went off without a hitch, and few malfunctions were anticipated for future firing squad executions. However; none followed.

H.L. Bartlett, an Elko County assemblyman, was the person responsible for bringing lethal gas into the nation's death chambers. Bartlett deplored Nevada's use of the gallows or firing squad, and set about to find an alternative. After much thought and research, he announced a much better method would be the use lethal gas. Gas, he argued, would be much cleaner, would spare the condemned the agony of a botched hanging, and could be done with total confidence of success. He, at first thought it could be done simply by having a volunteer creep up on the condemned's cell while he was asleep, slide the mixture inside the cell, and then get back out as quickly as possible. He was to learn that it would take much more than this.

Bartlett contacted the prison warden, Denver Dickerson, who in turn got in touch with the state food and drug commissioner, S. C. Dinsmore. The plan they worked out was to use a small, two-room stone house near the northwest corner of the prison yard. The house, built in 1888, of quarry stone and concrete, was fairly well preserved. One room, they reasoned, could be sealed off air tight and would serve as the gas chamber where a stiff-backed wooden chair with leg and arm straps, could be secured to the floor. The other room would hold the heavy gas tanks. This is where the person chosen to dispatch the gas, would be stationed.

Once the condemned was strapped into the chair, the guards would back out and seal the room airtight. Pipes leading from the tanks would carry the gas into the chamber where it would be released directly under the chair where the condemned was seated. To clear the air afterwards, a one-half foot hole which was to be cut in the roof, would vent the gas adequately. This of course would be kept sealed during the execution. Another sealed hole, near the floor, would be opened to allow fresh air in after the condemned were dead. This was the plan, and it was all contingent upon using a highly lethal gas, a gas that essentially had to be lighter than air, so that it would rise and not gather along the floor.

E. B. Wallker, described as a gas expert from Reno, was retained to start the necessary preparations. The building to be used for the execution, he said, was too old, and not suitable for execution by poisonous gas. Nevertheless, he was told, he would have to work with this structure; there were no others available. The most suitable poison to use then, he said, would be hydrocyanic acid—HCN. HCN is produced by combining hydrogen and cyanogen, and exists as a colorless liquid with the smell of peach blossoms or bitter almonds. Converting the HCN into highly lethal hydrocyanic gas, he explained, could only be achieved if a constant temperature of 75 degrees were maintained in the death chamber. If not, he said, the gas would fail to volatilize. And lastly, he told the others, only an expert with knowledge of the inherent dangers should be retained as executioner.

There was only one place known where this dangerous chemical mixture could be purchased and that was on the West Coast. And since the rail and express lines had very stringent regulations against transporting these dangerous chemicals across state lines, it would be up to prison officials to bring it in by automobile. S.C. Dinsmore, who also served as state chemist, was appointed to locate and secure the chemicals and bring them into Nevada.

Dinsmore went to San Francisco to make the purchase, but when the company learned what Nevada had in mind, they refused to sell the poisonous mixture to him. He then traveled to Los Angeles.

On January 22, 1924, Warden Dickerson received a telegram from Los Angeles and was informed the sale had been made. Sufficient gas producing chemicals had been purchased—enough to execute three men who were scheduled to die, the two Chinese Hop Sing tong men, and an Elko itinerant, who had been convicted of slaying an Indian girl named Mamie Johnny.

The immediate problem was how best to get the chemicals back to Carson City. Rumors had been circulating that certain tong men, and other opponents of the planned execution by lethal gas, were going to highjack the gas-carrying vehicle to prevent the execution from taking place. Dickerson then advised Dinsmore to come on back to Carson City, but cautioned him not to try transporting the gas. Another plan had to be worked out.

When Dinsmore arrived back at the prison, he was told three steel cages, each about seven-feet high, seven-feet long, and three-feet wide, each with an iron bunk, would be constructed to hold the three condemned men until the executions. The condemned would be held in these cages until the fateful hour when they would be shackled, and then, escorted to the death house. Inmate handymen were put to work building the cages. Everything went well until the workers started drawing heat from the other inmates who demanded they stop working on anything connected with the lethal gas executions.

Within a day, work on the cages came to an abrupt halt. The inmate workers went on strike and refused to finish the cages. They were ordered back to work, and when they balked, were tossed into the prison dungeon (an unlit natural cave fitted with a hinged, strap-iron gate, that dug into the cliff bordering the yard on the west side).

After a couple of days of bread and water in the cave, the inmate workers relented and agreed to come out and go back to work. Dreary looking and shielding their eyes from the sun, they emerged like bats, and after being fed, went back to work on the cages. Within a week, work on the cages and gas chamber had been completed. The inmate workers were rewarded with extra food rations and sent back to their cells. The administrative staff kicked back and waited for the appeals process to wind down, and the anticipated dates set for the three condemned men.

The Chinese Consulate in San Francisco, sent a strongly worded protest to the Nevada Board of Pardons urging them to use some other form of execution. Citing anti-Chinese sentiment, Chinese Consulate General, Koliang Yih, asserted the gas chamber was only an experiment to be tested on Chinese, with no guarantee that American criminals in the future would be put to death by the same method.

Koliang wrote, "I humbly beg you to substitute some other form of punishment. I appeal to you in the name of fairness and traditional international courtesy."

Other letters and petitions were sent by several Nevada residents. Charles Burrit, of Reno, contended that to use gas would be equivalent to the use of mustard gas during the first world war, when thousands of American soldiers who'd been gassed, came home only to live out the remainder of their lives severely disabled.

On the afternoon of January 26, the state pardons board met to consider the appeals of the two Chinese tong men. Taking into account Hughie Sing's young age (19) at the time of the murder, and the fact that he carried no weapon, the board commuted his sentence to life imprisonment. A few days later they also commuted the death sentence of the itinerant ranch worker, leaving only Gee Jon facing execution.

In a last ditch effort to stop Gee Jon's execution, attorneys argued feverishly before the Nevada Supreme Court, citing among other things, racism. However; Gee Jon was affirmed as the person who gunned down the other Chinese tong man in Mina, citing premeditation. Clemency was refused. He was ordered to die by lethal gas on February the 8th, 1924.

Back at the prison, the two Chinese tong men bid each other farewell. Sing was moved back to the general population, and was put to work Monday morning in the prison laundry. Gee Jon, could only lie on his bunk and stare upwards.

Warden Dickerson and state chemist Dinsmore, met with Governor, J. G. Scrugham, to work out a plan for bringing the gas to Nevada. They agreed the car used to transport the gas, should have the appearance of a private vehicle with no hint of its actual purpose. Therefore, an unmarked car with out-of- state license plates, should be the vehicle of choice. The lethal gas tanks should be concealed in the rear of the car, and to ensure the safety of the drivers, a rubber hose leading from the tanks to the outside rear of the car, should be used to vent the gas in the event it expanded inside the tanks while driving through the Mojave desert.

A civic minded, middle aged couple, Mr. and Mrs., Tom Pickett, were chosen to be the drivers, and were promised good pay ($25.00 a day) for their adventurous mission. They were presented with the car, which carried California license plates, and were given a brief outline to follow. They were cautioned that rumors were circulating in town that Chinese tong men planned to intercept their cargo to prevent the execution from taking place.

Under the strictest secrecy, they assumed the roles of a vacationing couple and set out for Los Angeles presumably to enjoy a pleasant weekend.

Five days later, on Monday night, February 4, the Picketts, both of whom appeared to be near panic, sped into Carson City carrying the tanks of lethal chemicals in the trunk of the car. Appearing grateful to have made the trip safely, they recounted a harrowing tale of being frightened throughout the return trip by the suspicious actions of other travelers.

Near Mojave, Mrs. Pickett said, two cars were seen parked by the roadside, and the drivers were carefully scrutinizing every passing vehicle. It was Mrs. Pickett's opinion, that the drivers were looking for a car-truck bearing Nevada plates, and when the Picketts passed with their California plates, no suspicion was aroused.

As the Picketts neared Minden in the evening, they spotted two automobiles parked in the shadows near the road. As the Pickett vehicle came into view, two men jumped from the leading car in a threatening manner. Mrs. Pickett, who was driving, accelerated to sixty miles an hour heading for Carson City. The two parked cars then came to life and roared after the Picketts, chasing them into Stewart. As they came into Stewart, the pursuers abruptly broke off the chase, and the Picketts arrived in Carson City, shaken, but safe. The Picketts, both agreed they thought the men were trying to stop them in order to steal the poisonous gas.

Less than three years after being convicted of the murder of a fellow Chinese, Gee Jon entered the annals of history by becoming the first person put to death by lethal gas in the United States, and quite possible, the world. Actually, Jon was something of a guinea pig. Since this method of execution had never been tried before, many questions arose and few answers ensued. It was to be an execution by trial and error.

On the appointed day, Feb. 8, 1924, Captain Joe Muller, and his three select guards, called to Jon, who was reclining on his bunk, and told him it was time. There was no response. Muller again called to the Chinaman, who this time, rose slowly and began to sob. He was then led across the yard and into the gas chamber where he was strapped into the chair.

Confident that he was well secured in the chair, the death watch crew backed out and closed the door. Air tight sealing around the door and windows was meticulously applied, and then double checked by the warden. At his post in the adjoining room, the appointed executioner stood ready to unleash the toxic mixture. He signaled to the warden that everything was in order.

The warden nodded, and a mist of death was seen to escape from a pipe under the chair holding Gee Jon, and begin to slowly fill the small room. Jon's eyes widened in panic. Within five seconds, Jon appeared to lose consciousness. His eyes however, remained open and his head moved spasmodically for what seemed an eternity, but which was actually six minutes. Then all movement ceased. The attending physician, who had previously taped a stethoscope to the man's chest and ran a tubing out through the wall, listened attentively, and then looked up at the warden who was standing nearby and pronounced the condemned man dead. Tong man, Gee Jon had made history.

The vents were opened and procedures to clear the gas from the chamber were effected. However, no one was anxious to enter.

After several hours, Capt. Muller, holding ammonia based smelling salts (an acid neutralizer) under his nose, cautiously entered the gas chamber. On the floor could be seen damp spots where the hydrocyanic gas had liquefied. Carefully, as if stepping through a minefield, he and the other guards removed the body from the chamber.

The next day, the body was placed in a pine box, and carried twenty-five yards across the yard to the prison cemetery by other inmates. Gee Jon was buried without ceremony.

Reactions to the execution varied. Captain Joe Muller, offered his opinion.

"I have observed several hangings and one shooting in the executions of prisoners at the Nevada State Prison, but the most humane method that I have ever witnessed is that by lethal gas."

Warden Dickerson had similar comments.

"The lethal gas method of execution is far more humane than the old methods of hanging and shooting, but I would not recommend lethal gas until the method of its application has been perfected, for there is the great danger to witnesses. There is no doubt but that death by this gas is painless. If some company should be able to eliminate the element of danger to the witnesses, I would unhesitatingly recommend its use for capital punishment."

Reverend, Dr. Goodwill, of the Church of Unity of Springfield, Massachusetts, had differing thoughts, He sent a furious letter to the Nevada Prison warden.

"Your revolting execution of a poor Chinaman," the letter stated, "has stirred the people of Massachusetts as no other incident of cruelty has done for a long time.

"Say! Are you civilized out there? You belong in the Middle Ages.

"The method of cutting off one's head as they do in China is much more humane than that execution. Oh well, I suppose you had to have a subject and the lone Chinaman had to stand for it.

"I shall trust you have that law repealed at once and let this be your last execution by such a cruel method."

Other states had been following these events set by Nevada, and began to weigh the possibilities of replacing their existing methods of execution with lethal gas.

When one of the prison doctors was asked to respond to an inquiry from another state, he sent a letter of explanation.

"I have witnessed hangings, shootings and electrocution, and I am sure that gas is to be preferred. The subject appears to suffer no pain, and it is my belief that he is no longer conscious after the first full inhalation of the gas. There was of course some little movement of the body, but it was reflex in character. From the standpoint of witnesses it does not have the brutality connected with it, that goes with the other forms of execution."

The prison warden though, continued to question the safety of the gas and the cost involved. But since it was now the law, he set about to find a safer way to use it. The gas he learned, could be handled and released much safer by using sulfuric acid and cyanide, both chemicals which could be held separately until the final moments. But the first priority was to put up a secure structure that would be designed for, and used only for a gas chamber.

But a year later, on April 6, 1925, the old stone building, was again the scene of a second execution. This time, Stanko Jukich, 29, was put to death for the slaying of Jennie Medak, a year earlier. Everything went fairly well, but again the warden was fearful that the gas could escape and threaten others nearby. He vowed not to use gas again until a chamber could be built that would be unquestionably safe.

After much research and consultations with various experts, plans were ultimately drawn up for the death house. The prison quarry had long been used as a source of stone material which was cut into blocks and used in construction of the cell house and other prison buildings. Inmates were now pressed into service cutting new blocks and transporting them to the proposed building site. The warden watched happily as work began and the place began to take shape.

The inmate workers did a commendable job in putting up the rough structure. The floor was poured using reinforced concrete, which when cured, was over a foot thick. The walls of stone and concrete, were two-feet thick, and supported a reinforced roof. A single, solid steel door provided entry into the building from the front, and the doorway and windows, were also fitted with steel bars. Two of the exterior walls were fitted with double glass insertions, window-like, but air tight, to serve as observation windows for the benefit of the attending physician, and other witnesses. One of these windows had a small hole through which passed the stethoscope tubing, where the attending physician, standing outside, could monitor the heart sounds of the condemned.

Inside, two barred cells, side-by-side, covered the space on the west side. Each cell was fitted with a steel bed and toilet accommodations. The gas chamber was situated on the east side, directly opposite the two cells. A well sealed room, it measured eight-feet long, six-feet wide, and six-feet, six-inches from floor to ceiling. The only necessary furniture was a stiff-backed chair made in the prison wood shop, and which was bolted to the floor. Heavy leather straps were fitted to the arms and legs. The seat of the chair was exactly twenty-four inches up from the concrete.

Another small, sealed off room near the gas chamber, called the observation and operations room is where the work of the executioner was carried out. This room shared a common airtight window with the gas chamber where everything was visible. Below this window, a copper pipe descended down the wall into the concrete floor coming up into the gas chamber. From here, it climbed up the chair's left leg terminating under the seat. A heavy cord ran inside this tubing.

When the gas chamber was to be used, a nest of cyanide eggs (fifteen ounces), held in a mesh bag, was suspended from under the seat, and which could be lowered by the person in the operations room releasing the cord. A two-gallon crock containing two pints of sulfuric acid and five pints of water, lie directly below. When the eggs contacted the mixture, gas generation was instant..

To clear the room, a small amount of ammonia was piped into the area which neutralized the gas. An overhead exhaust pump was then activated and whisked the fumes up through a roof mounted, high rising vent. It was said that this method could clear the room ten times in a four minute period. After much trial and error, ultimately, in 1929, the world's first designed for execution, lethal gas chamber was ready to be used.

Robert White, 41, had the dubious distinction of being the first person put to death in the new gas chamber. White's execution was broadcast as the news feature of the day. White, who had murdered an Elko gambler, was optimistic to the end. As he was being strapped securely into the chair, the warden approached and asked if he had any last requests. White looked up at the warden, and quipped, "Yes warden, let me have a gas mask!"

This efficient stonewalled gas chamber served for a number of years, and then in the early 1950s, another was built, this one being inside, on the upper tier of the cell block which housed death row. Two steel chairs, bolted to the floor, were installed in the event of a double execution (which happened only once, on July 15, 1954, when Frank Pedrini and Leroy Linden were put to death together for the strangulation death of a motorist who had given them a lift).

Thirty two persons in all, have been put to death by lethal gas in Nevada. Gee Jon, Chinese tong man, made history by being the first on February 8, 1924. Jesse Bishop, contract killer, and friend of Ross Brymer, who on October 22, 1979, was to become the last.

Portions of the chapter reprinted courtesy of the Carson City Daily Appeal, February 5, 1924.

Chapter Thirteen
THE EXECUTION OF JESSE BISHOP

Shortly after midnight, on October 22, 1978, Jesse Bishop, 46, lowered himself into the left chair of the two-seated gas chamber and commented, "This is just one more step down the road I've been walking all my life."

The long road, with many bumps and detours, began in Garden Grove, California, where Jesse was born and raised. During the formative years he had a few scrapes with the law, but none that were serious enough to keep him out of the Army during the Korean War.

At age 18, as a combat paratrooper with the 187th Airborne Regimental Combat Team, he found himself fighting for his life in the bloody undeclared war in Korea. To survive, he learned how to kill without remorse, a trait he was to carry for the rest of his life.

In 1951, he was hit during a fierce battle, and was given morphine in the field. During recovery, he, like many others, became addicted to the poppy's yield. In 1952, charged with possession of heroin, he was given a dishonorable discharge from the army,. and sent to Leavenworth Federal Prison, where he did two years. After being released, he returned to Southern California. Murder and narcotics were to play a major role in his life.

At age 25, in Southern California, Bishop was convicted of a first offense armed robbery and sentenced to prison. For the next 20 years, Bishop spent many years of confinement in prison, and records indicate that during the infrequent times he was on the streets, he was responsible for at least 25 armed robberies. At age 44, again released on parole from a California prison, he set his sights on the bright lights and easy money offered by the Las Vegas casinos.

On Tuesday night, December 20, 1977, while employees of

the El Morocco Casino, on the strip, were gathered for their annual Christmas party, a man wearing a blue nylon coat and blue jeans, charged into the casino and headed for the cashier's cage. Seeing a cash drawer open, the man reached in trying to get a handful of bills. The startled change girl shrieked wildly and slammed the drawer closed. The shift manager, alerted by the girl's screams, rushed over to see what was going on, and instinctively grabbed at the would be thief.

David A. Ballard, 22, a tourist from Baltimore, MD, who was playing the slots, had been married only three hours earlier. He and his newlywed wife, Kathy, 20, had come to the El Morocco to celebrate. When David heard the commotion, he jumped up from the slot he was playing and rushed over to help the shift manager. The would be thief broke from their grasp, jumped back and pulled out a short barreled revolver. Two rapid-fire shots followed and both the shift manager and Ballard crashed to the floor screaming they'd been hit. Other patrons and employees ducked for cover as the lone gunman jumped atop a change booth frantically grabbing for the money. The terror stricken bride ran outside and ducked down behind a parked car, still clutching the freshly inked marriage certificate in her hand.

Grasping a handful of bills, the shooter jumped down to the floor and raced outside through a doorway on the north side of the casino. Outside, he sprinted toward a restaurant and crashed through the front door, startling the patrons and staff, and raced out through the exit. Hot on his trail were three or four El Morocco employees screaming for him to stop.

The shooter pulled up slightly as he approached Las Vegas Boulevard, and then jumped from the curb and zigzagged across the heavy traffic heading for the parking lot of the Stardust Hotel. The pursuing employees saw him leap into a white car parked nearby and roar off.

The police and an ambulance were on the scene of the shooting within several minutes. The shift manager and David Ballard, were rushed to Sunrise Hospital. An all-points bulletin was put on the air alerting all jurisdictions of the robbery and shooting. Shotgun toting cops set up strategic roadblocks throughout the city, checking all traffic.

The dragnet quickly spread to other adjacent communities, but by Wednesday morning, it was thought the shooter had eluded his pursuers. Then, about 11:00 a.m., the police radios began crackling with reports of a man with a gun, trying to stop vehicles including a UPS service truck on a busy street south of town. Also, two reports of kidnapping by the same suspect were coming in. Eyewitness accounts were evaluated, and indications were the suspect was clawing his way south from Las Vegas towards Boulder City.

Heavily armed police from several agencies moved swiftly towards Boulder City. Police in that jurisdiction spent much of the afternoon and evening going house to house alerting the residents and conducting searches. By 10:20 p.m., when no trace of the man could be found, the manhunt was relaxed. And then, just before midnight, came the break needed.

Many of the residents of Boulder City, who had been following the events throughout the evening, continued to check their own yards and neighborhoods for anything out of the ordinary. One couple checking outside their home late at night, noticed that the hinges on the outside cellar door had been removed, and the door was ajar. Checking further, they could hear a man inside coughing. They called to the man, who responded and said he "was just sleeping." They hurriedly went back inside and notified the Boulder City police. Las Vegas Metro SWAT officers, and the Boulder City police were on the scene in minutes, but it appeared the man was on the move again.

Searching the cellar, patrolmen found it empty, but in a dusky corner, they could see where someone had been crouching in the dirt. Quickly a police-manned perimeter was set up to seal off the area, and the incident commander on the scene, amid the barking of scores of dogs, ordered all personnel to maintain their positions until daybreak.

As dawn began to break in the desert city, police from different jurisdictions renewed the search. One lady reported someone had stolen a blue bedspread from her clothesline, and then the prolonged barking of a dog alerted officers to a small travel trailer parked nearby. Probing cautiously under the trailer, Metro Swat and Boulder City patrolman, spotted a shivering figure huddled under the trailer wrapped in the blue bedspread. They knew it was a man by the sound of his coughing.

With guns drawn, the police ordered him to crawl out from under the trailer, and to keep his hands visible. As he emerged from under the trailer, a .38 caliber revolver fell to the ground. Roughly, the police pounced on him locking his arms behind his back and applying the cuffs. As he lie there in the dirt, with knees drawn, shivering and coughing, one of the patrolman covered him with the blue bedspread, leaving only his dirt splattered face and hair showing.

"I don't know how I made it through the night with all the cops around," he muttered. "I would sleep for a few minutes, and then wake up because it was so cold."

Fired up after having been on the alert all night, and confident they'd nailed the suspect in the shooting at the El Morocco, the police slapped each other on the back and talked excitedly among themselves. Two or three of them jerked the man to his feet and tore everything out of his pockets looking for other weapons. Confident he was clean, they shoved him into the back of a patrol car and took off for the Clark County Jail. There, he was identified as Jesse Bishop, ex-con from California, and was held without bail.

On Friday night, December 30, 1978, David Ballard, newlywed tourist from Baltimore, Maryland, and hero to the staff at the El Morocco, succumbed to wounds received when shot just three hours after his marriage.

Jesse Bishop, slammed in the Clark County Jail, was served with a multitude of felony charges including, two counts of kidnapping, three counts of robbery, one count of grand theft auto, one count of assault with a deadly weapon, one count of attempted murder, and one count of first degree murder. On January 11, 1978, a Clark County Grand Jury indicted Bishop on six felony counts including open murder. Bail was denied.

On January 27, a hearing was held before Judge Paul Goldman. Bishop attempted to plead guilty to all charges. Judge Goldman refused to accept the plea at that time. Instead, he ordered a psychiatric hearing for the defendant. Following the psyche hearing, which was conducted by three certified psychiatrists, Bishop was declared sane, competent to enter his plea, and would be allowed to fire his public defenders (he'd previously indicated he wanted to act as his own attorney).

Bishop then fired the two court appointed attorneys. The judge granted the motion, but ordered the two attorneys to remain as "standby" counsel. The judge then asked Bishop if he wanted to call any witnesses.

"I will call no one," Bishop answered. "I have no witnesses. I appreciate your concern."

Bishop then requested that he be sentenced on all charges at the same time.

On Friday, February 9, Judges Paul Goldman, of Las Vegas; William Forman, of Reno and Merlyn Hoyt, of Ely, convened in Judge Goldman's chambers to decide Bishop's fate on the murder charge. Bishop flanked by his two "standby" counselors, cross examined several of the 20 witnesses who were called during the day long hearing, but he called no one in his own defense, and made no argument.

Deputy District Attorney, Mel Harmon, assisted by Steve Gregory, called for the death penalty. He told the three judges that five "aggravating circumstances" have been proved, which under the new Nevada law warrant the death penalty. Outlining the prosecution's case, he explained that Bishop was on parole from California at the time of the murder; he previously had been convicted of violent felonies; he blatantly created a great risk of death to innocent persons; he killed while committing a robbery, and he was trying to avoid a lawful arrest.

"Jesse Bishop, in the state of California alone, has committed 25 robberies with a firearm," Harmon said. "Mr. Bishop has had a long life of crime. I think he's had his chance in society. It is simply our hope that what you do will be the final chapter for Jesse Bishop—the end, and not to be continued.

"We urge you not to give him the opportunity to add a sequel."

Bishop arose and faced the prosecutor.

"I'm a product of that society," he said. "I was made by the same people who made you. A poor person never has a chance. I stand before you as what you made me."

The next day, the three judges deliberated all morning, and at 3:08 p.m., that afternoon, called the defendant into the packed courtroom. Addressing Bishop, Judge Goldman said they were all in agreement that the five aggravating circumstances to warrant the death penalty had been proven "beyond a reasonable doubt."

At the conclusion of the hearing, Judge Goldman read the "warrant of execution" ordering the defendant to be put to death by lethal gas on April 24, 1978, "in the presence of the warden of the Nevada State Prison, at least six reputable citizens over the age of 21 years to be selected by said warden, and a competent physician."

Bishop was asked if he had anything to say. Emotionless, Bishop answered, "I have nothing to say."

Ex-combat paratrooper, Jesse Bishop, who had fought for his life in Korea, and for years afterwards along California's seamy drug trails and prisons, had apparently given up the fight. He said nothing in court that would have helped him stay alive.

On the following day, Bishop again stood before Judge Goldman, this time for sentencing on the charges accumulated during his crime spree following the shooting at the El Morocco. In addition to the penalty of death, Bishop was sentenced to 20 years for attempted murder (the El Morocco shift supervisor), 15 years each for three robberies, plus 15 years on each count for the use of a deadly weapon during the commission of a crime; 15 years each for two kidnappings, plus 15 years on each count for the use of a deadly weapon; 71/2 years for attempted kidnapping, plus 71/2 years for the use of a deadly weapon, and 10 years for grand larceny, a total of 195 years, all of which were to run consecutively to the penalty of death.

With the death penalty reinstated,[1] the Nevada State Prison was notified to get things in order. It was expected the gas chamber would again be put to use. Lethal gas, first used in 1924, had not been used since 1961, when Thayne Archibald, 22, was put to death. After so many years of idleness and neglect, serious repairs would have to be made ensuring an air tight chamber with no possibility of leakage into the observation room. A walk-through inspection of the chamber revealed crumbling caulking around the observation windows, and brittle seals around the weighty bulk head door (originally part of a naval submarine).

When he arrived at the Nevada State Prison, Bishop, was moved into a block with five other men, all of whom were killers recently condemned to death following reinstatement of the death penalty. Unlike Bishop, these five were filing active appeals. From the moment of his arrival, Bishop let it be known he'd reject all appeals. If the execution were carried out as expected, he would become the third person to be put to death in the United States, following the moratorium handed down by the Supreme Court. The other two were, Gary Gilmore, who was executed by firing squad in Utah in 1977, and John Spenkelink, who was electrocuted in Florida in 1979.

Under Nevada law, all capital murder cases are automatically reviewed by the Nevada Supreme Court. As expected, Bishop made no effort to appeal his conviction or the sentence of death. And unlike the five other condemned men with whom he shared death row, Bishop rejected efforts by attorneys on the outside, who tried to intervene. Yet, some of these inmate rights activists, were able to delay the execution for months.

Other attorneys, acting without his consent, were able to get his case before the United States Supreme Court. In late fall, 1979, the Court handed down a 7-2 decision which stated in effect that Nevada could go ahead with the execution. A final date was set. for October 22, 1979.

Speaking about one of these do-gooder attorneys, who had acted without his permission, an outraged Bishop told a cellblock officer, "If I were back on the street, I'd take out that no good son-of-a-bitch."

As the time drew nearer, the cigar chomping Bishop spoke freely with the prison officers. He said he would not fight the execution because it would just lead to endless anxiety and stress for everybody concerned.

What about a commutation to a life sentence?

Bishop said he would accept that type of sentence if so granted. But to remain on death row fighting endless appeals and making brief court appearances was something he said he would not go through. He said he knew he'd eventually wind up in the gas chamber anyway, and he reasoned the stays would only make it harder on his family.

He steadfastly refused to make excuses for his past. When speaking to the cellblock officers, he was candid about the things he had done, and where it had lead him.

"I make no excuses for being myself," he said, "I am what I am, and I have no regrets."

How did he want to be remembered?

"As a man who stood by his word," he quipped. He said for all the many years he'd been locked up, he'd never become a snitch or a bitch. He was still the same man, Jesse Bishop, gunman.

"No other person made me a criminal," he said, "That was my decision, and I never regretted it. There've been good times, and some not so good times. When rolling," he said, "I always had plenty of money, classy women, fast cars, and good whiskey. And I never lived under the bridge like a lot of cons have."

When asked how he felt about facing death, he said he'd never known fear at anytime in his life, "...and going to the gas chamber won't be any different."

During one *macabre rehearsal*, he had agreed to enter the gas chamber and allowed the officers to place him in the steel chair at the request of the administration.

"The seat's not too uncomfortable," he said, "but the banging and other noise they're making getting the thing in order, is annoying."

Once when a cellblock officer asked him if he believed in God, Jesse avoided the question to say he believed only in Jesse Bishop.

On Sunday, October 21, 1979, Jesse Walter Bishop was moved to one of the two *last-night cells*, both of which were windowless, with cold steel walls, and a sliding barred entry gate. Ahead, ten feet away, lie the gas chamber. Located on the third landing of the cell house, access to the area could only be achieved through a series of locked steel gates.

In the last night cell, isolated from the rest of the prison, Bishop had only the correctional officers who had been assigned to the "deathwatch," to converse with.

On the other side of the steel-barred cell gate, the deathwatch officers stood vigilant to prevent any last minute suicide attempts, or other violent disruptive behavior. They also had been given instructions to hand Bishop a phone in the event he wanted to call a lawyer and request a stay of execution.

State Prison Director, Charles Wolff Jr., who was charged with the responsibility of carrying out the execution, said Bishop would have an opportunity to seek an appeal up to the point just minutes before the cyanide pills were popped into the bucket of sulfuric acid secured below the death chair.

Wolff said a phone line to a defense lawyer would be available for Bishop to initiate a call to stop the execution if he had a change of heart. Even so, Wolff said, it would be up to Bishop to initiate the call, though the time element could become critical. There would have to be sufficient time to process the legalities.

A simple call by Bishop, would not in itself be enough to stop the execution, Wolff said. That could only be done by a written or verbal order from the judge. And this could take time to accomplish. Another possibility would be for the governor to relay a court order to the prison director, but under Nevada law, Governor Robert List could not by himself issue a stay of execution. That would be up to the Nevada Board of Pardons, which the governor chaired.

When asked whether he had second thoughts about not asking for an appeal, Bishop reminded the deathwatch crew that once a man makes a move, he should never back up. He said he was well aware that it would be up to him, and to no one else, to halt the proceedings. This he would not do, he repeated.

"I know that right now, I can call the attorneys, and stop these proceedings and move back to my cage on death row. But," he said icily, "that's not what I'm going to do. We're all going to walk in there tonight, and get it over with."

The officers were required to ask him what he wanted as a last meal. When queried, he winked and said, "... a fifth of Jack Daniels and a good woman." The officers chuckled, grateful for a humorous moment, though brief.

"Why not," Bishop said. "It's something any man would want."

Outside, night was falling. Two miles away, on the grounds of the State Legislature, a mingling of death penalty protesters was gathering to pray and speak to the news reporters.

"Why are we killing this man, when we're taught that killing is immoral?" one young woman repeated.

"Will our country be safer tomorrow?" another pleaded.

An unidentified voice rose above the crowd chanting, "..stop it, stop it,." though for the most part, the chilled crowd huddled together quietly.

.Three or four protesters stretched out a banner that read, "WHY DO WE KILL PEOPLE TO SHOW THAT KILLING IS WRONG?"

A few hecklers on the sidewalks countered with catcalls and name calling. One or two tried arguing.

"An eye for an eye," shouted one, "he killed, so he gets killed. Go on back home."

Citing questionable statistics, a bearded protester pleaded for others to join his protest.

"'It's a proven fact," he yelled, "that killing people doesn't do no good."

One man, clad in religious attire, spoke quietly to express his sorrow about the state once again firing up the gas chamber.

"We're going backward," he pleaded, "this is barbaric."

His views were supported by another.

"Violence breeds violence. Why do we perpetuate this?"

"Light your candles," came a soft voice from among the protesters, "it's time to mount our vigil."

The protesters, who now numbered about 75 persons of all ages, began lighting handheld candles, which began flickering in the cold night air. A solemn procession then began the slow march down Fifth Street, enroute to the Nevada State Prison. Inside the Legislature Building, another group of 75 persons, correctional officers held in reserve in the event of a major riot at one of the three local prisons, killed time by joking and sipping coffee.

Outside of the century old maximum security prison, Lt. Wayne Curry, commanded a task force of officers whose function was to maintain security in the front parking lot. As the candle-lighters neared the prison, he gave the officers instructions to position the group in one corner of the lot, and to leave them alone as long as they remained peaceful. His team was backed up by deputies from the Carson City Sheriff's Office.

The prison officer manning the top of One-tower, was there to maintain constant surveillance of the events below. If things turned to shit, he could provide necessary firepower.

As the execution witnesses began arriving, they were processed through the bottom of One-tower. Proof of identity and invitation was verified before they were allowed inside the yard past the barbed-wire topped fences. Cameras, weapons, and other items not allowed inside, was taken from them and secured in the upper deck of the tower. At 11:45 p.m., the 14 witnesses were escorted past the north side cell house, up an outside stairway under the watchful eye of the officer manning Two-tower, and finally, deposited in the observation room facing the windows that peered inside the gas chamber where the condemned would be seated. An exhaust fan rumbled in the ceiling causing several witnesses to look upward.

After adjusting to the hard seats, a few of the witnesses conversed in hushed tones. Others fidgeted nervously saying nothing. They all shifted their eyes when the door creaked open breaking the silence, and the attending physician strode in. Standing rigid, he faced the subdued group grimly.

"Using lethal gas is a very dangerous procedure," he began. "We've taken all necessary precautions, we've sealed the cracks tight, and we've checked for leaks. We think everything is in order, but," he informed those present, "anything can happen."

He went on to relate that it had been nearly 20 years since the gas chamber was last used for an execution. Repairs had been made, he told them, but there was still an element of danger.

"Over the years, because of normal deterioration—and especially because of misuse, maintenance on the gas chamber had been neglected," he explained. "And now, for the last couple of months, needed repairs have been made."

"However," he stressed, "we're still not 100 percent sure that everything will go according to plan. There is a possibility—though remote, that there could be a leak. And remember, people," he said, his voice rising markedly, "it doesn't take but a thimble full of this stuff to put you down."

"If," he stressed, "there is an accident, you should all hold your breath and the officers will usher you out of the room and out of danger."

And then to emphasize the point, he looked into their faces and barked, "I promise, I'll club the first one of you who panics!" This said, he turned and left the room and joined the prison superintendent in an adjoining observation room. The witnesses, many of whom had paled at his words, stared at each other in stunned silence.

The superintendent and the physician could be seen by the witnesses, speaking together in hushed tones, in the adjoining room What the witnesses could not see, was the physician stuffing the stethoscope earpieces with moistened tissue paper until they were tightly sealed.

A prison spokesman then entered the room and informed the group that ammonia capsules would be available for anyone who felt faint; a nearby plastic trash can could be used for if nauseated, and a medical team was standing by for any other problems. As he turned to leave, he noted the tension among the witnesses had peaked. Some had paled markedly, others were chatting rapidly among themselves. Still, others just stared ahead lost in thought.

Near midnight, the group of 14 were startled to see correctional officers enter the gas chamber from the rear bulk head door and pull down the window blinds obscuring the witnesses' view. This was followed by the rattle of heavy keys and steel doors opening and closing. Then abruptly, the blinds were raised revealing the condemned man seated in the left side death-chair. Dressed in a white shirt, blue jeans and white socks, he was bound to the chair by straps around his waist, arms and legs. He calmly peered back out at the witnesses, turned his head from side to side, and raised his hand slightly, as if to say he did not fear death.

Out of sight, three correctional officers who had volunteered to drop the cyanide eggs were poised to release three wall mounted switches. On a command from the prison superintendent, each would throw a switch, only one of which would set the lethal mechanism in motion. The system was designed this way so that the executioners could never know which switch actually released the cyanide eggs.

When the command came from the prison superintendent, the lethal linkage was put into motion and a sharp metallic clang jolted the apprehensive spectators, some of whom began holding their breath.

Hearing the metallic sound, Bishop glanced down at the floor, wrinkled his nose and looked back up at the witnesses. Then staring straight ahead through the lethal mist that was beginning to envelope the chamber, he drew in a deep breath and shuddered spasmodically several times. His skin flushed and he began gulping for air, staring up at the ceiling. Saliva trickled down his chin and his eyes closed as he pitched forward against the straps, his body moving in a series of convulsive jerks. His head pitched backwards and forwards in unison with his chest which was alternately expanding and contracting. And finally, what must have seemed like hours to the spectators, all movement ceased.

The attending physician, in the adjoining room, now appeared to be listening intently through the stethoscope earpieces for any sign of life. Actually, he could hear nothing, since he had previously sealed off the tubing with the packed tissue paper. Like the others, he too had feared leakage of the lethal gas. And since the other end of the stethoscope tubing ran inside the gas chamber, terminating on Bishop's chest, he reasoned the possibility of the gas escaping through the tubing into where he and the superintendent were, was a legitimate concern.

After all movement ceased inside the gas chamber, the physician graphically mimicked the movements of a doctor listening for vital sounds through the stethoscope. Satisfied, in his own mind, that the gas had done its lethal work, he casually informed the supervisor the condemned man was dead. The time was 12:17 a.m., the start of a new day, Monday, October 22, 1979. Just six minutes had elapsed since the cyanide eggs were dropped.

A correctional officer then entered the witnesses' observation room and read a prepared statement from the Director of Prisons affirming that justice had been served. The witnesses were then advised to begin filing out of the room.

As the witnesses started back down the outside stairway, the cellhouse came to life. Faceless inmates began calling from the darkness. Banging and shouting filled the night air.

"You just murdered one of ours, you bastards. How does it feel?" a voice yelled.

"Go home you rotten animals," came from nowhere.

"Phony hypocrites," screamed another nameless voice.

"Wait's I get out of here, punks," screamed another, "you'll get yours too!"

A correctional officer leading the witnesses back down the stairs, barked into his radio alerting the cellhouse officers. And peering through the windows into the darkened cellhouse, he warned the inmates to shut up.

"Knock it off!" He demanded. "We're gonna' be venting this gas in a minute so you all ought'ta shut your mouths and hold your breath 'case it blows back down through the windows."

Outside in the parking lot, Lt. Curry was pacing up and down keeping things pretty well under control. Suddenly he caught sight of a hulking figure arguing with one of the officers at the far end of the lot.

"Brymer!" he yelled, alerting the other officers. And turning to one of the sergeants, stammered, "Ross Brymer's here! This can only mean trouble. Come on!" The two charged toward the disruption.

Willard Ross Brymer, who had been released only months earlier after doing 15 months on the Oscar Bonavena slaying, was waving his arms wildly and screaming through clenched teeth..

"I'm not gonna' let you get him," and he swung wildly at a nearby officer.

Three deputy sheriffs bolted over to the melee as Brymer worked hands and feet in a frenzy, targeting any uniform in sight.

"I can't see you kill the son-of-a-bitch," he screamed. "You didn't get to me and I'm not gonna' let you get to him!"

It took the three deputies and several correctional officers to take the now, 280 pound Mustang Ranch, brothel bodyguard to the ground. Even after being handcuffed and hobbled at the ankles, he continued to scream and thrash about wildly. This continued even as he was stuffed into a patrol car and whisked away to be booked at the Carson City Jail on a charge of disorderly conduct, resisting arrest and trespassing.

After cooling off in a dank jail cell overnight, Brymer was released on $1,000 bail (and at the subsequent court hearing, was fined this same amount which closed the case).

At 12:24 a.m., Las Vegas Judge, Paul Goldman, was awakened from sleep by the persistent jingle of the telephone and informed that the execution had been carried out. Wiping the sleep from his eyes, he listened sadly. He was later to say the call was the most chilling phone call he had ever received, but did acknowledge that he had asked the warden to do so.

Judge Goldman, was originally assigned Bishop's case, and it was he who accepted Bishop's guilty plea. Along with judges William Forman, and Merlin Hoyt, the three-judge panel acted in unison to sentence Bishop to death. During two subsequent resentencing hearings, Judge Goldman sat as the sole reviewer. Totaled, he'd handed the convicted killer three death warrants.

Judge Goldman told the press the next day, that he and Bishop had got to know each other very well since being assigned to the case. In a sense, they were friends.

Sighing audibly, he tried to explain the tenuous relationship he had developed with the killer. He said it was possible only a judge could understand the gut wrenching events that one suffers while living through the trail that begins during the court trials and terminates in gas chamber.

"I knew Bishop well," the judge said. "He knew me well. When I sentenced him I think he looked at me as if we were old adversaries."

Judge Goldman said that during a resentencing procedure on August 2, Bishop complained of cockroaches and other filth that pervaded the death-row cells at the state prison in Carson City. A few days later, the judge said he made a surprise visit to the prison to follow up on Bishop's complaints.

Goldman said that after the surprise inspection, he did indeed find there were roaches in the block, but other than the roaches, the living conditions were satisfactory. And the administration had promised to bring in an exterminator to rid the area of the bugs.

Judge Goldman also revealed that Bishop had shown some remorse over the killing of David Ballard in Las Vegas. And, the judge said, Bishop had told of countless other killings he'd carried out during his infamous crime career. The judge revealed that Bishop had asked him not to make this public until after the execution.

Judge Goldman said he considered the death penalty distasteful but necessary. And he said Jesse Bishop's background makes a strong argument for capital punishment. As far as being a deterrent, the judge said, it certainly is with Bishop. "He'll never kill again."

What about the fact that Bishop was wounded in Korea, and became addicted to morphine. The judge was of the opinion that thousands of other military personnel were administered morphine in time of battle, and most of these never went on to a life of crime. Cigar-smoking, Jesse Walter Bishop, 46, of Garden Grove, California, who spent at least 20 years behind bars, liked to boast of being a successful hitman who enjoyed fast cars and fast women and plenty of narcotics. On October 22, 1979, he won the dubious distinction of being the last person put to death by lethal gas in Nevada, the state that had pioneered its use.

Between February 8, 1924, when Gee Jon became the first person to die by lethal gas in the nation, and October 22, 1979, when Bishop became the last in Nevada, a total of 32 persons had been put to death in Nevada's gas chambers. Following the death of Jesse Bishop, lethal gas was replaced by lethal injection.

EPILOGUE

Following the execution of Jesse Bishop, Ross Brymer became the focus of a narcotics investigation by Nevada authorities. On December 11, 1979, undercover agents accompanied by an informant, went to Brymer's Sun Valley mobile home hoping to buy a large quantity of Quaalude tablets. Unsure of the agents' identity, Brymer refused to let them into his home, allowing only the informant inside.

A young woman inside with them, spoke to Brymer and the informant in hushed tones, while the undercover agents watched from the curb. Nodding quietly, she slipped outside followed by the informant. Clenched tightly in her hand was a small package.

Facing the undercover agents, the girl whispered she had 600 Quaalude tablets to sell. An exchange was quickly made, with the agents receiving the small package and the girl receiving $600 in marked bills. The group then dispersed, and the agents hurried back to their department to book the evidence prior to handing over a sample to the lab for analysis. When it came, the pills, it was discovered, were not Quaaludes, but Valium, another prescription drug..

Ross Brymer was subsequently arrested and charged with illegal sales of a controlled substance, and for being an habitual criminal. In accordance with Nevada law, the latter charge was punishable by life in prison.

The authorities named as their star witnesses, the informant, and the young girl who had made the transaction. Fearing prison, she had agreed to testify for the state. In their depositions both the informant and the girl swore the drugs were taken from Brymer's home, and sold under his direction.

Ross Brymer soon made bail and hired Jerry Polaha, his longtime Reno attorney as defense counsel. Polaha was able to delay the trial for nearly two years until September, 1981, when they went to court. Chief Criminal Deputy District Attorney, Bruce Laxalt, was first named as prosecutor. When it was determined that Laxalt may be a potential witness, Deputy D.A., John Oakes was selected.

Oakes began by relating the events of the December night when the undercover officers made the purchase. The informant and girl both testified the drugs belonged to Brymer and were sold under his direction.

Polaha had little to use in defense. Unable to refute the testimony of the informants, he tried to discredit the prosecutors and alleged they had fabricated the case. The District Attorney's office, the local police and state narcotics agents "conspired to get Ross Brymer," he told the Washoe District mixed gender jury.

In closing arguments, Prosecutor Oaks said to the jury: "If you weigh the evidence and find him not guilty, you by inference, find us guilty."

It took the jury less than seven hours to return a verdict.

"Guilty as charged." Sentencing was tentatively set for November 12.

Outside in the corridor, pandemonium was erupting. Bruce Laxalt, angered at the allegations of a fabricated case unleashed by Polaha in the courtroom, was running back and forth yelling, "Where's Jerry, where's Jerry," referring to defense counsel, Polaha

As Polaha was about to go down the stairs, Laxalt caught up with him and spun him around screaming that Polaha had made untrue allegations of a frame-up inside the courtroom.

Polaha, startled, reacted quickly and started throwing punches in the direction of the prosecutor. Laxalt grabbed out and tried to wrestle him to the ground to no avail. Startled courtroom officers and spectators moved in quickly to separate the two.

"Don't be no punks!" Ross Brymer screamed, "I don't need this!"

Laxalt was quickly pinned against a wall by spectators but continued to curse Polaha, who was held back by his law partner, John Conner. Conner admonished him to back off, and abruptly, Polaha dropped his hands and backed away brushing off his clothing and straightening his tie. Along with Ross Brymer, the two hurried down the outside stairs and disappeared into the crowd.

The news reporters jammed Laxalt for an answer. He told them he resented the way Polaha tried to put the district attorney's office and staff on trial by the innuendoes he made. Laxalt said this wasn't the first time it happened. It was common whenever a high-profile client gets accused of a crime, he said.

The next day, Polaha and Brymer began the necessary paperwork to delay sentencing. But inevitably, Brymer was ordered back to court. And this time, the prosecutor made known his intentions to hit Brymer with the *bitch*.[2]

On March 3, 1982, Brymer again stood and faced Judge Peter Breen. Breen began by informing the court he would not go along with the prosecution who wanted to slap Brymer with the habitual criminal statute. Brymer remained motionless, but some of the spectators later said they could see him breathe a sigh of relief. But this was only short lived.

In his next breath, Judge Breen reviewed Brymer's past criminal record citing four felony convictions which included possession of marijuana, manslaughter and burglary, plus 15 misdemeanor convictions. He also made reference to the disturbance Brymer created at the Nevada State Prison, the night Jesse Bishop was executed.

Judge Breen continued to hammer the defendant when he brought up the three prison terms Brymer had already served at the Nevada State Prison. He concluded by informing the court there were other felony charges against Brymer in other state courts, charges which would have to be resolved by Brymer eventually.

Judge Breen then stared directed at Ross Brymer and handed down a sentence of life in prison, with the possibility of parole, for possession and sales of a controlled substance. Under this sentence, Brymer could be paroled in 7 1/2 to 10 years.

Jerry Polaha, immediately made known his feelings when he informed the judge a life sentence for possession and sales of a prescription drug was unheard of. And he stated vehemently that he would file an immediate appeal with the Nevada Supreme Court. Judge Breen nodded and ordered Brymer remanded to the custody of the Washoe County Jail authorities pending transfer to the Nevada State Prison.

Deputy Parole and Probation's Officer, Tom Bartley, who had asked for the life sentence,Back at the maximum security prison, Brymer settled in quietly asking only for continuing legal phone calls and visits from his attorney, Jerry Polaha.

Warden, George Sumner, a tough and wily administrator, learned that Brymer was trying to get a release from prison on an appeal bond, and Sumner vowed to keep this from happening. But on July 29, 1982, Warden Sumner was served with a certified appeal bond from Judge Peter Breen, which effectively allowed for Brymer's release from prison pending disposition of his appeal.

Warden Sumner questioned the legality of the $40,000 appeal bond, and contacted the attorney general's office. He was advised it was a legal court order which had to be followed.

Sumner was quick to vent his displeasure and said he had never heard of such a law and believed it should be changed. He said he also believed anyone convicted of a crime should remain in prison unless, and until, the conviction has been overturned. He said he planned to bring the matter up again before Attorney General Richard Bryan, and Governor Robert List. Nevertheless, Brymer again walked out the front gate of the century old Nevada State Prison, grinning widely.

It was nearly two years later, On March 30, 1984, when Brymer again was compelled to face Judge Peter Breen, in Washoe County District Court. This time he was seeking a new trial on the life sentence he had received for possession and sales of a controlled substance.

Judge Breen referred to instructions he had received from the Nevada State Supreme Court. The Court ruled that district judges do have the right to order a new trial when they believe evidence in a case was not sufficient to support a guilty verdict by a jury. Referring to Brymer's case, the high court had sent his appeal back to Judge Breen to make a ruling on a new trial.

Judge Breen explained that the ruling sent back from the Supreme Court was unclear as to their intent. He said that in his interpretation, he could not agree with the defendant's position, that just because he differed from the jury's verdict, he was not compelled to overrule their findings and order a new trial.

He told the court the evidence on the first trial was "not overwhelming" and he may have voted differently, had he been a juror instead of a judge. But he also was quick to add that he did not feel he had a right to sit as a "13th juror" with veto power over the jury's verdict.

Brymer's attorney for this hearing was John Conner. Conner argued that if the judge personally believed the evidence did not support guilt beyond a reasonable doubt, he was required to order a new trial.

Deputy District Attorney, Ed Horn, was quick to jump up to counter this motion. He argued that there had to exist a "manifest injustice" before a a new trial could be ordered.

"I am not offended by the jury verdict," Judge Breen explained, "I think the jury could have reached it on the evidence and I don't think there was a miscarriage of justice in this case."

During closing arguments, Conner said the prosecution's case during the trial rested on the testimony of two questionable witnesses, the girl and the "maggot witness," the informant who agreed to "get Ross," and keep himself out of prison.

Ed Horn said the informant was "a maggot witness because he was a maggot," but that was the kind of people Brymer dealt with.

In denying the motion for a new trial, Judge Breen said, "Twelve reasonable people could have found him guilty from the evidence. Just because I would have come to a different conclusion, I don't think I can grant a new trial."

Ross Brymer was allowed to remain free on the $40,000 bond pending further appeals before the Nevada State Supreme Court.

On December 5, 1984, the high court handed down a ruling refusing to overturn the drug conviction against Ross Brymer. The court agreed with Brymer's attorney that the Washoe County prosecutor John Oakes, made improper remarks by telling jurors that an acquittal for Brymer would be an indictment of the state.

However, the court said the comments by Oakes, while "irrelevant and patently improper," were nullified by the trial judge's admonitions and jury instructions.

Brymer was again fighting for survival, but was rapidly running out of options.

On May 8, 1985, three and one half years after being arrested on the drug charge, Ross Brymer again faced Judge Peter Breen. Brymer's appeals to the Supreme Court had been heard and rejected. The Washoe County District Attorney's Office, represented by Mills Lane, said a "risk of flight" was a very distinct possibility. He argued Brymer should begin serving the life sentence immediately.

Brymer again reiterated his contention that he knew nothing of the Valium sales until he was arrested.

Judge Breen wasted little time in arguments. He ordered the $40,000 bond revoked immediately. Ross Brymer was placed in handcuffs and led from the courtroom to begin serving a life sentence.

After going through the routine fish-tank intake, Ross Brymer was again sent to the maximum security, Nevada State Prison.

During December of that year, Ross Brymer's 18 year old son, Willard Ross Jr., was sentenced to ten-years for armed robbery and burglary. Plans were begun to transfer the elder Brymer out of state.

A month later, in January, 1986, Ross Brymer made his first appearance before the State Parole Board (though no one could offer an explanation why he was able to appear for parole so soon).

Brymer told the board he wanted to pursue a career in music. He admitted to being an alcoholic and said most of his arrests occurred when he was drinking. He made no attempt to gloss over his violent past.

"Boxing and fighting were a family tradition," he told the board. "You get a reputation for it and it attracts violence."

Speaking of the current conviction for drug sales, Brymer told the board the drugs were sold by a woman he had ordered out of his home, a sale that had been arranged by a former prison inmate.

"I didn't sell any drugs to anybody," he stated. "I didn't need to sell drugs to anybody."

After careful consideration, the board handed Brymer an 18 month dump (he could make another appearance in 18 months). Not long after, he was transferred to a prison in the state of Iowa (on a prisoner exchange program).

July 24, 1987. Ross Brymer was returned to make his second appearance before the parole board. Citing his previous criminal history, a record of poor adjustment while on previous paroles, and an unsatisfactory adjustment to prison, the board again gave him an 18 month dump. He was told to come back again in September, 1988.

In 1988, Ross was again dumped by the board.

In 1991, however, the board agreed to release him on a lifetime parole.

For a few years, Ross was able to stay relatively trouble free. However, in 1995, he violated the terms of his parole and was again sent back to the Nevada State Prison.

The years behind bars had taken its toll on Ross Brymer. When he again was paroled in 1998, he was in poor health. However, he was fortunate to go back to his first love, playing guitar, singing country western, and song writing. He was soon a regular Friday night performer at the Fitzgerald's Hotel-Casino, in Reno.

On June 27, 2000, Ross Brymer was found dead in an apartment on Wells Avenue. Cause of death was listed as an overdose of morphine. He, along with Oscar Bonavena, and Jesse Bishop, were now playing on a higher sphere.

Chapter Fourteen

WHITE SANDY BEACHES

While Ross Brymer was doing time for the Argentine boxer's death, attorneys for Joe Conforte had been working frantically to keep their client out of prison. Joe was still looking at 20 years in a federal joint for the 1977 conviction of income tax evasion. During the lengthy appeals process, a motion for a new trial was reviewed by the Ninth Circuit Court of Appeals in San Francisco. After several months of deliberations, the Ninth Circuit refused to grant a new trial. The court did however, reduce the original sentence of 20 years, down to merely five years. This was in itself, a prodigious—if short lived—victory for Joe Conforte.

Following this ruling by the Ninth Circuit, the case was moved on up to the U.S. Supreme Court. In due time, the case was reviewed by the high court, which refused to hear arguments on a motion for retrial. The case was remanded back to U.S. District Court, in Reno.

Stan Brown, Conforte's lead attorney, grasped at one last straw and announced he would file for a rehearing of the case.

Despite the legal maneuvering by the attorneys, the ground beneath Joe Conforte was becoming increasingly unstable. And then abruptly, other local events brought on by his own doings, threatened to immerse the flamboyant brothel owner in a sea of self destruction.

On Tuesday morning, July 3, 1979, following the return of a grand jury indictment, Joe Conforte was picked up by Washoe County authorities and whisked away to the Washoe County Jail where he was booked on felony charges of bribery against a public official.

According to the indictment, Conforte had sought the assistance of Lyon County, District Attorney, John C. Giomi, in securing a brothel license in Lyon County. Conforte, it was alleged, enticed Giomi with promises of trips, money, women, the use of a Ferrari sports car, free cigars, the use of a Conforte ranch, and a partnership in a liquor distributorship. The indictment further alleged that when Conforte suggested these freebies during one of their meetings, he also said, "Remember John, my money never runs out."

Since most of the alleged meetings took place in Washoe County—specifically, at the Black Angus Restaurant, in Park Lane Mall, Harold's Club, in downtown Reno, and the Hyatt Hotel in Incline Village, the charges were filed in Washoe County.

What did the brothel owner expect of Giomi in return?

The indictment stated that Giomi was expected to assist Conforte in getting a Lyon County brothel license to operate the Starlight Ranch[1] in Moundhouse, and to put the squeeze on competitive brothels by filing nuisance suits against them.

As he was being booked into the jail, deputies discovered Conforte was carrying a concealed recording device. When asked about its purpose, he said he'd used it to tape his meetings with the Lyon County District Attorney, and said the tapes would show that he had only tried to hire Giomi as a personal attorney—there was no attempt at bribery. Everything was legitimate he told the deputies. It was all on tape.

Where were the tapes now?

Conforte said he had them in a secret location, but hinted they would be presented at court in his defense if formal charges were brought against him. When he refused to reveal their location, the authorities began the required paper work to secure a search warrant. In the meantime, Stan Brown, Conforte's attorney had arrived to begin bail negotiations.

Cal Dunlap, Washoe District Attorney hurried over to District Judge, Roy Torvinen's chambers to argue for a cash only, high bail. Dunlap reminded the judge that both Sally and Joe Conforte were currently out on appeal bonds of $40,000 each for federal income tax evasion charges. And, he noted, the feds had liens against Confortes' property amounting to five million dollars. If Conforte skipped, Dunlap told the judge, Washoe County would have to get in line behind the feds when it came to collecting.

Dunlap explained to the judge that because of these entanglements, bail should be posted as cash only, or at the least, in the form of a surety bond backed by an insurance company. Either way, Dunlap explained, the bail should not be secured by any properties owned by the Confortes. Judge Torvinen then announced the bail would be set in the amount of $200,000, cash only. Attorney Stan Brown, protested loudly, but to no avail. The bail would remain as ordered.

By the close of the day, the $200,000 had been raised, $100,000 of Conforte cash, and $100,000 put up by Mac Bail Bonds, of Reno. That afternoon, the same day he was booked, Conforte walked out of the Washoe County Jail accompanied by his attorney anticipating a next day, 4th of July celebration.

As they were leaving, a small crowd had gathered outside. He waved to them and said the bribery charge was just so much harassment.

"I will be acquitted," he said, "we'll prove there was no bribery."

Conforte, and his attorney then wished the crowd well and the two headed for Conforte's Sullivan Lane home where they tried to relax, yet anticipating a knock on the door at any minute by detectives waving a search warrant. They had not long to wait. Law enforcement personnel from Washoe and Lyon Counties, along with agents from the Internal Revenue Service, descended upon the house like scavengers. After the necessary advisements, they began to systematically move from room to room searching for recording tapes. Save for a few blank tapes, they came up empty handed. The IRS agents, however, confiscated an estimated $80,000 in cash and assorted jewelry items, which they seized to be held in abeyance until the Confortes' income tax problems were resolved.

While Conforte's house was being torn apart, law enforcement officers from several agencies had also converged on the Mustang Ranch, disrupting the nightly business and sending scores of johns scurrying back out into the night. The girls for the most part were cooperative, patiently wanting for them to finish and leave (no pun intended). In the end, the agents conducting the searches confiscated what they told the press were large quantities of recording tapes. These tapes subsequently proved to be blanks. Officers who searched the Conforte vehicles likewise came up empty handed.

Responding to their annoyance, Conforte said he still had the tapes in a secret place and he hinted they implicated the Lyon County D.A., John Giomi. Also, he said, he might make the tapes available to the media during the coming week so the public could learn of the political corruption that existed in Lyon County.

Before the law officers prepared to leave, they warned Conforte that if he didn't present the tapes, a court order would be issued demanding he did. He played this remark off and turned back to huddle with his attorney.

The next morning, Cal Dunlap, the Washoe D.A. wasted no time in filing a court order demanding Conforte turn over the missing tapes.

In the meantime, Conforte was contacted by the press, and seemed eager to respond to their questions. Conforte said the tapes would show he was innocent of the bribery charge, and when they were played before an unbiased audience would unveil the scope of corruption that was so pervasive in Lyon County.

He said the tapes would confirm he attempted hire Giomi only as a private attorney; there was absolutely nothing on the tapes that even hinted at bribery. Everything was above board, he said.

"And," he said, "I did this only after receiving several demands for payoffs from a 'bag man' in Lyon County."

What is a bag man?

"A bag man," he said, "is someone who collects money and delivers it to 'certain officials.'"

He said he was told that if he made the payoffs, he would be permitted back into the brothel business in Lyon County.

Who was the bag man?

Conforte named a local figure. and stated that he could back up what he said. This bag man collects money from all the brothel owners locally, Conforte said, and hands it off to a number of officials, all of whom are on the take.

Speaking of Giomi, Conforte said he first went to him only to retain his services as an attorney. And only as a private attorney, yet an attorney who was well established Lyon County.

During the meeting, Conforte said he gave Giomi $1,000—only as a retainer—and certainly not as a bribe. And, Conforte said he was given a receipt, which is a legitimate business transaction. Now, Conforte wanted to kow, who gets a receipt in return of a bribe?

Why did he pick Giomi as his personal attorney? He already had Stan Brown and others.

Conforte said those kind of questions should be answered in court. And Conforte hinted of widespred corruption in Lyon County, and promised that it would all be revealed in due time.

"The tapes will prove it," he said

Biting the end off of a large Cuban cigar, he lit up and resumed his quasi-defense for the benefit of the news people. He then brought up the actions o fthe authorities who tore his house apart looking for the tapes and said the only reason they wanted the tapes was so they could be altered and used to refute his defense. The tapes, he said, were so well hidden that nobody could have found them.

On Thursday morning, District Attorney Cal Dunlap and Conforte's attorney, Stan Brown appeared before Judge Peter Breen in Washoe District Court, to resolve the question of the missing tapes.

Dunlap presented his case and explained to the judge he just wanted the tapes deposited with the court to prevent anyone from tampering with the recordings.

"We just want to make certain these tapes are preserved and their integrity is preserved," he told the judge.

Conforte's attorney, Stan Brown then stood and addressed the judge protesting the demands of the district attorney to present the tapes.. Referring to the eight-page grand jury indictment, he said, "The tapes are entirely at variance with the matters contained in the indictment."

Where were the tapes now, the judge wanted to know.

Brown conceded he had received three cassette tapes from Conforte with instructions to keep them confidential. He stressed the point that if the tapes were left intact, when played before the court, they would reflect the belief by Conforte that he was hiring Giomi as a private attorney to represent him in obtaining the brothel license. If true, this would exonerate his client from charges of bribery.

At the conclusion of the arguments, Judge Breen ordered Brown to turn over the tapes no later than 4:45 p.m., Friday afternoon. He granted the attorney's request to duplicate the tapes before surrendering them.

When Conforte was contacted by the news people he said he had felt it necessary to record his meetings with Giomi to protect himself and to ensure the truth of corruption in Lyon County could be brought to the attention of the people and officials of the state.

Commenting on the Lyon County officials, he said every time they approached him, they had their hands out. An endless situation.

On Monday morning, September 17, 1979, Conforte and his attorney again appeared in court, this time in front of Judge John Barrett, in an effort to quash the upcoming bribery trial. During questioning by Cal Dunlap, Conforte maintained an air of innocence and repeated his stated defense that the $1,000 money paid to Giomi was a legitimate retainer.

"I contacted him only as a private attorney," Conforte repeated. "I offered him nothing that I did not offer other attorneys."

His next statement brought loud chuckles from the spectators when he said he told Giomi the $1,000 was "gas money,"

Turning to smile at the seated spectators, Conforte said they shouldn't consider this unusual, he also gave "gas money" to his attorney, Stan Brown who was here defending him. And again he repeated what he'd testified to earlier that he had asked Giomi for a receipt for income tax purposes.

"Nobody gives a public official a bribe and asks for a receipt," Brown hammered away at the judge, and questioned why Conforte's request for a receipt had never been brought up during the grand jury hearing.

Brown said the request for a receipt was exculpatory evidence in favor of his client and had the grand jury known about it, the indictment may never have been presented.

Brown then brought up the question of Giomi's accountability. Giomi should have told Conforte that he could not represent him because of a conflict of interest between his position as district attorney, and Conforte's position of seeking a brothel license.

"Given all the facts," Brown argued, "the defendant is entitled to in that star-chamber, the grand jury won't indict."

Dunlap then stood and told the judge the defendant's story was preposterous. The only reason Conforte asked for a receipt was to lend an air of propriety to the whole sordid mess he said

"This is the way we'll fool the folks," Dunlap mocked the

defense. "This is the way we'll cover our tracks,"

On Wednesday, September 19, Judge John Barrett ruled that sufficient evidence had been presented to the grand jurors to support the bribery charge against Joe Conforte. A tentative trial date was set for sometime in March, 1980. Conforte's attorney wasted no time in filing for an extension.

Into 1980, Conforte had apparently gone underground. He suddenly was no longer seeking media attention, nor was he being seen in town with his girls as was usually the case. Word on the street was that he'd fled to South America to avoid going to prison on the federal income tax rap, and the impending Lyon County bribery trial. Under Nevada law, another conviction could send him back to prison for life under the habitual criminal act.

Early in July, U.S. District Judge Ed Reed Jr. heard arguments from U.S. Attorney, Phil Pro, on a motion to revoke Conforte's passport, along with the $40,000 bail and force the elusive brothel owner to begin serving the five-year sentence on the income tax charge. If not done, the U.S. attorney said, there was a good chance Conforte would flee the country.

Attorney Stan Brown working under orders to block efforts to have his client pinned down, countered by saying his client had a history of "total compliance" with court orders.

"This man has too much at stake to flee," Brown insisted.

Any deterrent to Conforte's fleeing the country which might result in tougher release conditions, would far outweigh the "criticism my government will take for picking on this man while he still has a chance to win this case,." Brown stressed.

Sgt. Marv Pennington, with the Reno Police Department Intelligence Division, testified that he'd been told by a local businessman that Conforte had offered to go into a partnership with the businessman as operators of a casino in Ipanema, Brazil.

Attorney Brown then produced a letter from this same businessman which stated that he and Conforte had never discussed such a venture. The businessman refuted Sgt. Pennington's assertions and said the two had never spoken together. Brown wrapped up the argument by informing the judge that there is no legal gambling in Brazil.

Pro jumped up in defense of the sergeant.

"The government will stand by Sgt. Pennington's testimony as truthful," Pro argued. "Sgt. Pennington has no reason to lie."

Taken aback by the conflicting testimony, Judge Reed asked Conforte's attorney to file another motion to vacate the passport revocation. The judge said he wanted time to weigh the testimonies and the letter's revelations. He did grant a motion to revoke the passport, but then granted Conforte an extension on the time required to surrender the document

By the end of July, doubts about Conforte's whereabouts were no longer circulating. Stan Brown notified Judge Reed that his client was in Colombia where he was trying to promote a heavyweight boxing match between Colombia's Bernardo Mercado who, he said, Conforte managed, and Muhammad Ali. Brown said he had every reason to believe that Conforte would be back as promised.

True to his word, Conforte flew back to Reno and in August, surrendered his passport to Judge Ed Reed. He was admonished not to try leaving the country again and to report to his attorney every week.

Back in Reno, Conforte announced he had a signed contract for Bernardo Mercado to fight Leon Spinks on the same card as the Muhammad Ali—Larry Holmes championship fight to be held at Caesar's Palace, Las Vegas, on October 2, 1980.

On September, 15, 1980, it was back in court. This time during a hearing on pretrial motions. For this hearing, Conforte had augmented his defense with the addition of two other attorneys, Jerry Polaha, of Reno, and San Francisco attorney, James L. Brosnahan. These two, along with Stan Brown, presented a formidable defense team.

During the proceedings, Lyon County District Attorney, John Giomi, testified that he feared for the safety of himself and his family when he first became involved with Joe Conforte's adventures in Lyon County. He cited past Conforte adversaries—Bill Raggio, who Conforte tried to set up with an underage girl, and Oscar Bonavena, who was gunned down outside the Mustang Ranch, on May 22, 1976.

How did he deal with the fear and continue to do his work as district attorney?

"I put myself with my God, and had no more anxieties," he testified..

And then he revealed to the court that he too, had been wired during the meetings with Conforte. The judge asked him to repeat what he'd said. Had he too, rolled tape during their meetings?

He told the court that he had first been contacted by phone by a "Mr. Jones," who wanted information on acquiring a brothel license in Lyon County. Mr. Jones suggested a meeting between the two at Harold's Club, in Reno, to discuss a matter of "mutual benefit." Suspicious, Giomi contacted state agents who planted a wire on him prior to the first meeting.

Giomi testified that when he learned the true identity of Mr. Jones, he knew he'd made the right decision in going to the state investigators. During the first meeting, Giomi said Conforte tried right away to compromise the D.A.s position. As they were talking, Conforte casually took out a wad of bills, and reached across the table.

"He stuck it all in my left front pocket," Giomi said, and quoted the brothel owner who told him, 'Go ahead and take it. It's only gas money.'"

"Later on, when the state agents took the money out of my pocket with tweezers, much to my surprise, it was 10, one hundred dollar bills"

During the following meetings, at which time he was always wired, Conforte gave lavishly of cigars and other gifts. Giomi testified that Conforte always tried to patronize the D.A. by telling him he was "a big man...the boss; what a great person I was being the district attorney."

Conforte's defense team, upon learning the D.A. had rolled tape on their client, huddled together to revamp their tactics. Should they cast doubt on Giomi and the law enforcement personnel. What other strategy was there?

Brosnahan contended that Giomi's conduct was outrageous. He did not follow an American Bar Association cannon of ethics, Brosnahan began. There would have been an absolute conflict of interest, he explained. Because of his official capacity as district attorney, he was automatically excluded from representing Conforte in securing a brothel license.

On the stand, Giomi countered and said in his opinion a conflict of interest did not exist.

Why not?

"Mr. Conforte contacted me as a district attorney," he said. "Each and everything he asked me to do were things only a district attorney could do."

Brosnahan hammered away at the judge, and insisted that his client's due process was denied when the Nevada Division of Investigation agents, along with officers from the Washoe County Sheriff's Office, used Giomi to "get Joe Conforte."

As the hearing concluded, a follow up continuation was scheduled for October 9, 1980, before Judge Roy Torvinen in Washoe District Court.

On the appointed day, Conforte's defense team again filed two pretrial motions seeking to have the bribery charge thrown out because the indictment did not adequately state the charge, and because of the suppression of exculpatory evidence (evidence which would tend to clear the defendant of the alleged crime) during grand jury proceedings

Brosnahan argued that the indictment did not state what official act Conforte allegedly attempted to bribe Giomi to perform. And, he said, the Washoe County District Attorney, Cal Dunlap, never told the grand jury that Giomi, in addition to acting as district attorney, also had a private law practice, or that Conforte had asked for, yet did not receive, a receipt for the $1,000 "retainer."

Brosnahan continued his counterattack and made a point that this information would have supported Conforte's assertion that when he slipped Giomi the $1,000, and made offers of other gifts, he thought he was retaining Giomi as his personal attorney.

As the hearing concluded, Judge Torvinen announced his decision.

"A careful review of the indictment discloses that it contains substantial factual allegations that Conforte attempted to influence the district attorney's powers or functions as a peace officer."

He then bound a stunned Conforte over for trial.

Judge Torvinen's clerk scanned the court docket and set a trial date early in March, 1981.Court was adjourned. As Conforte and his defense team slipped out of the courtroom, gray clouds were forming on the horizon. The feds, who had been waiting impatiently since 1977, were ready to exact their due. Things were looking darker for Joe Conforte.

On December 1, the U.S. Supreme Court refused to review Conforte's tax evasion charge, leaving the conviction intact. He was ordered to appear in U.S. District Court, in Reno, on December 23, 1980, for a bail revocation hearing.

Had he appeared for this final court action, bail would surely have been revoked, and Conforte would have been taken into custody and held for transport to a federal prison to begin a five-year stretch on the tax evasion rap. But he made no such appearance. He had vanished.

Conforte's attorney, Stan Brown, assisted by two income tax attorneys, Bruce Hochman and Harvey Tack, appeared in his place. Brown made a futile effort to stall the proceedings, causing the U.S. prosecutor, Alan Freedman, to jump up vehemently.

"Your honor," he blurted, "No one knows where he is."

Freedman then reminded the judge that Conforte's attorneys had been informed of today's bail revocation hearing two weeks ago.

"...he (Conforte) could have been planning this for the past two weeks," Freedman said.

"He was facing the position of imposition of sentencing today," Freedman insisted. "I'm sure Mr. Conforte knew there was a possibility he would have been taken into custody.

"It's easy to speculate and say he never intended to serve a prison term," Freedman went on, "but his attorney stated in court he (Conforte) was under duress and was not himself. It might very well be that he is sitting in Reno, scared and has every intention of showing up."

Conforte's attorneys then added more doubt to the proceedings. They were in agreement when they said they had received two recent phone calls from the brothel owner. The first call seemed to indicate that Conforte was in the area, however, the second call came from out of the United States, they told the judge.

Judge Reed threw up his hands showing his exasperation and demanded to know whether information had been uncovered to document reports that Conforte had fled to Brazil.

IRS spokesman, Marty Bibb, was invited to speak.

"We know there is a statement on the (court) record to that extent," Bibb said, "We're aware of those things happening, and that is a possibility."

Judge Reed had heard enough. When Conforte's attorneys could offer no viable explanation for the absence of their client, the judge issued a federal arrest warrant, and revoked the $40,000 bail. Conforte was now a fugitive from justice. Talk on the street was that he was languishing on the white sandy beaches in South

America.

On January 24, 1981, a scheduled date for Conforte to appear for sentencing on the income tax evasion charge, again came and passed without the star defendant making an appearance. In U.S. District Court, Conforte's attorney, Stan Brown however, was there to represent him. Brown told the court, he was certain Conforte would soon return to Reno and face the sentencing.

Outside of the courtroom, Brown told reporters that Conforte was in a foreign country and would soon be back. Brown hinted that he had been conversing with Conforte by telephone, and indicated the brothel owner wanted to return to the United States and clear up his problems.

For the next few months a rash of rumors circulated on the streets and around the casinos and bordellos: Joe was hiding out in Brazil. No, Joe was in Colombia. No, he was in Chile or Belize. Or maybe he was actually hiding out at the Mustang Ranch. No, he'd fled the country forever. Not exactly; he'd been killed by Bonavena's fans, and his body dumped in the ocean.

The Washoe County Sheriff's Office continued to collect and disseminate this street chaff. And then a tip came in that he was actually hiding out right under their noses, holed up in the Mustang Ranch.

Around 3:00 p.m., on Wednesday, June 17, 1981, five Washoe County deputies along with an FBI agent, pulled a surprise visit to the Mustang Ranch where they were met by Sally Conforte. Sally screamed at them to get off the premises.

Armed with state and federal search warrants, they told her they were there looking for Joe. She was ordered to back off or face arrest. Her face hardened but she shook off their intimidating presence, and demanded she be allowed to accompany them into each area they searched.

The search party ignored her demands and split up into teams branching out in different directions pulling back curtains and opening doors. One thing they didn't need right now, was hindrance from Sally; after all, there were at least one hundred rooms to go through, some of which were king-size, and others no more than squeezed cubicles. The working girls and their johns for the most part took it all in stride, and kept out of the way while the officers did what they had to do.

After ninety minutes of searching with no results, the party had to admit they'd been given faulty information. Joe Conforte was not here. They apologized for the inconvenience they'd caused and began to leave together. A few of the girls were amicable enough, in fact a few even made passing comments,

"You're only a stranger here once; come again soon," and similar remarks.

When the papers got word of the search and started jamming people for answers, Mills Lane, chief investigator for the Washoe County D.A.s office (now a TV courtroom judge), quickly assembled a press conference and made a routine announcement in defense of the impromptu search.

He reminded those in attendance that local and federal law enforcement agencies had been following up on a plethora of leads that were coming in constantly relating to Joe Conforte's whereabouts. Rumors were circulating that he was either in Italy, Ecuador, or Brazil. Other reports had him living right here in Reno.

On July 1, 1981, Judge John Barrett, signed an order authorizing forfeiture of the $200,000 cash bail previously posted by Conforte and Mac's Bail Bonds of Reno, on the bribery charge. This and the $40,000 bail revoked by the U.S. District Court, on the tax evasion charge, along with the excessive attorney's fees, far exceeded a quarter of a million dollars the elusive brothel owner had shelled out.

Less than a year later, all doubt was removed regarding Joe Conforte's status. A Brazilian news weekly, Istoe, splashed a photo of Joe, along with a feature story about the flamboyant brothel owner, in a March, 1982 issue. Conforte was seen participating in the samba club parade in Rio de Janeiro, and later, dining on filet mignon during a midnight dinner.

Quoting the Istoe news article, Conforte was said to be one of the guests of honor seated in the carnival loge of Castor de Andrade, a reputed gambler and businessman. At one time, Castor is alleged to have been arrested on an illegal numbers game racket known as "jogo do bicho" or animal game.

The account went on to say the headline grabbing brothel owner was always accompanied by "two or three bodyguards." Besides his friendship with Castor, the article also quoted Conforte as saying he had other influential friends, and equated gambling with any legitimate business.

When confirmation of Conforte's presence in Brazil, was received in Reno, Cal Dunlap, Washoe County District Attorney, spoke with the U.S. Attorney, Lamond Mills, to discuss the possibility of bringing the brothel owner back for trial.

Contrary to popular opinion, the U.S. did have an extradition treaty with Brazil, however, the treaty was limited to 31 offenses. And, as a spokesman for the State Department in Washington noted, income tax evasion, was not one of them. However; bribery of a public official was. In short, Dunlap was advised, if Conforte were to be extradited back to Reno, it would have to be done by Washoe County, on the bribery charge. The feds could not do it on the income tax rap.

"If the local jurisdiction wants him badly enough it would be up to them," a State Department spokesman said.

Thus, the responsibility of bringing him back fell on the shoulders of the Washoe County authorities. They would have to initiate the process. Once they put together the necessary papers requesting extradition, the Department of Justice could relay the request to the U.S. Embassy in Brasilia, Brazil. Dunlap was urged to pursue this stratagem, since the feds were eager to get him back here to serve the five-year tax evasion sentence. The State Department spokesman made it clear they would help all they could.

During a press conference, Cal Dunlap had other thoughts.

"I don't think it's as easy as they make it sound," he said.

When asked for clarification, he placed the responsibility of extraditing Conforte on the back of the federal government. He explained that the Justice Department, with its embassies and State Department officials, had the resources and contacts, and it was they who should find a way to bring him back. It wasn't up to Washoe County. Besides, Dunlap reasoned, Conforte had forfeited the $200,000 bail posted in Washoe County, and the $40,000 posted in Lyon County. With him hiding out in Brazil, Dunlap said, Northern Nevada was better off.

In conclusion, Dunlap told the reporters that should Conforte ever again show up in Reno, additional charges would be filed against him, charging him with being a habitual criminal which could mean a life sentence in state prison.

With $200,000 in Washoe's, court's coffers, Dunlap had little incentive to renew court battles with Conforte. Good by and good luck. This was Dunlaps's hope—a hope that would soon be dashed.

Unknown to Cal Dunlap, for the past several months, Conforte had been engaging in secret talks with agents of the federal government trying to work out a deal to bring him back willingly.

When word of these negotiations were leaked to the press, most of the Washoe County officials were livid with anger. What was happening? They were soon to discover the feds had been negotiating with Conforte to return him to Nevada, not as a fugitive, but as a star witness in an entirely different case.

Not to place him in prison, but to persuade him to work with them on nailing one of their own. Not to harass him, nor to arrest him, but to work with him. The feds were going to use him as bait, to land a much larger fish, U.S. District Judge, Harry Claiborne.

Chapter Fifteen
JUDGE HARRY CLAIBORNE

At age 63, (in 1980) Judge Harry Claiborne could look back on a decades long stormy career in the courtroom. As a brilliant defense attorney, it was said he was colorful, cunning, intimidating, brutal with a bulldog's tenacity who would do anything to win a case. He was a master of cross examination and in creating courtroom drama which could electrify and win over jurors. His patented street-fighter tractics in the courtroom were legendary.

As a United States District Court Judge, in Nevada, it was said he was consistent; he was unpredictable; he was good; he was fair; unfair; excellent; trusted not to be trusted.

And because of an association with Joe Conforte, he would be called upon to use all of his ingrained talents in fighting for his very existence. The feds were preparing to indict him on charges that he took bribes from the brothel owner to squash several counts of income tax evasion.

Glimpses of his character may be gleaned from past statements attributed to him during confrontations with news people, government agencies, and adversaries.

When he leaarned he had become the target of the Justice Department's Organized Crime Strike Force, in Las Vegas, he denounced their investigation calling them "rotten bastards" and "crooks and liars," while accusing them of planting illegal wiretaps and making questionable arrests.

Prior to his appointment as U.S. District Judge, he had built a reputation as a defender of the people using his skills in courtroom antics. During one confrontation with Cal Dunlap, Washoe County prosecutor, he called Dunlap a "legal whore," and in court referred to him as a "boy."

During a trial in Las Vegas, when he faced Mills Lane and the arguments grew heated, he blurted, "Ah, sit down and quit your babbling."

Lane threw up his hands and objected, causing the judge to caution Claiborne.

It was courtroom antics like this that inspired Lane to refer to the gangling, craggy-faced Claiborne as "Harry the Horse."

"I call him Harry the Horse, because he comes right at you," Lane explained.

Peter Echeverria, a prominent Reno attorney, had high praise for the Arkansas bred attorney. He said there was no greater lawyer to work with, that Claiborne was an imaginative attorney who was thorough and who never quit working.

That was one side of the coin. His critics, and there were many, had other thoughts. One said the Razorback lawyer was highy vindictive, that he was a throwback to a different era, and that he frquenttly showed up unprepared.

Many of Claiborne's clients were notorious persons with mob ties, and when President Jimmy Carter appointed Claiborne to the U.S. Judiciary on September 1, 1978, many former adversaries were quick to show their displeasure. A former Nevada prosecutor and Claiborne adversary of long standing, expressed his feelings of President Carter's selection.

"When interviewed by the FBI," he said, "I told the investigator in no uncertain terms, that in my opinion, if Claiborne ever got the appointment, it would be a travesty of justice forced upon the American people.

Other stories circulated about Claiborne; some of which were praising his character and others denigrating it. One persistent rumor alleged he resorted to illegal tactics when defending a client. He once was accused of directing an investigator to install an illegal wiretap.

With this background, it was no wonder that Joe Conforte admired the man, and hired him as a defense lawyer years earlier. In 1967, when Washoe County authorities indicted Conforte on a white slavery charge, Claiborne was hired as defense counsel. Following a lurid trial which lasted several days, Conforte was acquitted. Claiborne was destined to be the only attorney ever, who was able to gain a felony acquittal for the notorious brothel owner. Thus began a long time friendship between Joe Conforte and Harry Claiborne.

When Claiborne was appointed to the federal judiciary in 1978, this friendship continued. And when the feds went after Conforte for income tax evasion a year later, Judge Claiborne was a visiting judge sitting on an impaneled grand jury, in Portland, Oregon, reviewing Conforte's income tax case.

Questions of a payoff circulated. There were accusations that Claiborne had taken $30,000 on one occasion from Conforte, and $50,000 on another.

"I never received one quarter in my life from Joe Conforte," Claiborne growled to a reporter, "except attorney fees when I represented him."

The feds continued to build a case against Claiborne on the basis of the alleged $80,000 payoff from Conforte, and Claiborne's illegal use of a wiretap when he was one of the most prominent defense attorney in Nevada. What the feds were lacking was a first person witness who could testify against Claiborne in court.

There was such a witness. A witness, who could put Claiborne in prison. And that witness, himself a fugitive from justice, was living lavishly in Rio de Janiero. His name? Joseph Conforte. Conforte made it known he could be bought if the price were right.

Would the feds actually make a deal with a notorious brothel owner, who was on the lam from his own tax evasion charges? On charges of bribery of a public official? Would they stoop this low in order to land a corrupt federal judge? You bet they would.

Would Joe Conforte, a fugitive from justice and a notorious brothel owner, turn against one of his long time friends and try to cut a deal with the feds? You bet he would.

Secret negotiations between the feds and Conforte had been going on for months. Would Conforte return to the states to help put the federal judge away? In return for what?

He sure would. In return for a reduced sentence on the income tax rap the feds were chasing him for, and on the bribery charge Washoe County wanted him on.

As word of the negotiations leaked out, Cal Dunlap, Washoe D.A., was pressed for answers. Were the rumors true? Would the feds bring Conforte back to testify against Claiborne? Would Dunlap himself, make a deal with the brothel owner?

"As far as I'm concerned," Dunlap said, "I've made no deals with Conforte. He is still a fugitive from justice."

The Lyon County D.A., John Giomi, the target of the alleged bribe, said he hadn't been contacted by anyone in authority regarding a deal with the brothel owner. He admitted hearing the same rumors for the past few months, but said the feds had not approached him about the possibility of bringing Conforte back.

In September, 1982, a second Portland, Oregon grand jury was impaneled, this time to investigate allegations of the Conforte payoff to Claiborne. The hearing had been transferred out of state to avoid undue publicity. Stan Brown, Conforte's long time attorney, was scheduled to make an appearance there. It was expected he would try to cut a deal which would allow the brothel owner to hang Claiborne in exchange for a reduced sentence.

The outcome of this grand jury hearing is sketchy at best. What followed though, was another federal grand jury held in Reno, in December, 1983. that targeted Judge Harry Claiborne specifically.

Brothel owner, Joe Conforte, who had been lured out of hiding, arrived in Miami, on December 4, 1983. He was immediately grabbed by FBI agents at the airport, and whisked away to Washington D.C. Two days later, he appeared before U.S. District Judge, John Smith, on bail jumping charges, and was ordered held in federal custody.

He emerged again in Reno under heavy guard, to testify against his one-time friend, and lawyer, federal judge, Harry Claiborne. Conforte's testimony before the grand jury was a smashing success. A seven-count indictment alleging Claiborne had tried to extort $100,000 from Conforte in return for dismissing the income tax charge against him, along with additional charges of bribery, tax evasion and obstruction of justice were handed down.. At least 17 of the jurors said later they felt the brothel owner had told the truth when he said he had made a payoff of $80,000 to Judge Claiborne.

Outside the courthouse, Claiborne, flanked by his attorney, Oscar Goldman, faced a battery of media personnel who had been standing by for his appearance. He spoke briefly and told them he would tackle this charge just as he'd faced other crises in his life. And that was to face them head-on. He said he was innocent of the charges, and would be acquitted.

"...I have faith in myself," he said, and added that he also had faith in God.

Before walking off, he indicated he would start preparations for the upcoming trial right away.

"I'll win," he shouted. "I'll win because of that fact. That's all I have to say."

Claiborne tipped his hat and sauntered off.

Questions were passed back and forth among the reporters.

What about Conforte. Would he benefit from his grand jury testimony?

That would soon be known.

Appearing before Judge James Guinan, in District Court on the bribery of a public official charge, Conforte was represented by Peter Perry, his new attorney. Perry told the judge his client was "not the same man" he was four-years ago. He was now very civic minded, judge. He willingly jeopardized himself by returning here from Brazil. In Brazil, he could have lived out his life as a king (Sally, his wife, was regularly sending him vast amounts of money from the Mustang Ranch's proceeds).

Conforte stood to address Judge Guinan.

"...if there is such a thing as paradise on earth, Brazil was it. But I still chose to come back. I am 58 and can't live much longer. I can't enjoy life like a young man anymore. It was a hard and tough decision. I took and I made it with whatever good sense I had."

What was not made public was the terms of the plea agreement made by Conforte's attorney, the Washoe County District Attorney's office, and the U.S. Justice Department.

Conforte and his attorney rose to their feet for sentencing.

Judge Guinan then sentenced the one-time fugitive brothel owner to 18 months in the Nevada State Prison for bribery.

Did he go back to prison?

No. Judge Guinan then announced the sentence was to run concurrently with the impending sentence expected on the federal charges. In lieu of going to prison, Guinan ruled that Conforte could serve the time in the Witness Protection Program, "to minimize the great peril and risk," he took in returning to Reno to testify.

Judge Guinan ruled that Conforte would have to pay a $10,000 fine, and could not seek to recover the more than $200,000 bail that was forfeited when he fled to Brazil.

Conforte next appeared in U.S. District Court in Reno, along with Peter Perry for sentencing on the tax evasion charge and flight to avoid prosecution. A plea negotiation had been worked out. In return for Conforte coming back to testify against Claiborne, he agreed to a 15 month sentence, concurrent with his Washoe County bribery trial sentence. He was to remain under heavy guard until the trial with Claiborne was resolved.

Before he was whisked away, the news reporters jammed him for his opinion of the Claiborne charges. Conforte's attorney cautioned him not to say a word. Conforte, though, brushed this aside and spoke briefly with the reporters, complaining about what he termed, the "...slanted news coverage of the events."

Before he could explain further, his attorney grabbed him by the arm and hustled him away.

On Monday, March 5, 1984, the Ninth Circuit Court of Appeals in San Francisco, heard an appeal by Claiborne's attorney to dismiss the federal charges against his client. The attorney argued that under the constitution, a life-tenured judge cannot be prosecuted unless he is first impeached by Congress and removed from office. This argument derives from the separation of powers doctrine intended to keep the executive branch from interfering with judicial functions.

The plea was ruled on by an appellate panel of three judges selected from other circuit courts because all of the Ninth Circuit's judges had disqualified themselves from the Claiborne case. In their ruling to reject the plea, the panel made their decision clear.

"No man in this country is so big that he is above the law. A judge, no less than any other man is subject to the processes of the criminal law."

The panel by their ruling cleared the way for the trial to begin on March 15, 1984, in U.S. District Court, in Reno. They also noted that this was only the second time felony charges had been brought against a sitting U.S. Federal judge.

Opening arguments began as scheduled on Thursday morning, March 15. William Hendricks, an experienced prosecutor, began by telling the jury he would present evidence that Claiborne received $85,000 in bribes from brothel owner, Joe Conforte, to quash a Storey County voter fraud investigation and to reverse Conforte's 1977 income tax conviction. Other charges levied against the judge were accusations of hiding large sums of earned income from the Internal Revenue Service and government investigators.

Speaking of the bribery charges, Hendricks told the jury that the government's star witness would be the infamous local brothel owner, Joe Conforte, a fugitive who'd recently returned from Rio de Janeiro, to testify against his former friend and attorney. Hendricks went on to detail the friendship between the two that had its start in 1967, when Claiborne, then a renowned Nevada attorney, was hired by Conforte to defend him against a charge of white slavery.

"For the next decade, not only a legal relationship but a close personal relationship developed between them," Hendricks said.

Hendricks continued to explain to the attentive jurors that this cemented relationship led to bribery and payoffs given to Claiborne after he was appointed as a federal judge by President Jimmy Carter, in September, 1978.

The jurors listened as Hendricks sought their response when he told them that Conforte would testify about a meeting between the two in Claiborne's apartment in Reno, during December, 1978. During this meeting, Hendricks said the judge accepted a $30,000 bribe to quash an illegal voter registration charge lobbed against Conforte. Specifically, he was charged with forcing his working girls to fraudulently claim permanent residency in Storey County for the purpose of voting for local candidates friendly to the brothel owner.

Allegedly, when the two met in Claiborne's apartment, Claiborne pointed to the ceiling and held a finger to his lips as if to signal the presence of a wiretap. Hendricks then told the jurors the judge scribbled on a piece of paper, "I need $30,000...don't worry about your case."

"What case?" Conforte allegedly scribbled back.

"The subpoena," scribbled the judge.

During the scribbling back and forth, Conforte pried into Claiborne's personal troubles, suspecting that other persons may have been squeezing the judge for money.

"Is anyone bothering you? Extorting money?" Conforte wanted to know. "Tell me. I'll take care of it."

When the judge told him no, Conforte winked and then gestured that he didn't have the money on him, but would get it. As he was turning to leave, he paused to watch the judge crumple up the piles of notes and set them on fire. Conforte then left the apartment.

"On or about" the tenth of December, Hendricks said, Conforte returned and again met with Claiborne. This time he had $30,000 in $100 dollar bills which he handed over. Conforte then scribbled on a legal pad and held it for Claiborne to read.

"You are a very smart person to deal with me directly, instead of going through Stan Brown (Conforte's attorney).

Hendricks then looked sternly at the 12 jurors and told them that of all the prostitutes who were subpoenaed, none had ever been called to testify before the grand jury looking into the case. The investigation was stalled and then died a quiet death.

"Conforte," Hendricks said, "was delighted."

The second large money bribe was consummated in the garage of the Portland Motor Inn (Oregon), in March, 1979, where Claiborne was staying while presiding over a trial. During this bribe, Hendricks said the two huddled in the shadows of the garage to discuss terms for Claiborne's assistance in reversing an income tax conviction against Conforte. A conviction that threatened to slam the brothel owner in a federal prison for as long as 20 years.

"I think I can do that for you," Claiborne allegedly told Conforte. "In case I can't, don't worry about the appeal."

Claiborne then allegedly asked Conforte how much he could pay.

"The sky's the limit," Conforte replied.

According to Hendricks, Claiborne then asked for $100,000 "to get things started." Following this conversation, Hendricks said Conforte counted out $50,000 in $100 dollar bills which he gave to Claiborne. This was followed by another $5,000 which he stuffed into the federal judge's coat pocket.

Business completed, the two men turned and silently walked away in opposite directions.

The reason the two long time friends eventually fell out, Hendricks said, was that Claiborne did not have enough clout to reverse the conviction. In reality, there was nothing he could do. Hendricks said this was the government's position. Claiborne had taken the bribe with no intention of carrying out his side of the agreement.

Conforte had paid out $55,000 to get the tax conviction overturned, but all he got for his money was a smile and a promise. The con-wise notorious brothel owner had been flim- flammed by a down home Arkansas boy. The conviction and the five-year prison term hanging over his head was carved in concrete. Conforte was looking at hard time. And because of this, he had agreed to become a government witness. Hendricks sat down and turned the floor over to defense counsel.

Claiborne's lead attorney, immaculately suited for the occasion, stood and rose to his feet. Whispers among the surprised spectators confirmed that he was none other than State Senator, Bill Raggio, a long time adversary of Joe Conforte. This was the same Raggio, who during his tenure as Washoe County District Attorney, had been the target of a sexual setup engineered by Joe Conforte. And a setup for which the brothel owner had done time in the Nevada State Prison.

Once again, the long time adversaries were to meet in court. However—and this boggled the mind of many of those in attendance, the notorious brothel owner—ex-con Joe Conforte, would be there as a protected witness to testify for the United States Government. The clean-as-a-pin Raggio, now an elected State Senator, would try to refute the government's case and prove the brothel owner was a liar. Claiborne's career held in the balance.

Raggio began by trying to tear down Conforte's credibility. He described the government's star witness as nothing more than "...a pimp who has been a pimp all his adult life—a whore monger."

Hendricks jumped to his feet to protest loudly, but Raggio cut him off and shouted, "I'm going to call a spade a spade."

Raggio continued to denounce Conforte's credibility and said the meeting described by the prosecutor between the brothel owner and Joe Conforte, never took place. Claiborne had never accepted a bribe in his career, Raggio said.

"It is a lie on the part of Joe Conforte."

Raggio told the courtroom the government's case against his client stemmed from a vendetta to get the federal judge because of a "resentment" of Claiborne by federal prosecutors and the FBI who had been denigrated by the judge in the past.

As Raggio sat down, he had made in clear to those present, that Conforte would be on trial as much as would Claiborne

On the following day, Friday, March 16, Hendricks addressed the jurors accusing Claiborne of laundering untold thousands of dollars through the Las Vegas casinos while he was still a practicing attorney. This was money, Hendricks explained to the jury, that was never reported as income by Claiborne.

As a practicing attorney, Claiborne's estimated income was in the neighborhood of $375,000 a year, Hendricks stated. After being appointed to the federal judiciary, his salary as a federal judge, plummeted to around $55,000 a year. How did Claiborne make up the difference? According to Hendricks, he did this by collecting legal fees still owed him and by accepting payoffs, specifically from Joe Conforte, and evasion of income taxes.

Hendricks then turned back to Claiborne's relationship with Conforte, and accused the judge of accepting not only money from the brothel owner, but also the services of Mustang Ranch prostitutes. He was also accused of acting as the brothel's "conduit" for other local politicians.

Throughout the rest of the day, the federal prosecutor put several people on the stand in an attempt to bolster the accusations lodged against Claiborne.

During a Saturday interview with the Las Vegas Sun, Claiborne angrily told the reporters the government was trying to vilify him in public, because their case against him was weak.

"It's a damn lie," he said. "I'm not surprised at this move because they've been taking these cheap shots at me for three and a half years. And apparently they recognize that their case against me is weak in court so they intend to publicly vilify me."

On Monday when the trial resumed, the prosecutor announced his star witness, Joe Conforte would take the stand. Visiting Judge, Walter Hoffman, of Virginia, scanned the courtroom and was appalled at the sight of the heavily armed government agents sent as Conforte bodyguards. Fearing their presence could affect Conforte's testimony, he ordered them out of the courtroom.

Muttering among themselves, they reluctantly complied and filed out. Judge Hoffman then explained to the crowded spectators, that because of security precautions, they would not be allowed to leave the courtroom except during recesses, or until Conforte had finished testifying.

After being sworn in, Conforte began his testimony and set out to destroy his onetime friend. He testified he gave Judge Claiborne $85,000 to overturn the tax evasion conviction, and to fix a Storey County voter fraud charge.

What were the dates, the prosecutor wanted to know.

Conforte answered he first bribed Claiborne on December 13, 1978, when he gave the judge $30,000 to toss out the voter fraud charge.

When was the second payoff?

Conforte was uncertain of the exact date but said it occurred in March, 1979, in Portland, Oregon. Conforte said this is when he gave the judge the $55,000.

The prosecutor hesitantly acknowledged the government was of the opinion that even though Claiborne took the money from Conforte, he had no intention of trying to overturn the tax case. He just wanted the money.

Conforte related how he and the judge had been good friends for many years. During their frequent meetings, they discussed many things including which politicians deserved their financial support. Conforte was quoted as saying he wanted to elect people "who would not outlaw prostitution."

Continuing his testimony, Conforte said he once gave his attorney, Stan Brown, $5,000 to forward to Claiborne as a gift. "I wanted to keep Claiborne happy," he said, "and I was happy to give it to him."

During the periods when Raggio tore into him on cross examination, Conforte's memory at times fell apart. He struggled with details of their frequent meetings where money was allegedly exchanged.

Other times, his memory was razor sharp. After handing over the first payoff of $55,000, Conforte quoted Claiborne: "...it's in the bag, it's positive, don't worry about it, you don't got to worry about it no more."

Did he get his moneys worth?

He told the court he was outraged, when after paying out $55,000, the appellate judges from the Ninth Circuit Court, ruled against him. He'd paid for an empty promise, and was now looking at a five-year stretch in a federal joint. He told the court his blood would boil when he thought of Judge Claiborne. It was then he decided he'd have to flee the country. Within a few days, he put together $500,000, and told Sally to run things at the Mustang (which she'd been doing most of the time anyway).

Before he jumped across the border into Mexico, which was to be his first stop on the way to Brazil, he said he phoned the Las

Vegas Strike Force, and told them he could deliver Claiborne to them on a "silver platter," if granted immunity.

The head of the strike force, Geoffrey Anderson, recalled how Claiborne had once referred to them as "rotten bastards, crooks and liars." He was intrigued by the phone call, Conforte said, but did nothing. Conforte told the court he then made his way to Colombia, and from there to Rio.

After three days of testimony, Conforte was excused. The prosecution then called several government witnesses they'd dug up to corroborate Conforte's story.

John Colletti, a former Conforte bodyguard and driver (and witness to the Oscar Bonavena slaying in May, 1976) took the stand. Colletti told the court he had been with Conforte on December 12, 1978. During the day, he said he had taken the brothel owner to the bank "to conduct some business," and later on that night he watched Conforte stuff bundles of money into his pockets. His pockets bulging, Colletti said Conforte drove away by himself and did not say where he was going.

Hendricks asked the witness how much money Conforte was carrying. Wasn't it unusual for a person to carry around large amounts of cash?

"How much is usual or large?" Colletti stared back at Hendricks.

After pondering his remark for a few seconds, Colletti then acknowledged that it was not normal for Conforte to carry around that much cash.

Court was then adjourned for the week.

On Monday, March 26, 1984, Stan Brown, a Conforte attorney for 15 years took the stand. He was there as a prosecution witness to affirm Conforte's testimony.

In response to questioning, Brown testified he and Claiborne had met in the attorney's office once to discuss the grand jury trial in Portland, in which Brown was to be a witness. During the meeting, he said Claiborne begged him to lie about his (Claiborne's) efforts to reverse the tax conviction against Conforte. And showing a lingering paranoia, Claiborne scribbled on a piece of paper, "Don't tell them that, it's a matter of my life."

"I told him I couldn't do that (lie) because in the first place it wasn't the truth, and in the second place, Joe Conforte had already told the government about what I had said. There was nothing I could do about it."

Claiborne's co-counsel, Oscar Goodman, then attacked Brown during cross examination.

Targeting the attorney's ethics, Goodman accused Brown of handling Conforte's legal affairs "knowing full well that he was wanted by federal authorities, and that didn't cause you any ethical problems, did it?"

"No. He had to be defended." Brown went on to say that Conforte had been victimized by the government and cited the 20 years sentence which was initially handed down on the tax conviction as "savage."

Goodman then brought up the question of a $5,000 monthly fee paid by Conforte to Brown's law office. And Goodman wanted to hear about Brown's future financial transactions with the brothel owner, and his motivation for testifying.

"What did you owe to Conforte?" Goodman demanded.

"Friendship," Brown shot back. "I felt he had been severely injured by our system, and I stood by him. I am still standing by him." Brown did acknowledge that the Conforte account amounted to about 20 percent of his office's billing.

Brown reaffirmed his loyalty to Conforte.

"What happens during this trial has no bearing on Mr. Conforte's and my relationship," Brown stated.

The witness was then excused and court adjourned for the day. As they prepared to leave Raggio and Goodman were pressed for answers by the waiting reporters.

"We will move at the appropriate time for dismissal," Raggio quipped.

The government thus rested its case. If found guilty, Claiborne would become the first sitting federal judge to be convicted of a felony.

In the afternoon, Bill Raggio began the defense by asking Judge Hoffman for a subpoena to bring an unnamed State Department worker from New York City to Reno. Raggio explained to the judge that Conforte had testified, under oath, that he had met with Claiborne on December 13, a Wednesday. But, Raggio said, this date was refuted by the testimony given by John Colletti. Colletti had told the court it was on the 12th of December that Conforte made a mysterious trip carrying a large amount of cash.

Raggio told the judge that on December 12, Conforte was in New York picking up his passport.

Who was telling the truth? Had he been in New York on that date? In Reno? Conflicting testimony accomplished one thing: It cast doubt upon the minds of Judge Hoffman and the jurors.

Raggio continued to work on Judge Hoffman:

"The information and documents sought are for the purpose of establishing that the witness Joseph Conforte was in New York City on December 12, 1978, and personally received his passport and was leaving on a scheduled trip for Brazil within a few days. The court will note that this is the same date on which John Colletti testified Conforte was in Reno all day when he gave a bribe to the defendant, Judge Claiborne."

Raggio's unexpected request to bring a witness to Reno who could verify that Conforte was in New York on the day the prosecution said he was in Reno bribing Claiborne, jolted Judge Hoffman as well as the government's prosecutors. The jurors were scratching their heads.

After careful consideration, Judge Hoffman explained to Raggio that the application for a court order commanding the State Department official to appear was reasonable, but he refused to keep the government in the dark.

"What I'm being asked to do," he stated, "in effect, is to join with counsel for the defense to act as co-counsel. I can't do it gentlemen, and I know of no law that would permit me to do it."

Raggio responded, "The evidence involved is so crucial that, if that's the only way, I'll accept it."

He explained to Judge Hoffman that the information didn't come to light until Conforte began testifying. And he stressed the only way the State Department would honor a subpoena would be if it had been signed by a federal judge.

"Time is of the essence," Raggio stated.

A brief recess was called while the judge pondered the request. Returning to the bench, Judge Hoffman told the court he had signed the order for the subpoena. He went on to explain to the court the order called for a "custodial" witness to appear for the defense with passport information on Conforte. The subpoena required the unnamed official to fly to Reno with all records dealing with a passport issued to Conforte December 12.

Bill Raggio had another surprise for the court. He brought

out a video tape taken of Claiborne's apartment where the alleged $30,000 bribe had taken place. Raggio reminded the court that Conforte had testified the apartment had a kitchen bar where the two men met and exchanged the money. But, Raggio pointed out, the video confirms that the apartment did not have a kitchen bar. Raggio explained that in the apartment complex, the only units that had a kitchen bar, were the studio apartments. Claiborne's apartment was a one-bedroom unit.

"Mr. Conforte is describing and has been describing what obviously is a studio apartment, and not Claiborne's apartment," again casting doubt on Conforte's testimony.

On Thursday, March 29, John Scott Rholf, of the State Department's passport division, and who had flown out from New York to testify, told the court, a passport application signed by Joseph Conforte, had been submitted to his office on December 12, 1978, and had been issued in four hours.

Rholf said the passport in question carried a code "indicating urgent...expedite." He went on to explain that when an applicant fills out a form and provides proof that he needs the passport immediately, it gets top priority. In this case, Rholf explained the applicant had presented an airline ticket showing a December 13, 1978 departure from Miami, Florida, to Brazil.

Under cross examination, Rholf said the application could have been filled out earlier, pre-signed and sent to a person in New York, to be delivered to his office.

While it was not necessary for Conforte to pick up the passport, Rholf said, the person who could pick it up would have to have a letter signed by the applicant authorizing them to do so. There were no records that would indicate this occurred, he said.

Oscar Goodman, Claiborne's co-counsel, then arose and told the court the testimony of Rholf did not prove conclusively that Conforte was in New York on December 12, but it did cast serious doubt on the brothel owner's truthfulness.

Other discrepancies were entered next which showed the original indictments listed the date of the bribery to be "...on or about December 14 or 15." This was subsequently changed to the 12th, after the prosecution learned that Claiborne was in Las Vegas on the 15th.

The first character witness, one who threw even more doubt on Conforte's testimony, was a renowned Supreme Court Justice, one who had been on the court for 14 years, and was twice Chief Justice.

Nevada Supreme Court Justice, Al Gunderson, was sworn in. As questioning got under way, he told the jurors on the evening of December 12, 1978—the time of the alleged bribe, he and Claiborne were together in Reno. He testified the two met about 7:30 p.m., at the Holiday Hotel-Casino in downtown Reno. There they spent the evening eating and talking until about 11:00 p.m.

Under questioning, Gunderson had another surprise. He told the court that he and Claiborne had got together in Las Vegas on the 15th. This was the same date entered on the original indictment which said Claiborne was in Reno accepting a bribe from Conforte..

Under cross examination, Gunderson never wavered.

Following his testimony, court was adjourned.

As the jurors filed out for the day, they couldn't help but notice the challenging headlines of the Las Vegas Sun, strategically placed in a news rack outside the courthouse: "CONFORTE'S STORY CRUMBLES."

On Friday, Judge Claiborne took the stand in his own defense. He began to speak in his patented southern drawl by choosing his words calmly while outlining his legal career and his association with Joe Conforte. He said when he first arrived in Nevada, he joined the Las Vegas police force where he reached the rank of detective sergeant. In 1946, he passed the bar and left the police department to go with the District Attorney's Office.

He compiled an impressive record of convictions, he told the court, and then left to go into private practice.

"Back then," he drawled, "there were only 16,000 people living in Las Vegas. You would have starved to death as a specialist. I took everything."

Claiborne continued to say his practice grew, right along with Las Vegas. He soon had built a reputation as a formidable trial lawyer, and handled several high profile cases.

He said he first met Joe Conforte in 1967 when he successfully defended him against a charge of white slavery. This was the only felony acquittal ever won by Conforte he said. He said he later defended Sally Conforte on a tax evasion charge.

Claiborne related how he had taken on many unpopular cases of notorious individuals that drew undue publicity, "...some of it good, some of it bad."

Could this have earned him enemies?

"I'm sure I made many," he said.

He continued to speak of himself, however, pulled up short before reaching the dates of the alleged bribes. Nearing 5:00 p.m., Judge Hoffman announced court was adjourned for the weekend. Claiborne could resume on Monday, Judge Hoffman said..

Outside of court, Claiborne told the reporters he was glad to take the stand.

"It's hard to sit there when everybody is talking about your life," he said.

Standing beside him, Bill Raggio said, "He's got a good memory. I think he's a good witness."

The two thanked the reporters and smiled before turning away. It had been a good day for the defense.

On Monday, April 2, 1984, the trial was beginning its fourth week. Claiborne again took the stand in his own defense. He stated emphatically that Conforte had never been over to his Reno apartment, and he had never taken a bribe from him.

About the alleged $55,000 bribe in Portland, Oregon, Claiborne said this was a lie. He said nobody knew where he was staying in Portland because he had been forced out of the Portland Hilton, his initial destination, because of a convention. He was then compelled to look for another hotel. Nobody could have known where he found other accommodations.

The allegations of hiding income from the IRS, Claiborne said, this never occurred. All of his income statements had been given to his tax accountant for disposition.

He reaffirmed what Supreme Court Justice, Al Gunderson had testified to. The two men were together during the evening of December 12, when Conforte said he'd given Claiborne $30,000 to quash an illegal voter registration charge.

Claiborne told the jury the only time he saw Conforte in Portland, was on March 8, in the courthouse shortly before the trial. Claiborne said he remembered the incident because they rode the elevator together along with several other persons. Conforte, he said was unshaven and was smoking a dirty cigar that was annoying to the elevator patrons.

Another date in question, December 13; Claiborne said he dined with his secretary and the two spent the evening together.

During cross examination, Hendricks hammered away at Claiborne trying to trip him up. Claiborne remained calm, with his usual down home folksy attitude, smiling when responding.

Hendricks suggested that Claiborne lived on the edge squandering large amounts of money in the casinos, and that because of this, he was "desperate for money."

Claiborne conceded this suggestion, but told the jurors he wasn't desperate enough to turn to Conforte for $85,000 in bribes.

Hendricks then tore into the tax evasion counts.

"After you became a federal judge, your income dropped substantially, didn't it?"

"Drastically."

"After you became a judge, you started cashing a number of income checks, did you not?"

"Yes. I cashed many."

Hendricks then presented to the jury a series of checks cashed at the Golden Nugget, Benny Binion's horseshoe, and other local clubs.

"Were you trying to hide anything by cashing these checks?"

"Of course not!"

"Judge Claiborne, were you desperate for money at this time?"

"I don't know."

Hendricks reminded the jurors that in his opening arguments, he had told them Claiborne could not adapt to the relatively paltry salary he was making as a federal judge. As a renowned criminal lawyer, he had enjoyed a lavish lifestyle.

Referring to one check cashed for $3,000, Hendricks wanted to know why it was cashed and not deposited in the bank.

"I probably cashed the check, took some of it and left the remainder at home. In those days, I would probably walk around with $1,000 or $1,500. I cashed them at my own whim, at my own convenience."

"Were you desperate for cash as of August, 1980?"

"Yes I was," Claiborne answered. And he was quick to add that a real estate deal he engaged in had left him drained financially

"But, if I had taken the $85,000 from Joe Conforte, I wouldn't have needed the money."

Hendricks then surprised the court when he asked Claiborne about $75,000 the judge used to pay off an income tax settlement, but which had never been entered as income.

Claiborne said he got the money wrapped in a shoe box as a Christmas gift, given to him by a well known local gambler and Dunes casino mogul. When he opened the box, he was startled to see it contained $100,000 in bills. Not sure what to do, he went to see his friend Benny Binion at the Horseshoe Club. Binion suggested they store it in one of his vaults, which they did, and it stayed there for six-years. During this time, he said he drew money out twice to pay accumulated interest on his tax bill. When he became a federal judge, he retrieved the money and deposited it in his bank account. This same day, he sent the IRS a check for $76,413, which settled his overdue tax debt..

A government accountant was called later in the day and testified that Claiborne could have earned in excess of $37,000 in interest had he placed the money in a bank when he first got it.

On Wednesday, Claiborne was again placed on the stand. Oscar Goodman wanted to bring out more details of the $100,000 "gift" given to Claiborne, and stored in a vault in the Horseshoe Club.

Claiborne reiterated that the money was a gift and not a loan.

Goodman then wanted to know if the benefactor who gave Claiborne the money, had reported the transaction to the IRS.

"No."

"Did you borrow the money from the person?"

"No."

Did you tell anyone you had received a gift from the person?"

"No."

When the prosecution began summation, Hendricks told the court the 66 year old Claiborne was a man driven by greed, who was willing to sell his robes for $85,000 bribery money, taken from an ex-con brothel owner, and who had been a fugitive from justice for many years. .

The other government co-prosecutor, Steven Shaw rose to deliver his coup de grace. "I've been waiting a long time for this," he started and then described a "cash relationship that endured for many years between Judge Claiborne and Joe Conforte."

He said that when Judge Claiborne came to the stark realization that he couldn't continue his lavish lifestyle on the salary of a federal judge, he sought other sources of income.

"It does not startle the imagination to realize what is going through Judge Claiborne's mind," he said. "What is going through Judge Claiborne's mind is getting money from Joe Conforte."

Referring to the $55,000 bribe Claiborne allegedly took from Conforte to reverse the tax evasion conviction, Shaw said it was nothing but a scam and tried to explain to the court how Claiborne felt. Claiborne took the money, Shaw said, but never planned to have the case reversed.

"Judge Claiborne thinks the case is going to be reversed anyway, and he thinks, 'I might as well let this sucker think I'm the one doing it.'"

"The fact that Judge Claiborne failed in the larger scheme doesn't matter here," Shaw said. "What matters is there was a scheme to defraud." He explained to the jurors that a charge of wire fraud was added to the indictments because of an interstate phone call Claiborne made to Stan Brown. At the time of the call, which was made to discuss the case, Claiborne was in California, and Brown was in Nevada.

Shaw praised his star witness, Joe Conforte, as having a "remarkable, accurate memory" of the events going back five-years.

"I suggest he has no reason to lie," Shaw said, adding that he had already kept his part of the plea bargain by testifying. "As long as he tells the truth, the deal stands."

Shaw then went on to describe the paranoia surrounding Judge Claiborne. When he realized he was being looked at by federal authorities, Shaw said, the judge was constantly peering over his shoulder, looking for wiretaps and informants. Many times he ushered his friends out into the street to talk, fearful that his own quarters were bugged.

"Imagine," Shaw said, "a U.S. Judge being worried about bugs in his own courtroom.

"Judge Claiborne is the only person who has a personal interest in the case," Shaw said. "And he has the ability to do it in a convincing way—he is the only one to hear every other witness before him testify.

"It gives him the ability to lie. He virtually told everybody in the courtroom he based his testimony on what other people said."

Turning to the "gift" of $100,000, Shaw told the court the money was actually a loan, and following protocol, should have been entered on Claiborne's judicial ethics report. It wasn't.

"For Judge Claiborne to have the audacity and arrogance to come into this court and say it was a gift, is so outrageous as to defeat any credibility he had on the witness stand."

Referring to the transaction, Shaw sneered and called it Claiborne's "shoe box" defense.

Bill Raggio was the first defense attorney to speak from the podium.

Raggio said of his long time courtroom adversary, Joe Conforte, "He's a liar! And if any count is to be believed, it's that Joe Conforte committed perjury and it's he who should be on trial."

"Look at someone of the nature of Joe Conforte, and his confederates," Raggio said, trying to get across to the jury. "Because if you strip that away, there isn't anything left in this case."

"Joe Conforte was desperate," Raggio said. "He was on the lam and knew there was no love lost between (Las Vegas Strike Force Chief) Geoffrey Anderson" Raggio reminded the jurors of earlier testimony when Conforte had testified he could deliver Claiborne's head to them on a "silver platter."

"But I submit to you ladies and gentlemen, that after four weeks (of testimony), Joe Conforte didn't deliver anything on a platter. He delivered it on a sieve, because it's full of holes and when you shed any light on it, it disintegrates into nothing.

"Who is Joe Conforte? If you haven't figured out who Joe Conforte is by now, then we've wasted four weeks in the courtroom. He is an ex-felon. He's never had to work a day in his life in Nevada. He's run brothels all over the state of Nevada, and not always legally. In one of the brothels, he was bugging the rooms. He's lived off the earnings of prostitutes all of his life.

"This is the individual with whom the government made a deal, a deal with the devil."

Raggio continued to hammer Conforte's credibility. He said Conforte jumped at the chance to return from exile as a government witness, so he could lie against his former friend and attorney, Judge Claiborne.

"As a result of this very convenient deal, Mr. Conforte is now joyfully going to be with us soon...he'll be home by Christmas. Mr. Conforte is the one here who has a motive to come here and testify falsely."

Raggio said Conforte's testimony of the alleged bribe at Claiborne's apartment, fell apart many times: when Conforte slipped on the description of the apartment, when Chief Justice Gunderson testified Claiborne was with him the night Conforte said he had made the payoff, and when a federal passport official had testified Conforte was in New York City, on the night in question.

As the case fell apart, the government panicked, and they changed the dates on the indictments, "but it fell flat."

"I can't believe the government wants you to believe Judge Claiborne was in his apartment accepting a bribe from Joe Conforte," Raggio said, "It's a complete and absolute lie, and if that's a lie, then the whole case is a lie."

What did Raggio have to say about Stan Brown, the long time Conforte attorney who testified as a character witness?

"He's such an ethical guy," Raggio told the jurors, "who's been willing to represent this low-life all his life because he (Conforte} is his meal ticket."

He labeled the prosecution's case a rash of omissions and loopholes. He accused the government of branding Claiborne corrupt before they had any proof.

Raggio moved up and down in front of the jurors while punctuating his words with hand gestures. .He told the jurors the government had bought Conforte's line without question, and then let the brothel owner trample on the U.S. Judiciary while languishing in Brazil. Once back in the states, he continued to patronize the government by agreeing to testify against his one time friend and attorney.

Raggio was particularly critical of the plea bargain arranged by the Justice Department. He said the department's case was built on lies dished out by Joe Conforte, "the devil incarnate."

"They make it (the plea bargain) sound like something you should hang up on the wall next to the Mayflower Compact of the Declaration of Independence," Raggio yelled. "He had a lot of time to fabricate a story. He got a deal and he worked on it for a long time."

Raggio admonished the jurors not to accept the testimony of

brothel owner Joe Conforte. "Don't believe him when he said he went to Claiborne's apartment to pay the bribe.

It's a complete and absolute lie, ladies and gentlemen, and if that's a lie, the whole case is a lie. It's the keystone of the government's case, and you cut that keystone out, everything else crumbles."

It was Oscar Goodman's turn next. Waving his arms, his voice rising in timbre, Goodman told the jurors the Justice Department's case was "predicated on lies and dishonesty."

Goodman continued to alternately raise and lower his voice for effect. Commenting on Stan Brown, Goodman said, "You see two liars lying to each other," referring to Brown and Conforte.

"Stan Brown became Conforte's man, his puppet, his marionette. Brown," he said, "sold his soul to this purveyor of flesh, against his friend (Claiborne) of a lifetime." He referred to Brown as a "Judas."

Goodman then turned to face Judge Hoffman.

"Your honor," he said, "With that, the defense rests."

To the surprise of the courtroom, Goodman declined to ask for a motion for dismissal (which is almost routine in this kind of trial). He gave no indication why.

Speaking to reporters, Goodman said, "Right now, I feel confident with what we have."

Prosecutor Hendricks was asked why the defense attorney had not sought a dismissal. "He's a good lawyer. I'm sure he has a reason," Hendricks replied.

As the four-week trial concluded on Thursday, April 5, Judge Hoffman spoke to the jurors and told them to prepare for an overnight trip to an undisclosed Reno hotel. They were informed they would have single rooms, with no television, and would be accorded no more than two alcoholic drinks a night. Security would be provided by federal marshals.

For Claiborne, the waiting game began.

On Wednesday, April 11, after a week of deliberations, the six-men, six-women jury trudged into the courtroom, some with coats draped over their arms, others wearing spring jackets, all weary. The jury foreman remained standing and advised the judge the jury had reached a decision.

Judge Hoffman began to scan the paper handed to him and then looked up incredulously. "You have not agreed on any count?"

The sleepy eyed jury foreman rubbed his eyes and said, "Yes your honor, we were unable to reach a verdict on either not guilty or guilty on each of the seven counts."

Spectators and government prosecutors rose to their feet clamoring for an explanation.

"In a case as important as this," Judge Hoffman said, "I cannot accept a blank verdict form. I'll have to ask you to return for further deliberations."

The jurors slowly pulled themselves together and began to file out of the courtroom, under the watchful eye of the federal marshals.

Claiborne, along with his two attorneys, Bill Raggio and Oscar Goodman, huddled together to discuss the events. None of them had ever heard of a jury handing in a blank verdict form. This one was especially bewildering because it contained seven counts. And the jurors couldn't resolve even one? The trio shook their heads and slowly walked out of the courthouse and began a stroll along the Truckee River, waving off the horde of reporters.

Judge Hoffman noted that since being sequestered away from their families for a week, the jury had been dining on steak and lobster and other high-priced meals. They normally began deliberations at 9:00 a.m., breaking a couple of hours for lunch, and never worked past 6:00 p.m. Arriving at a verdict was becoming expensive for the tax payers.

The weary jury, after being directed by Judge Hoffman to get back to work, again began deliberations Wednesday afternoon, and resumed Thursday morning at 9:00 a.m.

Some of the jurors were battling problems other than reaching a verdict. Many had not yet filed their own income tax forms, and now the April 15 deadline threatened to make tax cheats out of them too. Hurriedly, one of the prosecutors sent out for a supply of IRS form 4868, which could be filled out by the jurors, granting them an extension—as long as the forms were in the mail by Monday.

With the added stress hanging over some of the jurors, Friday the 13th promised to be a risky day. But for whom?

At 2:30 p.m., the jurors, showing signs of strain and frustration, filed into the courtroom. The jury foreman passed a note to Judge Hoffman that said, "We are hopelessly deadlocked."

"I take it you are deadlocked on any and all counts?"

Looking dejectedly, the foreman answered, "Yes sir, we are."

"You think in your opinion, Mr. Foreman, there is no reasonable likelihood this jury will ever get together and agree on any counts?"

"I can't see it your honor."

Judge Hoffman then sent the jury out of the room so he could speak to both sides to find out if they wanted a mistrial.

Speaking for the defense, Oscar Goodman said, "Unfortunately, your honor, it's our position that, based on the explanations of the jury, and the indications of the foreman, it would be the only reasonable course at this time."

Facing the prosecutor, Judge Hoffman said, "And the government?"

"We agree, your honor."

Judge Hoffman then called for the jury.

"Ladies and gentlemen of the jury, in view of your foreman's report, it becomes impossible of course to do anything but retry this case. I will declare a mistrial.

"This case, in my opinion, was not a complex case, but that's neither here nor there. I had hopes that at least some of the counts would have been handled differently by you, but that's the way the ball bounces."

The judge then cautioned the jurors not to divulge their deliberations to the news media, "...you can get into trouble by talking too much."

Looking at the calendar, Judge Hoffman set the retrial for 9:30 a.m., on July 31, 1984. A new jury would have to be selected and Hoffman indicated they were to be locked up as long as the trial went on—not just during deliberations like this panel was. Also, he said the retrial would be extended to six days a week.

Outside of the courtroom, Judge Claiborne had little time for the pressing reporters. How did he feel about the mistrial they wanted to know.

"How would you feel?" he retorted. "I expected to be acquitted here, today. Sure I'm disappointed."

How did he feel about the judge, the jurors?

"Obviously, they gave a lot of attention to the case. It was a strain on them too."

Would the Justice Department go with the same seven counts

on the retrial? Or would they drop some of the weaker charges?

Claiborne said he had no idea what the feds would do. What could they do? They spent hundreds of thousands of dollars on this case without winning. What more could they try?

Did he get a fair hearing from Judge Hoffman? Would he ask for a different judge for the retrial?

Claiborne dodged this question, but his attorney, Oscar Goodman left no doubt about his feelings to ask for a different judge. Would he?

"You bet," Goodman snapped.

Claiborne continued to make his thoughts known to those around him. He said coming into the case he was confident of a victory. Now, with this unusual turn of events, he said he planned to enjoy his grandchildren, to take them fishing, and play as much as he could with them. This he thought would get his mind off his problems. Looking ahead to the retrial, he said he was confident he would yet be vindicated. He was a fighter, he said, and would remain a fighter until the end.

"And I'll win this case, because I'm a fighter and because I'm right," he said.

Joe Conforte, fugitive from justice, government witness and convicted felon, was whisked away to an undisclosed federal prison, to begin the reduced sentence of 15 months for income tax evasion. He couldn't sit still.

In June, he contacted the Associated Press by phone to express his feelings about the trial. He demanded a polygraph test to prove his truthfulness. He told the press it was he who was telling the truth; it was Claiborne who had lied on the witness stand.

"We can all solve this matter in one day, and avoid a new trial," he protested.. "I challenge Judge Claiborne to take a polygraph test with me.

When the Justice Department heard of the phone interview, they refused to make any comments.

Oscar Goodman, however, gave his opinion calling it a foolish proposition. Questionable results arise, he said, "when a sociopath takes a polygraph."

The Justice Department, on June 27, 1984, showed their hand when a spokesman announced the government prosecutors had dropped four of the original seven charges filed against

Claiborne. By doing this, they confirmed what the defense had known all along: the original counts had been *stacked* against Claiborne.

Stacked counts usually are done when a government agency loads up an indictment with the hope the accused will agree to a plea bargain in order to avoid defending against multiple charges. Does this work with naive criminals? Frequently.

But to try this against an experienced trial lawyer, shows naiveté on the part of the Justice Department. Did they think it would work? Apparently, but the mistrial proved it didn't.

Which counts were dropped?

The most important ones. The two bribery charges against Claiborne were thrown out the window, along with one count of tax evasion and one count of obstruction of justice.

What did this mean?

It meant that the jury didn't buy Conforte's testimony. It meant that the Justice Department had made a bad decision. They had enticed a fugitive back from Brazil with the promise of a reduced sentence for tax evasion, in return for testimony against a federal judge.

In the end, the fugitive received his reduced sentence, but the Justice Department had bought a pig-in-a-poke. Oh well....

Oscar Goodman and Bill Raggio were delighted. Goodman called the action "a vindication of Judge Claiborne." And then said he might reject the proposition of the government to drop the four charges, as a "tactical maneuver." Forcing them to go back to court with the original seven counts, Goodman reasoned, would vindicate his client.

The government—in this case, the taxpayers, had spent hundreds of thousands of dollars to bring Conforte back from Brazil, and to develop a case against Claiborne. Justice Department officials were spurred on by the promise of letters of commendations stuffed into their personnel files, leading to promotions. But when one looks objectively at the case, everything was dependent upon the testimony of Conforte, ex-con, brothel owner, fugitive from justice.

What did Conforte's testimony achieve? Absolutely nothing. Unless it is looked at from Conforte's perspective. He was welcomed back into the United States. He bargained for a reduced sentence on his income tax conviction, along with a concurrent sentence on the bribery charge, which he was handed on a golden platter. He was once again, back in control of his brothel, the Mustang Ranch.

What about the jurors? They were put up in private hotel rooms, dining on steak and lobster, and two drinks in the evening. Again, compliments of the U.S. taxpayers. Had the Justice Department erred? Of course, in their over eagerness to nail one of their own, they made a dubious compact with a dubious witness. Who was the loser in this case? Again, the taxpayers.

After Conforte's media interview, many of the jurors surfaced, and despite being warned not to speak to the media, they felt that if Conforte could call a press interview, so could they. Grouped together during a meeting, they rehashed the events during the deliberations. All agreed that no matter how long Judge Hoffman had kept them in seclusion, they could have never reached a verdict. A few supported Judge Hoffman's actions throughout the trial. Others accused him of withholding information that would have been favorable to Claiborne.

Another felt the Justice Department had gone after Claiborne unfairly.

"They tried to set him up," one lady voluteered. "They wanted to bury him at any cost. it was nothing more than cheap entrapment."

"The prosecutors acted like they were on a mission to get him because of his independence," voiced another."He wouldn't fall into line like they wanted to they went looking for his head, one way or another. They'll never get a conviction. If this goes to trial again they'll still lose."

One juror who said he voted for acquittal on all seven counts supported the others. "The best the government could do was to bring a fugitive—an ex-con brothel owner—back here as a stellar witness and expect us to buy his story. It stinks."

Another Claiborne supporter said the government would have to come up with much better evidence, and a more credible witness, if they had any intentions of getting a conviction the next time around.

Others voiced a different view.

"Each side had strong feelings," said one middle-aged man. "Some of us felt quite strongly that he was guilty, while others felt just as strongly that he was not. With such strong emotions during deliberations, there was no chance at all that the twelve of us could agree on anything."

"I felt strongly he was guilty," said another, "and so did some of the others, but some of the others felt just as strongly that he was innocent. Could we have all reached a verdict with continuing deliberations? Never!"

One juror said he felt the retrial should be moved out of Nevada.

"Take it to California, or maybe Washington or Oregon," he said, "but not in Nevada. There is too much emotion here centered around Conforte and his ranch."

Could the trial be held in Las Vegas?

"No," shouted another juror. "Claiborne has this same kind of influence down there."

Other jurors were resentful of Judge Hoffman's remarks when he stated the case was not that difficult.

One middle-aged woman tried to explain her feelings.

"It was a very difficult trial," she said, "and it took a lot out of all of us. There were arguments and disagreements. I only hope the next trial is not so demanding on the jurors. And I'm thankful I won't have to go through this again."

Another juror supported her feelings and said he too, could not go through another trial like this one.

"It was complicated," he said, "and in the end, the government based their entire case on the ramblings of Joe Conforte, their star witness. "Who can believe him?""

Apparently the jurors paid scant attention to the different character witnesses, including Chief Justice Gunderson who testified he and Claiborne had dined together the night Conforte testified he was with Claiborne.

"We didn't really pay much attention to his testimony," said a young man. "We felt that he and Claiborne were old friends, and so it was difficult to say whether his testimony was that important. In the end, it boiled down to a battle between Conforte and Claiborne. And which one of them you believed."

On Monday, July 2, Claiborne's attorneys called a press conference to explain they had agreed not to protest the government's plan to drop four of the seven charges lodged against their client. This was a change of stance, since earlier they had stated they were going to force the government to go ahead with all seven charges, just so they could vindicate their client. By agreeing to the government's motion, the only charges scheduled for the retrial would be reduced down to two counts of failure to file correct tax returns, and one count of submitting a false judicial ethics statement.

At 9:30 a.m., Tuesday, July 31, 1984, jury selection for the retrial began. Of the 32 who showed up, the attorneys selected 22 as potential jurors. As preemptory challenges began, more were weeded out and sent home.

Of these, several admitted to having a bias against the judge, in part due to television coverage of the case. One woman who was questioned stated flatly that she regarded Claiborne as guilty.

"I think he's guilty," she answered the judge. "From what I've seen on television and read in the papers, he is guilty!"

Another said she was terribly disappointed that Claiborne had not been convicted during the first trial.

Other prospective jurors felt that cheating on taxes should not be punishable. One lady said most people did it all the time.

"I have absolutely no love for the IRS," she told Judge Hoffman., "And I know many persons who cheat on taxes just like Judge Claiborne is accused of doing."

One man when questioned, responded saying he thought Claiborne was innocent because of Joe Conforte's questionable testimony during the first trial.

Judge Hoffman angrily reminded him that Joe Conforte was now out of the picture, and the prospective jurors should not bring up his name.

"Now," Judge Hoffman roared for the benefit of all those present in the courtroom, "Joe Conforte's gone to the winds as far as this case is concerned."

Inevitably, a jury was paneled consisting of six men, six women and two alternates. Hoffman then went into his chambers and called in attorneys from both sides. He confided in them that he was in fear for the safety of the jurors. He said during the first trial, one alternate juror had received a death threat scribbled on a piece of paper and placed on the windshield of her car. To protect this jury, Hoffman had ordered them sequestered for the duration of the trial, not just during deliberations. He finished by saying they would be housed in an undisclosed Reno hotel.

On Thursday morning, August 3, 1984, trial got under way.

Without the specter of Joe Conforte's notoriety influencing the courtroom, prosecutors envisioned this trial going much smoother and quicker.

Prosecution attorneys labeled Judge Claiborne a man "desperate for money," after relinquishing his lucrative law practice to become a federal judge. Wayne Hendricks told the jury Claiborne's income dropped from around $375,000 a year, down to $55,000, which is typical for a federal judge. To compensate, Hendricks said, Claiborne hid at least $100,000 he received as late payments from his private practice. When this was discovered, Claiborne lied and said this money had been a "Christmas gift."

Many other checks that Claiborne received, were cashed at local casinos and never reported as income, Hendricks said.

Oscar Goodman countered these arguments and told the jury Claiborne had turned all his income reports over to his tax accountant, who worked within the law, balancing the income against losses incurred when Claiborne moved out.

"Claiborne's being an outspoken protector of the little man," Goodman said, "as a defense attorney and deputy district attorney, made him a target of government agencies.

"It is not enough if you find Judge Claiborne was careless or negligent, but whether or not he intended to violate the law," Goodman told the jurors.

Following the opening arguments, the government's prosecutors hammered away at Claiborne's admitted act of stashing $100,000 in a vault of Benny Binion's Horseshoe Club in Las Vegas. Hendricks told the jury that had the money been deposited in the bank, it would have drawn $37,000 in interest during the six years it lie in limbo. Why would a person do this? To hide it from the IRS, Hendricks pounded away at the jury.

"There is no written record anywhere, is there," he queried, "of keeping this money for six years."

A government tax auditor was called in who testified Claiborne failed to report $106,000 in legal fees collected during the years 1979, 1980. He continued to say that most of the checks that failed to turn up on Claiborne's tax returns, were cashed in casinos rather than as deposits in Claiborne's bank account.

Horseshoe Club official, Teddy Binion, testified Claiborne brought two envelopes to the casino six years ago which contained $100,000. The money was placed in the vault, as Claiborne admitted, Binion said, and conceded the government's claim that Claiborne had not been given a receipt.

Various other government witnesses were called in Friday and Saturday morning, but offered little more to bolster the prosecution's case. Hendricks then told the court the government rested its case.

Oscar Goodman took over for the defense. He immediately demanded Judge Hoffman dismiss the two counts of tax evasion and the other count of lying on a judicial statement, for lack of evidence. Hoffman quickly refused this suggestion and told Goodman to get on with his defense. The two began a heated argument, and Goodman accused the judge of prejudice against his client.

Judge Hoffman boiled over and shouted, "I say you haven't a right to get up in this court and say I am biased and prejudiced. You keep your mouth shut from here on out! Is that clear?"

Goodman backed off and replied, "I understand what the court is saying."

At the conclusion of Saturday's hearings, Judge Hoffman acknowledged working on Saturday was unique, however he said the six-day weeks would continue until the trial was completed. With that he dismissed the court until Monday.

On Monday, a parade of defense witnesses were called in one by one to reinforce the defense's contention the money that had been secreted in the vault was a gift—not proceeds from Claiborne's private practice.

Claiborne was guilty of no more than carelessness, maybe negligence, the defense asserted. But certainly, he was not guilty of intention to defraud the government.

Oscar Goodman went on to lay the blame on Claiborne's tax accountant, and called it "frightening and disturbing" that the Justice Department would seek a conviction on such "paper-thin evidence."

Closing arguments began on Wednesday, when Hendricks, the stellar government prosecutor told jurors, Claiborne "admits to being desperate for money, not just in need of money." There was "ample evidence that shows Claiborne was acting in a knowing fashion" when he filed his 1979 and 1980 income tax returns, Hendricks said.

The other government prosecutor, Steven Shaw, told the

jurors Claiborne "made false statements to the IRS, made false statements to his fellow judges, and he lied to you in several instances. He treats the truth as his personal toy."

Co-defense attorney, J. Richard Johnston said the judge was guilty of nothing more than being careless. "...he was negligent. But that's not willfulness."

The case then went to the jury. After ninety minutes of deliberations on Thursday afternoon, the jury recessed until the next day.

On Friday, after 3 1/2 hours of deliberation, the jury foreman sent a note to Judge Hoffman stating they had arrived at a verdict.

Before calling in the jury, Judge Hoffman told the courtroom there would be no "outcries of any kind," when the verdict was read. He then told the jury to come in.

A verdict of guilty on two counts of income tax evasion, was read to the court, along with a verdict of innocent on the charge of lying on a judicial ethics report. Judge Hoffman asked each member of the jury if that was in effect their verdict. Each answered, "yes." He thanked each one and commented that they had done an admirable job in considering these matters." They were then excused and admonished not to speak to the reporters.

"It will save you a lot of headaches," he said as they were filing out.

So, the government had finally been victorious in winning two of the seven original charges against Claiborne. Conforte, who was serving his reduced sentence in an undisclosed federal prison, had been of no help. His name was not even brought up during the retrial.

Presiding Judge, Walter E. Hoffman set October 3, for sentencing. He noted later the defendant could receive a maximum of six years imprisonment and a $10,000 fine.

Claiborne appeared stoic in defeat, and when questioned by reporters admitted he was let down.

"I am of course disappointed," he told them. "I think that goes without saying."

Oscar Goodman jumped in to say he would seek to have the jury's verdict overturned, or possibly seek a new trial.

In response to further prodding by the reporters, Claiborne said he'd always judged a man by the way he dealt with adversity.

As for himself, he said he would handle this setback like he had always done, head-on.

Bill Raggio, co-counsel nodded. "I think he said it all."

William Hendricks, the chief prosecutor, was not strutting. He said he felt very sad about the verdict from the standpoint of the federal judiciary. Convicting a sitting federal judge of felonies, is not something you brag about, he said.

His partner, Steven Shaw, had mixed emotions. He said he felt satisfied they had garnered a conviction, yet on the other hand, was sad it had to be a federal judge.

"This is a sad as well as satisfying day for us," he said.

Government prosecutors then got to work preparing statements for the sentencing hearing. In a memorandum filed in U.S. District Court, they were to ask for "a significant term of incarceration" for Claiborne. The paper noted that Claiborne owed $160,000 in back taxes, interest and penalties, in addition to partial costs of the two trials.

"The defendant, as a federal judge, should have a special respect for the law as in his position, he is charged with the just administration of law in his courtroom," the prosecutors wrote. "Society is entitled to expect that those appointed to the judiciary will obey the laws they are entrusted to administer and that they will act with honesty and integrity, both in and out of the courtroom. For a man in this position to engage in a pattern of deception, and lies in the conduct of his personal affairs is an affront to the society which has entrusted him with the solemn responsibilities of the judicial office.

"Such conduct by a visible public official merits a strong statement of community condemnation through the imposition of a significant term of incarceration,"

Additionally, the prosecutors wrote, Claiborne should be assessed $32,737, costs incurred for the expense of witnesses, court reporters and others.

Claiborne's attorneys were quick to protest this charge lobbed against their client. This bloated sum included expenses for witnesses who never appeared and for useless transcripts, they complained.

On October 3, 1984, Claiborne and his attorneys filed into U.S. District Court, in Reno, this time for sentencing on the two counts of income tax evasion. They again stood before Judge

Walter E. Hoffman.

Addressing the court, Claiborne stood and faced the judge.

"I'm sorry I can't say I'm remorseful for these acts."

He told Judge Hoffman he "did nothing wrong. I'm guilty—not of the charges in this indictment. I'm guilty of being reckless with my own personal affairs," he said, "and I guess the reason I was a good lawyer and a good judge—and I defy any man to say I wasn't—was because I spent all my time there (in court). Money meant nothing to me."

Before he could continue, Judge Hoffman interrupted and demanded to know why he was speech making.

Stiffening, Claiborne's voice hardened, when he told the judge, "You are about to hand down and make a decision—a decision on my whole life. I definitely should have the opportunity to speak my piece fully and completely."

Steven Shaw then spoke for the prosecution and reminded Judge Hoffman that the two tax counts against Claiborne "were basic perjuries, intentionally false statements under oath for the purpose of personal gain. This is not a situation of negligence."

The prosecutors then made it known they felt a "significant term of incarceration" was warranted because of the accused's position within the federal judiciary.

Judge Hoffman then faced Claiborne and his attorneys and sentenced the accused to two years on each count, plus a $10,000 fine. He then ruled the counts were to run concurrently which amounted to two years behind bars. The accused, he said, would serve his sentence in a lightweight prison on the grounds of Maxwell Air Force base, near Montgomery, Alabama.

William Raggio immediately said a notice of appeal would be filed with the court. With this action, the case would be sent to the Ninth Circuit Court of Appeals, in San Francisco, which would have to select a panel of judges to hear the case. Claiborne was allowed to remain free pending a decision by the appeals board.

On December, 1984, the Federal Bureau of Prisons advised the courts Joe Conforte had served his prison term and was eligible for release. Strolling out of the lightweight federal prison near San Diego, again a free man, Conforte looked upward into the blue sky, inhaled deeply, and then drew in deeply on a long cigar he had just lit. Reno, and the Mustang Ranch, next stop.

During January, 1985, Judge Claiborne's attorneys filed a 48 page appeal with the Ninth Circuit Court of Appeals in San Francisco, citing illegal acts on the part of the federal government. The brief accused the Justice Department of embarking on a head hunting mission, pulling out all stops to bring down a federal judge. The charges against Claiborne, the brief stated, were "the product of a three-year war" by federal agents "to drive him from the bench." And the brief noted, their client was the only federal judge in this century to be convicted of felonies while in office. Essentially, the basis of the appeal was:

That the government illegally coaxed testimony out of Joe Conforte, an ex-con and notorious brothel owner, to help them gain a bribery conviction against Judge Claiborne. That the testimony later proved to be erroneous and uncorroborated. That the government prosecutors did reduce Conforte's own tax conviction sentence, from five years, down to 15 months as a reward.

That two simultaneous grand juries were paneled, one in Nevada, the other in Oregon, both targeting Judge Claiborne, which is in violation of federal rules.

That Claiborne's tax returns were obtained illegally, and therefore not admissible as evidence.

That federal agents were illegally acting as grand jury investigators, and roamed the country securing evidence and serving subpoenas, all the time misrepresenting themselves as agents of the grand jury.

That there was insufficient evidence presented in the second trial to warrant convictions on the tax counts.

That presiding Judge Hoffman, wrongly forced the defense to use "preemptory juror challenges (those that are arbitrarily not supported by factual grounds for dismissal) even though some of the jurors responding displayed outright hostility towards Judge Claiborne.

That a key witness, Claiborne's secretary, was improperly shielded from defense attorneys during a crucial recess in the second trial.

That evidence available to the defense was not made available to Claiborne's attorneys.

That Claiborne was tried illegally, because the Constitution's separation of powers doctrine requires a federal judge to be impeached by Congress before being subjected to criminal prosecution.

In the appeal, Oscar Goodman also noted that in the first trial, the government placed most of the responsibility for a conviction upon the testimony of Joe Conforte. The result was a hung jury because the jurors didn't believe his testimony. Consequently, the government had to drop four of the charges for the second trial. And without the Conforte-related charges, Claiborne would never have been indicted and gone to trial.

"If the jury in an adversary proceeding with a judge presiding, was distracted by the Conforte counts, then how much more was the indicting grand jury...distracted by the presentation of Conforte's false testimony?"

Goodman also said Conforte was enticed by the promise of a reduced sentence on his own tax problems, to the extent that the government had presented the brothel owner with an invitation to commit perjury.

"He (Claiborne) has not resigned and does not intend to resign from office until he has obtained vindication in the courts or in the House and Senate," Goodman said.

On Monday, July 8, 1985, a three-judge panel of the Ninth Circuit Court of Appeals in San Francisco, upheld the two tax evasion convictions of Judge Harry Claiborne. By doing so, they rejected Claiborne's contentions that a federal judge is immune from prosecution. The prison sentence of two years was left intact. Following this action, Claiborne's attorneys announced they would seek a rehearing in front of a larger panel of the appeals court.

On December 10, 1985, the full panel of the Ninth Circuit refused to consider an appeal of Claiborne's 1984 conviction. Oscar Goodman said he was disappointed by the decision, but said when the nation's highest court heard the case, his client would be vindicated. The appeals process which had been on a long arduous trip, was winding down. Next stop, the United States Supreme Court. Until then, Claiborne was to remain free on bond.

Claiborne clung to his appointed judiciary refusing to resign from the $73,000 a year post. Authorities then began the necessary preparations to impeach Claiborne before Congress. Representative, Barbara Vucanovich, R-Nevada, told the papers she believed Claiborne was looking foreward to this procedure.

"The judge himself, would like to go through the impeachment process in that it would give him the opportunity to present more of his case," she said.

Senator Harry Reid D-Nevada, said that Claiborne faced inevitable impeachment if he did not resign. Reid said despite his sadness that a federal judge had been convicted of felonies, he was after all convicted by a jury, and the Supreme Court had ruled.

"We should follow the law," Reid said.

Should the judge be impeached?

Reid had no answer for this, though he did make it clear if it came to impeachment proceeedings, he Reid, may have to vote on the issue.

Oscar Goodman, who continued to lead Claiborne's defense, was asked his comments about what Representative Vucanovich said about the inevitability of impeachment. He repeated what he had said many times that his client had been the target of an overzealous government prosecution.

Claiborne was advised to get his affairs in order. He was given 15 days to report voluntarily to the federal prison on the grounds of Maxwell Air Force Base, Alabama.

Oscar Goodman next filed two more motions on May 8, in a last ditch effort to keep his client out of prison. He stated in one motion that Claiborne could not go to an Alabama prison because federal law prohibits a sitting judge from residing away from the district in which he was appointed.

In the other motion, Goodman asked the Attorney General's Office to investigate his allegations of prosecutorial misconduct against Claiborne.

These last gasp efforts by Goodman were summarily dismissed by Federal Judge Walter Hoffman, who had presided over Claiborne's two Reno criminal trials.

Goodman was not yet finished. On Tuesday, May 13, 1986, he pressed for an emergency appeal before a three-judge panel of the Ninth Circuit Court of Appeals. The court took less than two hours to rebut the motion.

Following the hearing, Claiborne told reporters he would continue to fight whether he went to prison or not.

In San Francisco, attorneys from both sides argued the merits of the case over the telephone. The issue was whether or not Claiborne should surrender to the federal prison in Alabama, while awaiting other decisions from the Ninth Circuit.

Terry Anderson, a University of Miami law professor conscripted to assist Goodman in Claiborne's defense had a strong argument.

"In 200 years," he said, "no federal judge has ever been incarcerated. We are dealing with the fabric of our Constitution."

He asked the court to block Claiborne's imprisonment at least until resolution of the issues of whether a judge can be imprisoned before impeachment, and whether the outside appellate panel should have been appointed.

"Judge Claiborne has not been treated like other citizens in the Ninth Circuit," he argued.

Justice Department lawyer, Jan Little, said the defense's arguments were "completely meritless" and did not justify blocking Claiborne's imprisonment.

"At this point, it is time for him to report to prison," she said. "The Constitution does not immunize a sitting federal judge from the process of criminal law."

Claiborne was ordered to surrender to the U.S. Marshals in Las Vegas, or to the minimum security prison on the grounds of Maxwell Air Force base by Friday, May 16. He would continue to draw his $78,000 salary until duly impeached. He indicated he would report to the base.

In Las Vegas, prior to catching his flight, the 68 year old Claiborne looked confident. Responding to questions from the congregating newspeople, he showed he was still a fighter. Looking fit and trim in a short sleeved shirt and sharply creased trousers, he told them he was looking forward to the impeachment hearings where he expected to retain his judgeship.

When asked how he felt now, following in the footsteps of many criminals he had sent to prison, he admitted it was scary. But he said, he had to follow the law and would meet any challenges head-on.

Claiborne was asked if he had received a fair trial and fair treatment in the government's efforts to convict him. He just shook his head somberly and looked down at the ground in thought. Uplifting his head, he told the reporters that the last

three years of uncertainty
had taught him some valuable lessons. He learned who his real friends—and enemies—were.

He said he'd received more than 5,000 letters and cards of encouragement, not only from his friends, but from people he'd never met.

"You have no idea how encouraging that is," he said.

Again casting his gaze downward, he murmured softly to himself, recounting the greatest goal in his life had been to secure a seat on the the U.S. Supreme Court, a realistic goal, which had been in sight, up and until this conviction..

On May 16, 1986, a taxi rolled up to the gate of the Maxwell Air Force Base, in Montgomery, Alabama. The door opened and out walked Federal Judge Harry Claiborne, resigned to begin serving his two year sentence.

As he was ushered onto the base and entered the federal prison, he was met by Prison Superintendent, Tom Kindt. Kindt explained to him the orientation phase would start Monday. There would be a battery of tests, psychological, physical, and educational. When this phase was completed, he would be assigned a prison job, which could be anything from a clerical position to a groundskeeper on the golf course.

The Maxwell Air Force base prison was a minimum security facility, devoid of fencing or razor wire. Housing was provided by a series of one-story, white dormitories complete with double bunks, color television, a card room, and a common bathroom-shower. The facility boasted of having an extensive law library and a movie theater. During the Nixon era, John Mitchell, the U.S. Attorney General, and other Watergate notables had done their time here. The prison, if it could be called that, had been dubbed a "country club" by law and order advocates.

One large multi-use building was described as an "opera house." For physical conditioning, the *clients* could make use of up-to-date facilities for weight lifting, boxing, jogging, tennis and hand ball. There was also a large swimming pool complete with bath house.

The most visible fence was one three-feet high that bordered the outfield of the regulation sized baseball diamond. If a ball was hit over this fence, the clients were forbidden to go after it. To do so, amounted to an escape. Other balls could be purchased from the canteen.

Claiborne was told by the superintendent that the prison housed only white collar criminals, errant politicians and some lightweight drugs offenders. Claiborne could roam the grounds as he pleased, could make use of all the other facilities for clients, and could host picnics for visitors. If anything could be regarded as prison security, it was the inmate body count done at 4:00 p.m., when each inmate had to be standing by his bedside. Mail was also handed out at this time.

Claiborne was told that with good behavior he could be out in as little as eight months.

And until his case was brought before Congress and resolved, he would continue to draw his $78,000 salary as a federal judge.

During this election year, the politicians were quick to take advantage of Claiborne's case.

F. James Sensenbrenner, R-Wisconsin, stated his feelings on the floor of the House.

"Every day Judge Claiborne continues to draw his salary," he said. "It makes a mockery of our judicial system." He stated he would give the judge until June 4, to resign. If not, he said he would introduce an impeachment resolution.

In a letter mailed to Claiborne, Sensenbrenner said, "I hereby request that you resign immediately from your position as judge for the U.S. District Court of Nevada."

Barbara Vucanovich, R-Nevada, also called for Claiborne to resign.

"I really believe that the best thing that can be done to resolve this very difficult situation," she said, "is for Judge Claiborne to resign immediately. I have been informed by members of the House Committee on the Judiciary that impeachment proceedings will begin next month if there is no resignation. I do not personally believe that Judge Claiborne should be drawing a salary while serving a prison term, and I think that it is bad for our state to be the first to have a sitting federal judge in prison."

Judge Claiborne, #22709-048, who had been assigned a janitorial position at Maxwell, refused to grant media interviews. His attorney, Oscar Goodman spoke for him and said his client had no plans whatsoever of resigning.

"They're trying to speak of a judge misbehaving in office," he said. "That shows a lack of sensitivity to the entire judicial process."

On July 22, 1986, the House of Representatives, by a unanimous vote of 406-0, voted to impeach Judge Harry Claiborne, thereby forcing a trial in the Senate. During the hearings, none of the representatives defended his contention of innocence. Many ridiculed him for what they termed was his insistence on making a mockery of the judicial system.

On Monday, the fifteenth of September, 1986, Judge Harry Claiborne returned to the floor of the Senate, where eight years ago to the month, his appointment to one of the highest judicial offices in the United States had been affirmed unanimously.

He now sat facing a 12-person panel, which under the glare of television lights, accused him of "high crimes and misdemeanors" for failing to report $106,000 in income on his 1979 and 1980 tax returns. With him, were his long time attorney, Oscar Goodman, and former Nevada Senator, Howard Cannon, serving as special counsel.

House Judiciary Committee Chairman, Peter W. Rodino D-New Jersey, discounted Claiborne's stated defense that it was actually his accountants who were at fault, and not himself.

"It is simply impossible to believe a federal judge would be so ignorant of the facts and his responsibilities," Rodino began. "We simply cannot let a convicted felon sit on the federal bench and make judgments on others."

Another member of the prosecution team, Rep. Dan Glickman, D-Kansas, urged the Senate panel to bar Claiborne's lawyers from trying to prove that government prosecutors cooked up evidence against the judge as part of a vendetta.

"This is an impeachment trial," he said. "It should not serve as a forum where Judge Claiborne can search for evidence to substantiate wild and paranoid theories of government oppression."

Oscar Goodman stood up to portray Claiborne as a victim of Justice Department Strike Force prosecutors with whom he had often battled in court.

Goodman said Strike Force members had pressured witnesses into testifying against Claiborne. In their Nevada office, he said Strike Force members had caricatures pasted on their office wall depicting Claiborne as the Ayatollah Khomeini. Another judge, Goodman said, had been portrayed as a Ku Klux Klan night rider.

And so, on this the first day of the impeachment process,

punches and counter punches were lobbed for the benefit of the impeachment panel, whose job is was to gather all the relevant evidence, and when completed, pass it on the full Senate.

The next few days saw more of the same. And then on Friday, Claiborne took the stand. After being sworn in, he told a story of government harassment, and named the Strike Force Commander, FBI Agent, Joseph Yablonsky, as the man responsible.

Yablonsky was on a vendetta, Claiborne testified, he was out "to get rid of a lot of people, and unfortunately for me, I was foremost in his path."

Claiborne portrayed Yablonsky as "a very ambitious man who came into Las Vegas with the idea, in his words, of planting the American flag in the Nevada desert."

Claiborne testified that Yablonsky "recognized he'd have to deal with me in order to accomplish the things he wanted to do, but he didn't know me very well. To them, I was a threat because I was a criminal (defense) lawyer."

In his pursuit to get me, Claiborne testified, "Yobo Joe" was willing to cut a deal with the notorious brothel owner fugitive, Joe Conforte. And to bring Joe back from Brazil, he had to cut illegal or questionable deals with him. And other witnesses were bullied and threatened into telling pro-government yarns, he said.

Oscar Goodman said Claiborne's testimony was important, because were it not for the clouded testimony of the brothel owner, his client would never have been indicted on the bribery charges which subsequently were dismissed.

Without the bribery charges, Goodman said, the government's case fell apart. All they could grasp then, was the income tax charges, which initially had been nothing more than frosting on the cake.

On Monday, Claiborne again took the stand, this time to explain his failure to file proper tax returns. He placed most of the blame on his tax preparers. He said he did not willfully violate U.S. Tax laws. He said the discrepancies arose because of his carelessness.

""I'm sloppy, not greedy," he said. "I often signed blank returns over the years. I never should have been as careless with my returns as I was. I plead guilty to being careless in my own personal business."

He was questioned about his habit of cashing legal fee checks in the casinos, rather than making deposits in the bank. He replied that he had a large force of transient workers who were remodeling his house, and they wanted to be paid in cash.

On Tuesday, the last day of the hearings, Claiborne told the panel he had been stripped of "everything but my courage"

The panel wanted to hear from him why he continued to resist resigning his $78,000 federal judgeship.

"I've been stripped of my freedom, my good name and my honor," he said, "and I have three grandchildren, so maybe all I can leave is my heritage of courage so they can say, 'At least old grandpa had guts.'"

At the conclusion of the hearing, Claiborne agreed to put his yearly salary into a trust fund until the Senate rendered a decision on whether to remove him from office. If the Senate voted to acquit him, his salary would be returned. He would still have to complete the prison term.

In closing, the feisty federal judge told the court he didn't know the word quit.

"If I lose here," he said, "I will continue to fight until my good name is cleared.

The next day, Claiborne was back at the minimum security prison where he was warmly greeted by the other white collar inmates. For the next several days he tried to busy himself working at the menial janitorial duties he had been assigned.

On October 9, 1986, Claiborne was again transferred to Washington D.C., this time to appear before the full Senate. Facing the Senate, Claiborne stood tall and appeared fit and healthy. As roll call was effected, each Senator was required to stand at their seat and intone "guilty" or "not guilty" in answer to the charges levied against the judge standing before them.

When the voting concluded, Strom Thurmond, R-South Carolina, tallied the votes and announced the impeachment had been upheld. Harry Claiborne was stripped of his judicial post. He was then unceremoniously led out of the Capitol by armed federal marshals and returned to Maxwell Air Force Base, Alabama, to complete his two-year prison sentence.

A year later, on October 19, 1987, Harry Claiborne, after serving 17 months of a two year sentence, was released back to the streets from a halfway house in Las Vegas.

Prior to Claiborne's imprisonment, Joe Conforte again made the papers. On Friday 13, December, 1985 the flesh peddler was arrested on a charge of contributing to the delinquency of a minor. The charge contained allegations that on the evening of November 7, 1985, Conforte was in the company of a 17 year old girl at a Reno Hilton craps table.

The girl was charged with being a minor in possession of an alcoholic beverage, and for being in the gaming area of the hotel.

Conforte was released on $1,000 bail. The girl was held in Juvenile Hall.

On March 28, 1986, Judge pro tem, Robert Bell, with the consent of the attorney general's office, dismissed the charge against Conforte.

The Reno Police Department, which had made the initial arrest, was not informed of the dismissal until after it had been completed. They were furious.

Chapter Sixteen

BORDELLO FOR SALE

After Conforte was released from federal prison in 1984 on the income tax conviction, his troubles were far from being forgotten. The feds were still simmering over the entire case. Bringing him back from Brazil to testify against Claiborne had raised many judicial eyebrows. And after his testimony against the federal judge on the bribery charge proved to be worthless, upper echelons in the Justice Department, tried furiously to wipe the egg off their faces.

They planned once again to lop off his egotistical head.

How best to go about it?

Though he had served out his prison sentence, he was still responsible for millions of dollars in unpaid federal taxes and penalties. And this was the feds' next move. They could bring down upon him the unlimited power of the IRS. Rumors began circulating on the streets of Reno that the feds were again going to take over the Mustang Ranch.

Conforte was picking up the rumors but paid scant attention. He was being seen nightly frequenting the Reno area night spots, usually with a large Cuban cigar stuck between his teeth, and a couple of the Mustang girls draped across his arms.

Sally Conforte, who had always been the driving force behind running the Mustang, had put the ranch in Chapter 11 bankruptcy about the time Joe began serving his 15 month sentence. Under this arrangement, the Mustang was free to continue operating as a business in order to pay off the creditors. The largest creditor of course being the federal government which was seeking in excess of $13 million dollars in tax debts.

During this period of time, several attempts to sell the ranch failed, as did a $10 million stock offering. In 1990, a $5 million offer to buy the ranch fell through when the IRS demanded to do a background check on the potential buyer. Conforte refused to reveal the person's identity.

On September 18, 1990, the Mustang Ranch was converted to Chapter 7 bankruptcy. Under this law, the ranch was ordered to be sold with the receipts going to pay off creditors—the United States Government. Agents from the IRS swooped down upon the property armed with court orders and padlocks. The shocked working girls hurriedly bundled up their meager belongings, called their boyfriends or taxis and began a mass pullout.

Jerri Coppa, a federal bankruptcy trustee from Reno, who had been positioned at the Mustang, tried to fend off questions posed by the media. She said it would be in everybody's best interest to keep the brothel in operation. But she left no doubt that Conforte's role in the Mustang had come to an end. The Mustang Ranch was now under federal ownership.

In an attempt to placate the working girls who were frantically boxing up their belongings and leaving, she said nothing had changed regarding them. They still had jobs as far as she was concerned. The brothel was to remain open, and again she stressed, it would be under the control of the federal government.

Some of the girls began conversing quietly among themselves, and then a middle-aged woman turned to face Coppa.

"The madam told us the IRS was coming," she said, "and told us we had to get out fast or we'd be locked up. Any truth to that?"

Coppa tried to allay her fears and said the only person who faced immediate charges, was Joe Conforte—if he could be found. She said the status of the working girls would have to be worked out by the IRS, but she said, they have a vital interest in keeping the place open.

"If it remains open," she told the woman, "they get their money."

Coppa called for a meeting on Wednesday, and urged the people around her to notify the others who had already left.

When this word got back to the girls, many called the IRS to inquire about the possibility of their going back to work. The girls were invited back to the Mustang to discuss the situation.

On Wednesday, in the foyer of the Mustang Ranch, Jerri Coppa addressed scores of Mustang employees. She was there in an attempt to lure the girls back to work and emphasized the new employer would be the federal government. The girls nodded their approval.

Coppa started out by saying under federal control, the house would take less and the girls would take more. She said that Conforte owed millions of dollars to the IRS, and that under federal control, there was a chance of them collecting everything. But only if the girls agreed to stay.

Another middle-aged prostitute whose heavy makeup failed to cover her course features, looked up from her seat.

"Now let's see if I got this right," she said, "we're gonna be working for you, for the government, and you say we're gonna make more money than you. Is that right?"

Coppa explained that with the split, which could work out to be 60-40 in favor of the girls, they would in effect reap the greater percentage. However, she said out of their 60 percent, the government would of course take out income tax and Social Security.

"Income tax? Social Security?'"

Those in attendance squirmed nervously in the their chairs when the issue of payroll deductions was brought up. Under Conforte's arrangement, the girls were all classified as independent contractors. And as such, split their earnings 50-50 with the house. They were responsible for their own tax obligations. Now, under the government's plan, they would be classified as employees, and therefore, income tax and Social Security would be withheld from their earnings.

Many of the girls blurted out their displeasure while Coppa hurriedly tried to assuage their fears. She told them that under the government's plan the working women could get as much as 60-65 percent of the take. After the government took their share, she said, they would still realize a 50-50 split, the same as they did working for Conforte.

As this new development began to sink in, many of the girls voiced an opinion that they really didn't care who ran the place as long as they continued working.

"I don't care who I work for, "a bleached blond offered.. "Paying taxes is okay as long as I make as much as I did working for Joe."

Another was quick to voice her opinion.

"I'll probably stay here," she told the others, "I'm patriotic, I don't care if the U.S. does runs the place."

In the background, a high-mileage prostitute who had been standing and listening quietly, was quick to step in and defend

Conforte.

"If I can't work for Joe," she whined, "then I'm not working. What the hell does the federal government know about running a bawdy house."

"They've been screwing the tax payers for years," quipped another.

Another flashed her dark eyes and jumped to her feet to denounce the federal government.

"They don't know the business," she said, speaking of the IRS officials. "They try to act like they do, but they don't know shit."

A young blond who looked no more than 20-years old, looked up from her chair and reminded the girls that the Mustang Ranch was not the only place they could work.

"There's the Moonlight, the Starlight, the Old Bridge...."

Another young girl who admitted she was broke, said she was eager to start working again.

"I just want to work," she said, "I've got a four year old daughter and I need the money."

A part time prostitute, who was married to an unsuspecting husband, placed the blame on Joe Conforte.

"He knew this was going to happen," she lamented, "he knew the feds were going to roll in on us like this. Where the hell is he now? I feel betrayed."

Jerri Coppa, who had been listening to the remarks, tried several times to interject her thoughts and to assuage their rising anxiety. She told the girls again, that when they went to work for the government, they would be free of the uncertainties they were experiencing now because of Joe Conforte.

Shirley Colletti, a tall, gaunt, Storey County Commissioner for the past two years—but who had also worked for Conforte at the Mustang in a managerial position off and on for 13 years, rose to her feet to challenge Jerri Coppa's qualifications. She told Coppa running a brothel was fraught with problems. For one thing, she said, the health of the workers was of primary concern. She questioned Coppa's or any novice's ability to do this as it had been done under Conforte's supervision.

Coppa, obviously taken aback by this slur, stared at Colletti and said running a brothel was probably no different from running any other retail endeavor.

Commissioner Colletti then informed Coppa that the Mustang no longer could meet the fire and safety codes of Storey County. Conforte had grandfathered the structure in, Colletti said, but with a change of ownership, major modifications would have to be completed before the county would issue a license. In addition, since the prostitutes had left the premises for over 24 hours, they would now have to be tested for HIV and venereal disease again.

Colletti, nearing sixty years old, was a small voice for a tiny county. But she was not being intimidated by the power of the federal government. She stressed that Storey County was the licensing bureau, and they had the right to issue—or deny—the brothel license. The federal government would have to adhere to all the regulations, just as a private party would. Health certificates and work cards would have to be applied for on all prospective workers.

Storey County Sheriff, Bob Del Carlo, who was in attendance, then spoke to Jerri Coppa in private. He informed her that since she was presumed to be the government's appointed figure to run the brothel, she would have to file an application with Storey County. This would require a lengthy investigation and background check which would take about 90 days he said.

Obviously, the Storey County officials had no love for the feds operating a brothel in their county.

Responding to questions from the media later in the day, Coppa said that as a bankruptcy trustee, she was entitled to the same privileges as Joe Conforte. She would seek a court order immediately, she said, to force the county to permit her to operate under the existing license.

She said she thought Conforte was behind the roadblocks thrown up at her, but insisted the brothel would soon open under the banner of the federal government.

Sheriff Del Carlo and Shirley Colletti then huddled together for a few minutes and waved good-bye as they departed for their Storey County offices in Virginia City.

Peter Perry, Conforte's attorney, responding to media questions, placed the brothel's problems squarely on the federal government. He reiterated it was they who quashed the potential $5 million sale that had been offered previously. He added they also placed obstacles in front of a $10 million stock offer.

An IRS chief of special procedures for Nevada, denied Perry's allegations. He told a press conference that he makes an effort to treat all tax payers equally. His actions were solely done to protect the government's interest. Any talk of a vendetta was untenable.

The Old Bridge Ranch, a competing brothel just down the road, which was owned by David Burgess, a Conforte nephew, was happily filling the void left by the Mustang. A banner flowing from the iron gate read, "WELCOME AIR RACES," a reference to the annual Reno Air Races, which was drawing thousands of spectators from outside Nevada

Late night TV talk show hosts were quick to call attention to the prospect of the feds running a legal brothel.

David Letterman joked that running the brothel might be just the thing to get Washington D.C., Mayor Marion Barry interested in government work again.

Jay Leno, during his monologue, quipped that if anyone had the experience to run a brothel, the honor should go to Congress. Arsenio Hall had similar comments.

On Friday morning, U.S. Bankruptcy Judge James Thompson, rescinded his earlier ruling which would have allowed Jerri Coppa to run the Mustang Ranch for the federal government.

"We're not in the business here to run a business for just one creditor (the U.S. Government" Thompson said. "This is still the United States. We just can't run roughshod over people. They have to have time to prepare their pleadings."

At the same time, Judge Thompson lifted an order which prevented the IRS from foreclosing on the Mustang. What the judge's rulings effectively did, was to take the Mustang Ranch out of Jerri Coppa's hands entirely, and turn it over to the IRS to sell. The IRS could then sell the property through sealed bids, or through open bidding after setting a minimum amount.

This ruling also meant that the government would not again, go into the legal brothel business.

Under federal law, a person cannot wipe out an IRS debt through bankruptcy. And the IRS insisted the Conforte's owed as much as $13 million. So whatever the IRS got from the sale would be deducted from this amount. Estimates varied as to the value of the property and the Mustang name, but the feds said it could bring as much as $10 million. Even so, the Confortes would still have an outstanding tax bill in the millions.

Friday afternoon, the working girls and support personnel for the Mustang Ranch were told by the IRS to pack their bags. Some 200 workers began the gloomy retreat and by nightfall the place was vacated. The IRS placed tamper proof locks on all the doors. The Mustang Ranch, which for more than thirty years had been as much a part of Nevada as casinos and grazing cattle, was now officially out of business. And in so doing, the feds had successfully shut down Storey County's premier tax revenue. But Storey County authorities had a surprise for the feds.

On October 2, 1990, the Storey County commissioners voted to halt prostitution on the premises of the now closed Mustang Ranch. This meant that the property could no longer be used as a house of prostitution. The feds could go ahead with the sale, however; the Mustang could not now be sold as a brothel. What this vote did was to drastically reduce the value of the Mustang Ranch. The feds had hoped to sell the place for as much as $10 million. Now it's value would be far less.

Tiny Storey County, had stood face-to-face with emissaries of the federal government, and won the battle. If Storey couldn't retain control, then the feds could go to hell. There would be no Mustang brothel. And the feds could go sing for Conforte's back taxes. The Old Bridge Ranch, which had picked up the slack from the Mustang's closing, remained the sole licensed brothel operating in Storey County.

Reports from the Old Bridge brothel indicated that business was booming. Many of the girls who were formerly working at the Mustang, had eased on over to work at the Bridge.

Norma Lally, an IRS spokeswoman would not comment on Storey's decision to thwart efforts by the IRS to sell the property as a brothel. But it was pointed out that under a federal law, a person cannot wipe out an IRS debt through bankruptcy. And the IRS insisted the Conforte's owed as much as $13 million. So whatever the IRS got from the sale would be deducted from this amount. Estimates varied as to the value of the property and the Mustang name, but the feds admitted it could no longer bring in the earlier estimate of $10 million. Whatever it brought in though, would be deducted from the Conforte's tax bill. Even so, they would still be left with an outstanding tax debt totaling millions of dollars.

Federal agents next began to systematically inventory thousands of removable items scheduled for auction. Scores of signs were removed from over doorways and working rooms. A sampling of these read: "If you don't see what you want, ask for it." "You're only a stranger here once." "If you have any complaints about this girl, notify the management." "$2.00 per minute, 20 minute minimum. Unusual request, price varies." "Ask About Our Orgy Room," and similar phrases.

Truckloads of furniture, lamps, throw rugs, and other knick-knacks were prepared for sale. A framed portrait of Oscar Bonavena was expected to bring a tidy sum. A roomful of nude paintings promised the same. From the laundry room, thousands of used blankets and sheets, pillow cases, pillows, towels, wash cloths and mattresses were also laundered, disinfected, and made ready for the sale.

From the kitchen, a walk-in refrigerator, drinking glasses, dishes, bowls, eating utensils, and scores of pots and pans. One coffee mug was imprinted with the name "Sally," an obvious reference to Sally Conforte.

Other items dug up were clothing, thousands of condoms, two cases of stain remover, bleach, first aid supplies including nine canisters of oxygen, soft drink machines, exercise equipment, a tanning cubicle, costly Lladro ceramics, and crude X-rated ceramic figures. TVs and stereo equipment that looked to be in good working order were expected to sell quickly, as were five boxes of French perfumes, a cigarette machine, Mustang business cards, and Mustang security jackets.

The real property to be auctioned included the Mustang Ranch which actually was two adjoining buildings, 300 acres of land in Washoe and Storey Counties, several buildings and a 60 space trailer park.

The feds placed ads in the local papers inviting the public out for the auction. IRS Manager, Dierdre Pagni, went after the local garage sale crowd.

"We highly encourage the neighborhood yard sale enthusiast to come out and make a bid on anything they want," she said, referring to the thousands of items to be auctioned as memorabilia.

The main Mustang building was advertised in the Reno Gazette Journal as a fixer-upper house, with multi bedrooms and baths, and with a beautiful river view. Amenities included a large kitchen with a wet bar, spa, beam ceilings, and a state-of-the-art security alarm system with TV monitoring and other sophisticated electron security. Asking price was listed as $1.8 million. The seller was listed as the IRS, and a phone number was shown.

On Saturday, November 10, 1990, the feds conducted tours through the Mustang property starting at 9:00 a.m. Hundreds of curious people showed up—most of whom were women, and were systematically ushered through the brothel throughout the day. Most emerged from the 15 minute tours disappointed.

"There was more junk in there than I expected," said one woman. "Some of the furnishings were in poor condition. I expected it to be much classier."

"I expected to see more exotic stuff," commented another, "you know, stuff you'd expect to see in a working cat house. A lot of this here is just like the crap you see at garage sales. I'm disappointed."

Another envisioned the feds hanging onto the property and commercializing the name and location.

"They could have sold tickets and conducted tours," she said, "and by charging people to go through, could have made more money. Or, they could have rented out space for curio shops."

One Reno woman said it was "...a trip. We felt that by coming out here to look, we could let our out of state friends know what a working cat house actually looked like, she told a reporter.

"It's something that's deeply ingrained in Nevada history," her friend offered. "Whether you agree with it or not. It's part of the state's heritage."

Another couple, who drove in from Oregon, were concentrating on the silverware and crystal. Obviously knowledgeable about the items they were inspecting, the woman said they planned to bid on many of the more expensive items.

"We'll bid on the silverware, at least," she said, but she thought there would have been more elegant furnishings.

"A lot of the things being sold here," she commented, "are no different from things you can pick up just about anywhere. But, we came down here to spend a few days relaxing anyway, so whatever we take back will be worth the drive."

Another woman who had been listening to the comments said she had expected to see much more elegance.

"I expected to see fine French furniture and artwork," she noted. "But much of this furniture and decor is five-and-dime."

On Tuesday, November 13, the auction got underway in earnest. Reno attorney, Victor Perry, a brother of Peter Perry, Joe Conforte's attorney, was there to bid on the property for an unnamed party. He paid scant attention to the rapid fire staccato of the auctioneers barking like carnival hackers pushing the trophied memorabilia. His mission was to bid on the buildings and equipment..

"Bargains" abounded: A metal sign taken from the wall of the foyer that said, "Long Periods & Out Dates at Reduced Rates," went for $525. Another, a 2-by-10 inch red plastic sign that said, "Orgy Room," went for $170.

Former owner, Joe Conforte, who had been milling around with the crowd, remarked that the signs were being sold at highly inflated prices. He said the signs which were selling for hundreds of dollars, cost him no more than a "few bucks each."

The large round welcome sign that once graced the archway of the entrance to the Mustang brought in an expected $3,000. Sixteen cases of Mustang matches went for $575. A Nevada personalized license plate with the word "Mustang" went for $250. Sally Conforte's coffee mug brought $45. And a man selling Mustang Ranch caps out of the trunk of his car for $10 each, was doing a brisk business.

Conforte, obviously amused, circulated among the crowd to offer his opinions freely. He remarked that the items being auctioned were going for far more than they were worth. He cited an instance where the IRS agents sold two nude paintings by unknown artists, for $1,500 and $3,000 respectively, but which cost far less than that when new. He repeated that the people doing the bidding were "nuts."

Another man in the crowd was quick to support him.

"These people are in a frenzy," he said. "They have no common sense. Half the stuff being sold here could be picked up at any garage sale for a fraction of what they're paying."

Conforte was asked about the large welcome sign that went for $3,000, and which was a bonifide Mustang memorabilia. He said he believed the buyer got a very good deal. He said when he bought it new 20 years ago, it cost $2,000.

Other items, like a rubber stamp and ink that said, "Mustang Ranch," went for $225.

"I paid five dollars for it," Conforte quipped.

A Rolodex watch (not to be confused with a Rolex), brought $205.

"A cheap watch," Conforte offered, I paid maybe twenty dollars for it."

A young couple from Sacramento paid $240 for a blown up framed nude poster. Catching sight of Conforte, the pretty wife asked Conforte if he would autograph it for them. Conforte smiled and wrote something on the back of the poster. He handed it back and wished the couple well. Seeing this, others in the crowd pleaded with the couple to sell the poster to them—for a higher price than they had paid. They refused and said it was not for sale.

But others who had made purchases and watched as Conforte autographed the couple's photo, asked Conforte if he would sign their trophies. Again he took out his pen as a long line began to form around him. His bodyguard looked dismayed and grumbled as Conforte began autographing Mustang memorabilia for the happy patrons.

When the IRS got down to the business at hand, placing the Mustang Ranch property on the auction block, the auctioneer announced the minimum bid would start at $10 million. Loud guffaws rose from the crowd. Responding, the auctioneer then began dropping the amount in million dollar increments, until reluctantly, he bottomed out at $1.45 million. Still he got no offers. Slamming down the gavel, he sulked off and announced a short recess.

When the auctioneer returned about 30 minutes later, he asked the crowd for a minimum bid of $1 million and received an instant response. Several patrons then began outbidding each other until only two were left: Reno Attorney, Victor Perry, and a representative from Nevada Hydrocarbon Inc.

It appeared to the crowd that Perry was determined to buy the property as he continued to raise the bid by $100,000 increments. His opponent's raises were in $10,000 increments. At $1.49 million, it was all over. The gavel came down awarding the property to Perry for $1.49 million. Perry, who had been bidding for an unnamed client, refused to reveal his client's name. In addition to the brothel and several other buildings, the sale also included 330 acres of adjoining river front property. When the sale was announced final, reporters swarmed around Perry trying to find out who he represented. Perry clenched his jaws and again refused to reveal his client.

Was he fronting for Conforte?

He unequivocally denied this suggestion..

"When my client wants his name revealed, it will be," Perry said.

Victor's brother, Peter Perry who was Conforte's personal attorney, and who had also shown up to bid, drew a crowd when he outbid the others on every piece of heavy kitchen equipment. Walk-in freezers, restaurant style stoves, an ice maker, and other equipment was all snatched up by Peter.

Peter, too, denied he was fronting for Conforte, but refused to name his client. He told the crowd that some of the kitchen equipment he paid $100 dollars for, was actually worth over $1,000 dollars.

"It's an investment," he said,

What was he going to do with it, the press wanted to know.

He merely nodded and told them he was going to sell it to the unnamed client.

By dusk, the first day's historical auction was closed. It resumed the next morning promptly at 9:00 a.m., and continued on through Thursday. At the end of the three day auction, the IRS publicly announced they had taken in a total of $1.94 million, far less than the estimated $13 million the Conforte's owed in back taxes and penalties.

Did the IRS know the identity of the person or persons that Victor Perry had represented, the press wanted to know. Suspicions were running rampant. Rumors were flying. The Perry brothers weren't talking. Renoites were betting the unnamed client was Joe Conforte.

The IRS said their information was that the client was actually a hastily put together corporation named, "Mustang Properties Inc." Yet who the principle officers of the corporation were, continued to be shrouded in mystery.

The Perrys denied they had put up any money for the purchase, but told the press they were going to appear before the Storey County Commission to seek a rezoning of the property so that it could again be used as a brothel. Some of the IRS officials, when told of this, were livid. Again suspicion was cast upon Joe Conforte like a dark shadow.

Larry Prater, Storey County commission chairman, when

informed the Perry brothers were seeking a rezoning of the property to be used once again as a brothel, said the commission would have to know who the officers of Mustang Properties were before they would consider the request.

They would have to appear before the commission, he said, present their case, and identify those persons who were the legitimate owners. Prater said the commission would not license the property again as a brothel without knowing their identity. The license is always attached to the owner or owners, he said, and if Joe Conforte were no longer the owner, he could not transfer ownership.

Prater revealed that though the Mustang Ranch had been paying about $120,000 a year in taxes and license fees to Storey County, the property was now in arrears. Before a new license to operate the property as a brothel could be issued, he said, the new owners would have to pay $125,000 in back taxes and bring the building up to the present fire codes.

As this legal wrangling was going on, the open line on the betting in the Reno casinos, was giving odds that the Mustang Ranch would again be operating as a brothel, and that Joe Conforte would be calling the shots from the sidelines.

On Tuesday, December 18, 1990, Joe Conforte appeared again to be in charge of the brothel when he opened the doors to the Mustang Ranch and announced the place was again open for business. He notified the press that the military veterans of the Persian Gulf—if they were not married—could come in for a good time, compliments of the house.

When Storey County authorities got wind of the abrupt opening, they called an emergency session and ordered Conforte to present his case before them. After all, he was no longer the owner of the Mustang, and was being dogged by the IRS for millions in unpaid taxes and penalties. Who was he working for? What was his position?

Appearing before the commission, Conforte spoke as though the commission members were working for him. He told them the Mustang had reopened and was already serving clients. He said he had appeared before them only to make them aware of the opening. He puffed out his chest and smiled as though he were speaking to school children.

"The doors are already open," he began. "I'm here for one

reason and one reason only, as a common courtesy, to let you know how it is."

The commission members were flabbergasted.

The commission demanded to know if he were the unnamed buyer who had put up the $1.49 million to purchase back the Mustang Ranch though attorney Victor Perry.

"How could I?" He answered. "I have no money." He then told the commission he had been hired as general manager by the new owners. When the question of work permits for the girls came up, Conforte said they were all pre-IRS Mustang workers, and as such, did not need to apply for a new license.

Sheriff Bob Del Carlo, and Storey County District Attorney, Virgil Bucchianeri, were brought in to express their views. They were in agreement that in actuality, the property had not yet been rezoned, and that Conforte's license to operate the brothel had never been rescinded.

Conforte faced the commission and told them that nothing had changed. He said he could have reopened the place "five minutes after the IRS left," if he had wanted to.

"And the license," he smiled, "has never been revoked."

Larry Prater, conferred with the others for a few minutes and then told Conforte they would have to get a ruling from the attorney general.

Conforte then put out new bait. He said he planned to donate a new school bus to the local school district. In addition, he said the commissioners should consider raising the license fees for the Mustang Ranch and the Old Bridge Ranch, by $5,000 for each building.Councilwoman, Shirley Colletti, Conforte's longtime associate at the Mustang,, urged the others to allow the Mustang to reopen. She emphasized this point by reminding the others of the loss of revenue they'd suffered after the IRS shut down the place. And, she told them, Conforte had continued to pay the licensing fees to the county, "$15,000 plus $1,500 in late charges, quarterly fee to keep his license current.

Colletti reminded them that Conforte had always paid the required fees up front without protest; that indeed, the property had never been officially rezoned, and that the county could certainly use the revenue. It is still a licensed bordello, she said. And tossing a dig at the feds, she added only Storey County had the authority to revoke his license—not the IRS.

In town, nobody was betting against Joe Conforte. The Mustang Ranch was again in full swing. Troops returning from the Persian Gulf found their way to the brothel and wasted little time in praising patriotic Joe. And patriotic Joe was heard more than once to brag that the comps he was extending to the Gulf vets, was tax deductible—money the IRS could not get their hands on.

For the next few months, business was brisk at the Mustang Ranch. Joe Conforte, amiable when greeting patrons, was again back in the limelight—but not as the owner of the Mustang Ranch, but as a paid employee of Mustang Properties Inc., a murky corporation which was staffed by persons whose identity was obscure. Rumors persisted that the hidden owner was none other than Joe Conforte. The feds continued to pursue this premise.

When asked, Conforte said the names of the stockholders would be disclosed to Storey County officials by September 30, when the quarterly license expired. He said this would dispel rumors that he was the hidden owner.

And then on August 22, 1991, Joe Conforte surprised everybody when he announced his retirement. Ending a four-decade career of peddling sex throughout Nevada, Conforte told the press he was through. He said he planned to withdraw as general manager of the Mustang Ranch, and devote his time to playing bridge. He added that he would also work to push an initiative in California to legalize prostitution in that state.

Commenting on his belabored tax debt, Conforte assured his friends that he would eventually resolve all the tax obligations

Known as a crafty contract bridge player, Conforte said that is how he would like to enjoy the golden years. He said he had been looking for a good bridge partner—hopefully a pretty one—who would accompany him on the tournament circuit.

Conspicuously, the name of Conforte's wife, Sally, was never brought up. Was he still smarting from her affair with the late Argentine boxer, Oscar Bonavena?

Conforte played off this comment.

What about his hillside home in Sparks? The IRS had seized this too, at the same time they took the Mustang properties. It was reported he was still living there. Conforte cleared this up by saying his nephew, David Burgess, owner of the Old Bridge Ranch, had successfully bid on the house, along with a Danville, California summer home, for a reported $480,000.

On October 2, 1991, Peter Perry, Conforte's attorney, appeared before the Storey County commission to renew the brothel license. Perry named Conforte's nephew, David Burgess, as the person to succeed Conforte as general manager of the Mustang Ranch. Perry told the commission that when the final application was filed, he would name the stockholders of Mustang Properties.

Friendly, Shirley Colletti, said it mattered little to the commission who owned Mustang Properties. All we care about she said, is the name of the person who will be general manager, acknowledging it would be Conforte's nephew.

On Tuesday, February 4, 1992, Storey County commissioners licensed David Burgess as general manager of the Mustang Ranch. On the surface, Joe Conforte had no further interest in the property. Responding to questioning by the commission, Peter Perry, acting as attorney for Mustang Properties, informed the board that it was Conforte's wish to be taken off the license since he had retired.

Storey County commissioners pressed him to reveal the actual owners of Mustang Properties. Perry danced around a mine field refusing to divulge the names. The commissioners ostensibly contacted the attorney general's office and were advised they were entitled only to know the name of the person licensed—David Burgess.

The next day, Wednesday, brought even more surprises. Peter Perry announced that the Mustang Ranch, had been sold to a firm known as A.G.E. Enterprises. Who was A.G.E.?

"A Nevada corporation."

What was the sale price? Who were the principals?

Perry dodged this question to say the A.G.E. owners were not his clients.

The next day, Thursday, a retired local insurance executive came forward and announced he was the president of A.G.E. When pressed for details, he refused to name the investors, the officers of the company, nor the amount of the sale.

What did A.G.E. stand for?

This was not clarified.

The sports books in town were making odds that Joe Conforte was behind A.G.E. But Joe wasn't talking. He had disappeared from public view. Insiders said he had returned to Brazil. David Burgess continued to manage the Mustang Ranch for a few months, and then resigned to devote his time to the Old Bridge Ranch. His replacement at the Mustang was a longtime savvy woman, who had a sharp business head.

On Monday, September 7, 1992, an ambulance was called to the Conforte home in Sparks. Inside, 75 year old, Sally Conforte, lying comatose in soiled bed sheets, was quietly dying.. She was rushed to Washoe Medical Center, where she was pronounced D.O.A. Her husband, Joe Conforte, could not be reached. Friends, when contacted, said diabetes had taken its toll on her once proud spirit. For the last several years she had been receiving kidney dialysis three times a week.

The recently named Mustang Ranch manager, was contacted and told of Sally's death. Martin said she and Sally had been very close for the past five years.

Commenting on the Conforte's marriage, she said though their marriage wasn't a story book affair, they nevertheless cared a great deal about each other.

Had the Oscar Bonavena affair changed this?

This was an obvious question with an obvious answer.

On Friday, September 11, 1992, Sally Conforte was laid to rest. About 150 persons, some dressed in cowboy gear, others in stylish pinstriped suits, and others arriving on rumbling Harleys, along with scantily clad young women, and two Roman Catholic nuns, gathered to pay their last respects.

.Storey County's two brothels, the Mustang Ranch and the Old Bridge Ranch, were both closed for the day in honor of Sally Conforte.

Sally's husband of decades, Joe Conforte, had not bothered to attend the funeral.

Chapter Seventeen

THE LAST RIDE

Following the death of Sally Conforte, Joe languished in South America, ostensibly having nothing to do with the Mustang Ranch. The feds thought otherwise. Hundreds of thousands of dollars of tax payer money had been spent trying to tie him to the Mustang. And by 1996, the feds felt they had enough evidence. A federal grand jury released their findings in June, 1996.

An indictment handed down charged the brothel owner in exile, Joe Conforte, along with his attorney, Peter Perry, with three counts of bankruptcy fraud and one count of wire fraud. It was alleged in the indictment that Conforte and his attorney had conspired to defraud the IRS while the Mustang Ranch was in bankruptcy court.

The indictment said that as early as September, 1982, Conforte had opened a Swiss bank account, using the name, Jose C. Montoya, and had continued to build the account. Then during the mid 1990s, when the feds were breathing down his neck, he created a dummy corporation, Mustang Properties, which was to serve as a front, and which would allow him to retain control of the Mustang Ranch..

The lengthy indictment also charged that on August 14, 1990, $800,000 was funneled from the Swiss bank, through Valley Bank, in which Perry was an executive, and passed on to the newly formed Mustang Properties. Further, the indictment charged that on November 30, 1990, an additional $1 million was transferred through the same route. It was noted that Perry's brother, Victor, acting as a Mustang Properties representative, had been the successful bidder acquiring the Mustang Ranch on a high bid of $1.49 million.

To further confuse investigators, it was noted that that during 1992, Mustang Properties had been sold to A.G.E. Enterprises, another corporation of cloudy ownership.

Peter Perry was brought to court and entered a plea of innocent. Trial was set for August 12, 1996, in U.S. District Court, before Judge Howard McKibben. Perry was released on a personal recognizance bond.

With Conforte out of the country and again a fugitive from justice, the fate of the Mustang Ranch was questionable. It appeared the feds again would assume ownership of the brothel unless Joe Conforte returned and stood trial. Things again began to look gloomy for the working girls. But not for Storey County Commissioner, Shirley Colletti.

Colletti, it seems, in addition to her duties as Storey County Commissioner, had allegedly been on the payroll of A.G.E. Enterprises as a consultant. A political opponent of hers, Joe Haynes, who was also a part-time maintenance worker at the Mustang, stated publicly that in the past 18 months, Colletti had received $120,000 from A.G.E. in her capacity as a consultant. To support his allegations, Haynes produced copies of monthly checks received by Colletti from January 1995, through August, 1996. For the first six months of 1995, she was paid a monthly fee of $10,000; the remainder of the checks were for $5,000 monthly.

Commissioner Colletti denied allegations of impropriety and said there had never been any conflict of interest. She noted that while on the payroll of A.G.E., a prostitution related vote had never come before the commission. However cloudy the truth, questions of graft continued to surface.

And then, on November 7, 1996, the voters of Storey County had their say.

Shirley Colletti, was soundly beaten by challenger Carl Trink, for the position of Storey County Commissioner. Taking her defeat in stride, and despite the uncertain future of the Mustang Ranch, she subsequently hired on as one of the brothel's managers.

Sheriff Bob Del Carlo, after 26 years as Storey County Sheriff, elected to bow out of the race for sheriff. Instead, he ran for Storey County Commissioner, District Two. And he too lost. Del Carlo was soundly trounced by Greg J. "Bum" Hess. This was the first election in 30 years that Del Carlo lost. And he too, went to work at the Mustang Ranch.

Virgil Bucchianeri, Storey County District Attorney who had been in office during the Bonavena slaying, and through the trials of Ross Brymer, was also out polled by the voters. He lost his seat to newcomer, Janet Hess.

Whether the polls influenced Peter Perry is questionable. But what is known, is that he began to negotiate with the federal prosecutors. Following a series of secret meetings, the onetime friend and trusted attorney of Joe Conforte, rolled over.

On Monday, December 2, 1996, the feds announced that Perry had agreed to become a witness for the prosecution. In a previously sealed document made public, it was revealed that Perry had pleaded guilty to wire fraud, and would testify against Conforte and Colletti. The IRS further stated that Perry had agreed to divulge "the facts and circumstances surrounding his role and the role of others in the bankruptcy/wire fraud scheme."

According to the plea agreement, Perry admitted having knowledge that Conforte had a hidden Swiss bank account under the name of Jose C. Montoya. And that Conforte had transferred money from that account to buy back the Mustang Ranch after it had been seized by the IRS. Further, he also knew that Conforte and his wife Sally, would have an interest in the brothel despite their sworn testimony before the bankruptcy court to the contrary. And lastly, that he had assisted Conforte in purchasing additional property in the name of Conforte's daughter, Ruth Herd, and that these properties were hidden from the IRS.

For their part of the plea agreement, prosecutors agreed to file a special motion with U.S. District Court Judge, Howard McKibben, asking for probation for Perry with no prison time.

How much could Perry testify about his former client without violating attorney-client privilege?

Legally, a conspiracy to commit crimes plotted by an attorney and his client, are not protected under attorney client privilege. But, if a client confides to his lawyer about crimes committed in the past, that would be protected. And any good attorney knows this and respects this when talking with his client. Also, the client should never discuss future planned criminal activity. With all this then, it became a unique situation when Peter Perry agreed to testify against his former client, Joe Conforte and Shirley Colletti.

On Wednesday, December 4, the Reno Gazette-Journal ran a letter ostensibly initiated by Conforte, and published to portray him as a person in poor health, and as a homesick fugitive. In it, Conforte said he would return to Reno to face charges once his doctors cleared him for travel.

Reports at to Conforte's whereabouts differed. Some reports had him living in the country of his birth, Sicily. Others insisted he was still living the high life in Brazil. Inside sources though, said he was actually in Chile.

On January 28, 1997, the IRS filed two liens against Conforte, both in Washoe and Storey Counties. The documents stated that he owed $16.05 million for nine tax years beginning in 1977 and ending in 1992. The federal tax liens identified A.G.E. as the parent company of the Mustang Ranch brothel, and the "nominee, alter-ego and transferee of Joseph Conforte."

In late February, the feds confirmed Conforte was living in Chile. They explained that a treaty existed between the United States and Chile, that spelled out crimes for which a person could be extradited. Wire fraud and bankruptcy fraud were not among the extraditable offenses. Given this, it appeared Conforte could not be forced to return to the U.S.

However, reports kept circulating that the fugitive brothel owner wanted to return and clear his name, but because of health problems, was prevented from doing this.

Federal prosecutors were skeptical about the reports of Conforte's medical problems and said they would have to have him examined by their own medical staff in the U.S.—if and when—he could be brought back from Chile.

But then, the Chilean government intervened. On Friday, February 21, 1997, Chile labeled Conforte an "undesirable" and announced he faced deportation. The Chilean Supreme Court issued an order directing the federal police to detain the fugitive brothel owner.

For the next few months, federal prosecutors were kept busy preparing papers necessary to bring Conforte back to Reno for prosecution.

Conforte's attorneys were likewise kept busy appearing before U.S. District Court Judge, Howard Mckibben, arguing for bail for their client, once he was returned.

However, none of these actions were ever put into effect. The feds learned that Conforte had indeed been tossed into jail in Chile, however; he was released after only a few days, and was now confirmed to be living a life of luxury as a free person. And he had no intentions of returning to the states where he faced federal charges which could lead to federal prison.

By the close of 1997, the government's case against Joe Conforte, had ground to a halt. And rumors were circulating that the brothel owner in exile had applied for—and been granted—Chilean citizenship.

Not ready to admit defeat, the feds planned another costly grand jury for the coming year. Their main target would be fugitive Joe Conforte, though they had few expectations that he would be extradited. To set an example then, if not to gain a victory, they needed an alternate target, a person who had been closely associated with the brothel owner in years past. Enter, Shirley Colletti.

On July 5, 1998, a federal grand jury in Reno indicted Joe Conforte; Shirley Colletti; Joan Olcese, who was a Mustang Ranch bookkeeper; and Eduardo Neves, on a 33-count indictment alleging racketeering, money laundering, witness tampering, bankruptcy fraud, wire fraud and conspiracy. Neves was identified as a Brazilian citizen and airline pilot, and as a Conforte front man and seemingly the 80 percent owner of A.G.E. Corporation.

The charges which were made public on August 5, contained the following counts:

Count 1: Bankruptcy fraud; Aiding and Abetting. Indictment charges that from December 19, 1989, to at least May 6, 1992, Joseph Conforte fraudulently committed acts and transferred and concealed Washoe county property held in the name of Ruth Hurd.

Count 2: Bankruptcy Fraud; Aiding and Abetting. From September 28, 1990, to at least May 6, 1992, Joseph Conforte fraudulently transferred and concealed money deposited at PriMerit Bank in Sparks in an account under the name of Neva Tate-Starrett.

Count 3: Bankruptcy Fraud: Aiding and Abetting. From September 10, 1982, to at least May 6, 1992, Joseph Conforte fraudulently transferred and concealed money deposited at the Discount Bank and Trust Company, Geneva, Switzerland, in the name of Jose C. Montoya.

Count 4: Wire Fraud: Aiding and Abetting. From September 18, 1990, to at least May 6, 1992, Joseph Conforte and Peter A. Perry devised a scheme to defraud the Internal Revenue Service of Mustang Ranch property. On August 14, 1990,

$800,000 from Discount Bank and Trust, in Geneva, was transferred to Peter Perry c/o Mustang Properties at Valley Bank in Reno; on November 13, 1990, $1 million was transferred from the same Geneva bank to Mustang Properties at Valley Bank.

Count 5: Wire Fraud: Aiding and Abetting. From November 30, 1990, through December 3, 1990, Joseph Conforte and Peter A. Perry executed a scheme to defraud using interstate and foreign commerce transmission in transferring funds from the Discount Bank, through the Union de Banques Suisses in Geneva, Switzerland, to Valley Bank of Nevada.

Count 6: Money Laundering. On August 14, 1990, Joseph Conforte and others knowingly transferred $800,000 in funds from some form of unlawful activity under the name of Joseph C. Montoya from the Discount Bank in Geneva to the Valley Bank in Reno to conceal and disguise the source, ownership and control of the funds.

Count 7: Money Laundering. On December 3, 1990, Joseph Conforte and others knowingly transferred $1 million in funds from some source of unlawful activity from Union de Banqes Suisses in Geneva to Reno's Valley Bank to conceal the source, ownership and control of the funds.

Counts 8 through 28: Wire Fraud; Aiding and Abetting. From September 18, 1990, to at least May 6, 1992, Joseph Conforte, Shirley Colletti, Joann Olcese, Eduardo Neves, A.G.E. Enterprises Inc., A.G.E. Corporation Inc., and others devised a scheme to defraud the Internal Revenue Service. Through an elaborate scheme, the substantial Mustang Ranch income (more than $4 million) would be transferred via numerous transactions to Joseph Conforte without Conforte having to report the income to the IRS.

Count 29: Witness Tampering. In January 1995, Joseph Conforte used intimidation and threats to hinder, delay and prevent the communication to a law enforcement officer relating to the commission or possible commission of wire fraud, bankruptcy fraud, money laundering and racketeering. Conforte is charged with telling Peter Perry that he would kill him and members of his immediate family if Perry "talked" about Conforte's activities being investigated by a federal grand jury.

Count 30: Racketeering. Joseph Conforte, Joann Olcese, Eduardo Neves, Shirley Colletti, A.G.E. Corporation, A.G.E. Enterprises, Mustang Ranch, Mustang Properties and My Grange Ltd., and others were involved in a racketeering enterprise which affected interstate and foreign commerce. The enterprise enriched the members through wire fraud, money laundering, bribery and witness tampering; protected the power, territory and profits of the enterprise through the use of intimidation and threats of violence; and created national and international corporate shells for holding income from Mustang Ranch and illegally distributing income to Joseph Conforte.

Count 31: Conspiracy to Participate in an Enterprise through a Pattern of Racketeering. From about September 10, 1982, until the indictment, Joseph Conforte, Joann Olcese, Eduardo Neves, A.G.E. Enterprises, A.G.E. Corporation and Shirley Colletti knowingly conspired and participated in an enterprise through a pattern of racketeering activity.

Count 32: Money Laundering and Forfeiture. If convicted of Count 5 or 6, Joseph Conforte will forfeit any property, real or personal, involved in the offense or traceable to the offense, which would include $1.8 million in U.S. Currency.

Count 33: If convicted on either Count 30 or 31, the defendants will forfeit any interest in property and contractual rights which defendants obtained from racketeering activity. Included is Mustang Ranch, 264 acres surrounding it; Lockwood Mobile Home Park; the Cabin in the Sky restaurant in Gold Hill; and other land in Washoe and Storey counties. These are worth approximately $16 million.

The indictment charged that Conforte had arranged to purchase the Mustang Ranch and other assets by fraudulently using two companies—Mustang Properties Inc., and A.G.E. Corporation as fronts. It was alleged that employees of these two organizations were directed to make checks and wire transfers totaling more than $4 million to persons fronting for Conforte from 1993 through 1996.

Former Storey County Sheriff, Bob Del Carlo, along with an unnamed Storey County commissioner, were named as having received $3,000 a month for the past four years, money that was funneled down from Conforte "with the intent to influence them with respect to acts, decisions, votes and other proceedings in the exercise of their powers and functions." However; it was noted that neither Del Carlo nor the commissioner were indicted.

Del Carlo made a statement to the press in which he denied ever taking money from Conforte while he was the elected sheriff. Del Carlo said there was absolutely no way he could have helped Conforte in the brothel business, which he reminded the public, "was a legal business."

Shirley Colletti, the former Storey County commissioner, 61 years old at the time, was arrested by federal agents at the Mustang Ranch where she worked as a manager. She was booked into Washoe County Jail as a federal prisoner.

Olcese, the Mustang Ranch bookkeeper, surrendered to the U.S. Marshalls. The next day, U.S. Magistrate, Robert McQuaid released Olcese on her own recognizance. He was not so charitable with Shirley Colletti.

Assistant U.S. Attorney, Michael Barr argued for a high bail for Colletti. He told the magistrate that Colletti had received $760,000 in wire transfers. And Barr had learned that Colletti was co-owner of an ocean going yacht. In addition, Barr said that Marshal Bouvier, an A.G.E. Corporation president—*and a former Storey County District Attorney*—also in court today, had given Colletti $600,000 over the past several months. And when Bouvier asked her to return the money, she refused, Barr informed the magistrate. There was a very good possibility she would flee the country.

Marshall Bouvier, told things a little different. He told the magistrate that he had gathered together the $600,000 cash to meet his payrolls and pay the taxes. Since he had no safe out at the Mustang Ranch, he trusted Colletti to hold the money for him. In so doing, he told the magistrate, Shirley Colletti was appointed as an assistant director of A.G.E. Yet, when he wanted her to return the money, Bouvier said she refused to do so.

McQuaid questioned Bouvier about Conforte's role in A.G.E. Bouvier denied that Conforte had any financial interest in A.G.E. He insisted that Joe Conforte was no more than an unpaid consultant to the Mustang Ranch—not a hidden owner. He identified three foreign nationals as the A.G.E. stockholders. Eduardo Neves, a Brazilian citizen, who owned 80 percent; two Sicilian men, Emanuela Noe, and Augustino Conforte—a Joe Conforte nephew. Each of these two owned 10 percent, he said. And they hired Comforte because they didn't know anything about running a legitimate bordello.

Was Joe Conforte being paid?

"They hired him as a consultant," Bouvier answered, and "it was up to them. A.G.E. never paid him a dime."

"From time to time he (Conforte) calls and makes suggestions," Bouvier said to the magistrate, "but there's a clear understanding that I can accept or reject any suggestions made by Conforte, and I have rejected many."

Bouvier said that Conforte had called him on Thursday to find out what was going on.

"He wanted to know what the situation was and I told him they'd picked up Shirley, and I told him there would be a hearing at 3:00 p.m., this afternoon."

After the day's hearing had concluded, Bouvier tried to avoid media questions.

"I have no comment on this at this time," he said.

Bouvier was reminded that most of the charges stemmed from testimony given by one-time confidant and Conforte lawyer, Peter Perry. Perry, in effect, was the fed's stellar witness. And he had agreed to testify in a plea bargain in order to avoid a possible life sentence.

Bouvier cast a disdainful glance at the reporters and reminded them that Perry was now a convicted felon and had no credibility at all that could hold up in court.

On Monday, August 10, 1998, Shirley Colletti was released from Washoe County Jail on a cash only bond of $250,000. The money was said to have been posted by her husband.

On Monday, August 10, 1998, Shirley Colletti was released from Washoe County Jail on a cash only bond of $250,000.

The federal trial against A.G.E. Corporation, and Shirley Colletti—the only person present to stand trial—began on Monday, June 21, 1999. Judge Howard McKibben presided over the trial which was held in U.S. District Court, in Reno.

Eduardo Neves, a Brazilian citizen, and Joann Olcese, a former Mustang Ranch bookkeeper, though named in the indictment, were not going to trial. Neves, could not be brought back from

Brazil. And Olcese worked out a plea bargain with the feds in which she would plead guilty to her role in the money transfers, in exchange for her testimony against Conforte and Colletti.

Colletti was represented by two Reno attorneys, David Houston and Scott Freeman. These two attorneys were known locally by their weekly television show, "Lawyers, Guns and Money."

Richard G. Sherman, 61 (at the time), a Los Angeles based attorney, was there to represent A.G.E. Sherman, who was born in Chicago, received his law degree from the University of Southern California. After serving as an assistant U.S. Attorney for five years, he entered private practice specializing in federal prosecutions. He had been doing business with A.G.E. and Conforte for a number of years.

The prosecution's team was headed by U.S. Attorney, Michael Barr, 51 (at the time). Barr was a graduate of Northwestern University, in Boston, Massachusetts. For the past thirteen years, he had been assigned to the U.S. Attorney's office in Las Vegas.

During opening statements, Barr told the court he would present evidence that Joe Conforte was the hidden owner of the Mustang Ranch. Through A.G.E., Barr said, millions of dollars of Mustang proceeds were channeled down to Conforte who was living the high life in South America.

Conforte was named in the indictment as the mastermind of the money transactions through A.G.E. But because he fled the country in 1991 to live in South America—and because neither Brazil nor Chile would extradite him, the only defendant who would appear before the court, would be Shirley Colletti.

Lawyers for Colletti portrayed her as a kindly, 63 year old grandmother, who was a former Storey County commissioner, and currently a Mustang Ranch manager. She did nothing more than any other responsible employee would do, they told the jurors. She was an employee of A.G.E., which was the parent company of the Mustang Ranch, and she did their bidding, none of which was illegal.

On Tuesday, the prosecution presented their first witnesses, Peter Perry, Conforte's former attorney, and Cal Dardari, a Brazilian jeweler. These two testified that Conforte smuggled over $1 million abroad, and then when it was needed to buy back the

Mustang Ranch at auction, smuggled it back into this country.

Perry testified that while Shirley Colletti was a Storey County commissioner, Conforte had been making monthly payments to her, and also to Bob Del Carlo, while he was Storey County Sheriff (and who was now a general manager of the Mustang Ranch).

"He (Conforte) was amazed at how easily they could be bought," Perry testified, "and what they would do for the money.

"The main purpose was to keep a monopoly on the prostitution business, the brothel business in Storey County, so that nobody else need apply," Perry said.

Perry recalled a time in 1991, when he traveled to Sicily to meet with Conforte Conforte, then a fugitive, was fearful the feds were aware of his hidden ownership in the Mustang, and he wanted Perry to set up a dummy corporation.

Perry said following the meeting, he traveled to London and began a paper trail to throw the feds off balance. He bought several corporations on paper, eventually founding A.G.E. Corporation, designed to conceal Conforte's ownership.

"It would send the government traveling around the world trying to penetrate all these corporations before they could even get to who the true owner was," Perry testified.

And did it work?

Not for me, Perry stammered. "It destroyed my life."

"L I A R," defense lawyer Scott Freeman wrote on an easel in six-inch capital letters which he displayed to the jury as he rose to his feet. Judge McKibben ordered him to remove it which he did. Then followed hours of grueling cross examination.

Perry acknowledged surrendering his law license to the bar after he was indicted, and after he pled guilty to one count of wire fraud. He also admitted he committed perjury when he first lied to the judges about his involvement with the Mustang Ranch ownership. In addition, he admitted cheating the Internal Revenue Service when he accepted proceeds of theft. By pleading guilty to one felony, he said, he was able to escape prosecution on many other charges.

Scott Freeman cast his eyes derisively at Perry, and then looked up at the jurors and said it was a "huge reward" for Perry to get probation and not the 70 year sentence and the $1 million fine he could have been slapped with.

At one point, Perry tried to place himself in the role of a victim. He told the jury that when he cautioned Conforte that they were coming under increasing government scrutiny, the brothel owner scowled and threatened him.

"He said if I cooperated in any way, shape or form, he would have me killed, my family killed, right down to my cats and dogs."

Perry was to admit later there had been no attempts on his life.

Perry maintained his composure while the defense continued to hammer away at his character. He admitted he set up his brother, Victor Perry, as the front man to bid for and buy the Mustang Ranch for Conforte after the IRS had seized it and auctioned it for back taxes.

Richard Sherman, attorney for A.G.E., asked, "If you would do that to your brother, what would you do to this jury....?"

Barr jumped up to object, and Judge McKibben stopped Sherman from finishing the question.

Colletti's attorneys, David Houston and Scott Freeman, took turns to discredit the prosecution, and contended that the feds had a vendetta against Conforte for "thumbing his nose at them for years," and said they wanted to hurt him personally by destroying the business he built since they could not bring him to trial.

"It's my understanding," Houston said, "that it's the government's desire to seize and forfeit the property, not to sell the property for the taxpayers, but so they can turn it into a park.

"It's a personal issue with the government because quite honestly, it appears there has been a cat-and-mouse game with Joe Conforte for decades. I don't think the government has appreciated Mr. Conforte's choosing to leave the country in 1991.

"The government is left with trying to justify years of investigation by going after A.G.E. Corporation and Shirley Colletti. It's a tragic waste of time and effort."

Houston said it would be a shame to see a going commercial enterprise put out of business when it generates revenue flowing into the coffers of the federal and Storey County governments. Even if sex-for-sale is an unsavory business to some, it's a legal business in Nevada.

"If they can't get Joe Conforte," Houston said, "they're willing to get what they can, which is A.G.E. Corporation, and unfortunately, Shirley Colletti. This isn't about back taxes, this is about Joe Conforte."

Prosecutor Barr spoke up and said his forces had not been remiss in trying to bring Joe Conforte to trial.

"We have made every effort conceivable through the appropriate channels through the South American countries where he has lived and we have to rely on their systems of justice, their process. It's not like we have a court that has control over when we pick someone up and when they come back. We consistently check with the appropriate authorities to try and accomplish what needs to be done and we will consistently do it.

"If he lived in another country, that would be another story. He's just lived in places where the process has been lengthy."

"He (Conforte) has consistently used shills and front men," to continue operating the brothel from South America and has a "maniacal desire" to maintain control over it, Barr said.

And "he has continually refused to pay his taxes."

Barr portrayed Colletti as one of these fronts, and said she was Conforte's "right hand man."

Barr accused Colletti and Joann Olcese of stuffing money into their panties which they carried illegally to Mexico which was funneled to Conforte. At one time, Barr said, Shirley Colletti secretly carried $700,000 in cash to Acapulco, Mexico, for delivery to Conforte.

Car Dardari, the jeweler, testified that after the Mustang Ranch went into bankruptcy in the early 1980s, he helped Conforte open a Swiss bank account in which at least $1.5 million was deposited. He said under Conforte's direction, he deposited checks from the brothel owner to his currency exchange bank in New York, which then transferred the funds to Conforte's Swiss bank account. At the time, Dardari testified, Conforte was using a Honduran passport with the name, Joseph Conforte Montoya.

And so it went for the first two days of testimony. On Wednesday afternoon, Richard Sherman, representing A.G.E., asked Judge McKibben to sequester the jury, saying Reno was a small town and the jurors were beginning to appear as celebrities. Judge McKibben denied the request.

On Thursday, Joann Olcese, the former Mustang Ranch bookkeeper, did her best to bury her former boss. She testified that she and others moved hundreds of thousands of dollars out of the U.S. following orders of Joe Conforte.

"He would call and say the shareholders wanted to know how

much money was in the bank. He'd say, 'send 200-250 thousands.'"

Olcese went on to say that she and Shirley Colletti once hid $18,000 under their clothing which they took to Acapulco for Conforte.

Continuing her testimony, she told the jurors she wrote checks against the A.G.E. account which she used to buy a washing machine and television system for her home and to expand a carport.

She testified she took money from the brothel to pay for groceries, roof repairs, and utility bills for assorted Conforte girlfriends living in Nevada and California. In addition, other money she took went to pay off Shirley Colletti and other Storey County officials.

Besides Peter Perry, two other Conforte attorneys splattered their former client with smut. Herbert Ahlswede testified that Conforte was trying to portray himself as a minor consultant with A.G.E, however; he was truly calling the shots.

"I felt that he was in control," Ahlswede testified.

Marshall Bouvier, the former Storey County District Attorney, testified Conforte not only called the shots, but would become "furious" with them if they gave him advice he didn't want to hear.

During June and July of the previous year, Bouvier said Conforte wanted him to get rid of Joann Olcese.

"He said she was ratting to the feds."

Fugitive Joe Conforte, hiding out in South America, must have been chewing on nails when he learned his former attorneys and bookkeeper were testifying against him in federal court. It seemed the only person who remained loyal was Shirley Colletti, and she was, ironically, the only person on trial.

On Friday, Jeri Coppa, a U.S. bankruptcy trustee, who had presided over the closing of the Mustang Ranch nine years ago, was called to the stand. Coppa testified that when the place was taken over by the feds and put to auction, no money could be found on the premises.

"There was no cash on hand or in the safe," she testified. And that's when the feds retraced Conforte's known bank accounts, and put a freeze order on one.

Coppa said Joe Conforte was furious when he learned that the feds had frozen the account, which had in excess of $50,000 balance, preventing him from drawing out any of the money.

"He wanted his $50,000," she testified. "He said it was his money and that I had no right to it. He was very angry."

On a follow up visit to her office, she said, Conforte appealed with her to let him have the money, and she said he tried to bribe her.

"He offered me a job," she said, wide eyed. "He said if I was that tough, I could come out and operate the ranch."

Next up was a comely prostitute and part time porno star. She smiled briefly and testified that she applied for work at the Mustang Ranch, despite being advised by Peter Perry, that the place would soon close.

When she posed the question to Shirley Colletti, she said Colletti denied it. She quoted Colletti as saying, "Joe Conforte owns the place and it is not going to close."

Speaking of Peter Perry, the prostitute again quoted Colletti as saying, "...he created a lot of problems for them and would end up in a body bag."

On Thursday, July 1, the jurors were sent home for the 4th of July holiday weekend and both sides began preparations for final arguments.

When court resumed Tuesday, July 6, U.S. Attorney Michael Barr paraded in front of the jurors emphasizing his words with showy hand gestures. Joe Conforte, he stressed, continued to be the hidden owner of A.G.E. Corporation and the Mustang Ranch brothel.

He told the jurors that Shirley Colletti and others aided and abetted Conforte in defrauding the Internal Revenue Service. He referred to the testimony of the prostitute who quoted Colletti as saying Joe Conforte owned the Mustang Ranch.

"She (Colletti) was working for Joe Conforte. She was stealing for Joe Conforte. In her words, Joe Conforte was the boss, the owner," Barr hammered away.

He also cited evidence of a 1993 property option between A.G.E., and a brother of Colletti.

"A.G.E. agreed to conspire with Joe Conforte to keep the property from being liened by the I.R.S.," Barr said.

David Houston, trying to refute the prosecution's statements said Shirley Colletti showed innocence and strength when she took the stand to defend herself.

"So many people got up and lied," Houston said, "she had to set the record straight. The U.S. government has wasted ten years and thousands of man hours and dollars. If that was their best, it is woefully inadequate."

Houston said the government's stellar witness, Peter Perry, could not be believed because he pleaded guilty to wire fraud in 1996, and so is a convicted felon.

"Peter Perry is a liar, a trained liar," Houston impressed upon the juries. Sensing their attention, he continued in this vein for the next two hours, pausing only long enough to sip water. The case went to the jury the following day.

After thirteen hours of deliberations, the jury returned their verdicts on Thursday, July 8, 1999.

The court clerk began reading the verdicts against Shirley Colletti.

"Not guilty," he said somberly, on the first two counts.

Not waiting to hear more, a handful of persons in the courtroom burst into applause. However, this was to be short lived.

The court clerk continued with the other eleven counts of wire fraud and racketeering, and announced stoically, "guilty as charged," on all eleven counts The courtroom fell into stunned silence. And Shirley Colletti, teetering on her feet, broke out into sobs, and slumped to the floor.

After she recovered, she was assisted out of the courtroom, amid stares from those present..

Judge McKibben spoke to Scott Freeman, Colletti's attorney, to say that she would be allowed to remain free on bail pending appeal.

Freeman spoke briefly to the press saying he was "very disappointed" by the verdict. Richard Sherman, representing A.G.E. Corporation, sat stunned as the jurors returned guilty verdicts on all 23 counts lodged against the dummy corporation.

The jury then was given the responsibility of deciding whether A.G.E. should forfeit the brothel and other properties owned in Storey County. U.S. Attorney, Gregory Damm indicated he would seek all assets. In addition, Damm said the government would also seek a monetary judgment against Colletti, who also faced a prison term.

The hammer came down again on Friday when the jury voted to forfeit the Mustang Ranch to the federal government because it had been used as part of a criminal conspiracy orchestrated by fugitive Joe Conforte.

Judge Howard McKibben entered a preliminary order allowing the federal government to take over the brothel. But citing a need for the working girls and other employees to secure new employment, delayed the forfeiture for a month. August 9, 1999, would be the date of closure.

Shirley Colletti, who appeared shaken before Judge McKibben, was fined $220,000. Sentencing on the anticipated prison time was set for October 24.

Outside the courtroom, Colletti told the press the only reason she was singled out for prosecution was because she had been a county commissioner. That's why they came after me, she said. She said she'd earned her money the hard way, often putting in 24 hour shifts at the Mustang Ranch as one of the managers.

U.S. Assistant District Attorney, Gregory Damm said in addition to the fine levied against Colletti, fines totaling $20 million were assessed against A.G.E. Corporation, and A.G.E. Enterprises, though nobody knew how they were going to collect. And on the surface, it appeared Damm just wanted to bust them up regardless of money collected.

Damm explained that under the guidelines set forth by the federal government, asset forfeitures are done to disable a criminal enterprise, and to put out of business for a long time, big money criminals. Under the guidelines set forth by the federal government, the taking of the Mustang Ranch was not a seizure, but an asset forfeiture, which in effect meant it would not again be put up for auction.

Would the government put the brothel in mothballs?

Damm said he did not know what would become of the property, but was sure of one thing, that it would never again be used as a brothel..

Shirley Colletti said what many others were thinking, that the working girls would take to the streets, unregulated with no medical safeguards. She said she envisioned seeing unregulated prostitutes working the Reno area, spreading disease and being victimized by vicious street thugs.

But the biggest loser promised to be Storey County with its loss of revenue which amounted to hundreds of thousands of dollars annually.

The defense attorneys wasted little time in filing appeals. Scott Freeman, pointed out that Shirley Colletti was the only person who had been found guilty. And Colletti was only a paid employee, certainly not an owner. So how could the federal government seize the property when only an employee had been convicted?

"The government basically prosecuted the business entities that run the ranch, but not the people who own the ranch," he argued.

But insiders felt he had lost to the power of the federal government.

Barring any last minute favorable appeals for the defense, the government stated unequivocally that on August 9, 1999, the sordid career of the Mustang Ranch, the world famous purveyor of sex for the past 35 years, would take its last breath.

And this announcement, like a giant seductive magnet, reached out to the curious. Business was brisk.

On Sunday, August 8, which promised to be Mustang's last day, there was standing room only at the bar and in the parlor. Among those sipping drinks was an easily recognizable Hollywood celebrity, sandwiched in between three or four young girls vying for his attention. Though polite, "Craig," darkly handsome with flashing, well capped teeth, and green eyes, was looking past the giggling girls.

His gaze was on a middle-aged prostitute sitting quietly some distance from the bar who went by the name, "Dina." Dina was tall, about five-foot-eight inches, and weighed about 130 pounds. Traces of cellulite showing from her rump and the twinkling crows feet from the corners of her eyes when she smiled, hinted at her age. She could have been anybody's mother. She felt Craig's eyes, and knew from experience that many johns felt more comfortable talking with a mother figure, than they did with the younger girls. She smiled.

Craig finished his drink and excused himself. Working his way past the crowd he introduced himself to Dina. After several minutes of soft chatter, the two walked lightly toward Dina's crib, arm in arm. Casting a glance back at the rhinestone decked younger girls, she again smiled. Inside, with the door closed, a full length mirror reflected the small room's tasteful furnishings. A queen sized bed which occupied most of the room, was emblazoned with a flaming red satiny comforter (thought to excite). On the walls, which were devoid of pictures, hung several scanty costumes placed there for the same purpose. A lamp atop the dresser cast dim light on a few family photos, a reminder that the crib's occupant—emotionally—was not much different from other women.

Every bit the professional, Dina began small conversation to place Craig at ease.

"Did you drive in?"

"How long have you been an actor?"

"Do you like the Hollywood scene?"

"Do you gamble while you're here?"

"Have you been here before?"

Craig responded to each query with an out of character humbleness which surprised and pleased the woman, and which also told her she would have to direct the show.

"This is how we work here," she explained., "the girls are independent contractors. We have to go to the doctor once a week and we have to practice safe sex here."

She withdrew a "menu" from the dresser which she handed to Craig.

"The menu lists the activities which are available," she said, "along with the time limits and prices. Please feel free to ask questions and if you don't see what you're looking for here, we can discuss your needs."

"I'm not really the character portrayed on the screen," Craig told her. And glancing at the family photos on the dresser, said, "I have a difficult time living up to the studio hype."

Money exchanged hands which Dina placed on top of the dresser. She then took out clean linen which she used to cover the red comforter. She turned on soft music, lit some incense and turned the lamp down to a soft glow. She explained to Craig that she had to take the money up to the hostess, and suggested he take off his clothes and get comfortable

Up front, she was required to enter her name on the roster, her crib number, the time, the amount of money agreed upon, and under comments, she had to write down whether the john arrived at the brothel by private vehicle, taxi, limo, or helicopter. This done, she returned to face Craig.

Inside the room, Dina faced the mirror and asked Craig if he would like to help her undress. Standing close behind her, he placed his cheek next to hers as they both looked into the mirror, and he began to fumble with her blouse.

Outside in the parlor, the topic of discussion among some of the young girls was Craig and his choice of women.

"Can ya beat that," a petite redhead said, "in Hollywood you'd think he could have any girl he wanted to, yet he comes here and pays for it—and even picks an old lady. Go figure."

EPILOGUE

On December 21, 1996, a notice appeared in the Reno Gazette-Journal, offering 1,000 Christmas turkeys to be given away free to the needy. The benefactor was named as Joe Conforte.

The needy were not the only persons who paid heed to the paper. Local law enforcement intelligence officers were also scanning the announcement. The ad pictured Joe and Sally, arms around each other, obviously in happier days. But what caught the intel officers attention was the minuscule caption at the bottom of the ad which said the Renegades MC (Motorcycle Club) had paid for the ad.

Of further interest, was the use of red ink in some of the larger words.

Which motorcycle club is known as red and white?

Only one. The Hell's Angels. These are their colors.

So why would a local motorcycle club challenge the Hell's Angels, by using their colors.

The only viable conclusion was that the Renegades had been sanctioned by the H.A., and had been given permission to do so.

This fact was borne out not too much later, when the Renegades shed their own colors, and adopted those of the Hell's Angels. David Burgess, the Conforte nephew who was the owner of the Old Bridge Ranch, and former president of the Renegades, became the president of the Nevada chapter of the Hell's Angels.

Today, Joe and Sally's former home on Sullivan Lane, is now the clubhouse of the Hell's Angels. The white house is trimmed in red, and a blazing death's head patch on the east facing wall, proclaims, "HELL'S ANGELS, NEVADA CHAPTER (This can be seen from the street, and it is the author's opinion that the curious should not venture further.)

On Monday, August 10, 1999. federal agents swooped down on the Mustang Ranch with orders to close it down forever. Former Storey County Sheriff, Bob Del Carlo, who was listed as brothel manager and president of A.G.E., handed over all keys to

Customs Agent, Ron Mesberger. Del Carlo said that Joe Conforte, still a fugitive from justice living in Brazil, was dismayed about the takeover by the federal government.

Del Carlo told the press he wasn't sure what plans the feds had for the property, but their primary concern was that Conforte not again get his hands on it.

By nightfall, the brilliant lights decorating the property that for decades served as a beacon light for starved johns, were to be engulfed in the shadows.

The feds hadn't given up on bringing Joe Conforte back to the United States., whom they now confirmed was living in Brazil. A couple of months later, in October, agents hand carried a warrant for his arrest to Brazil which they presented to the authorities. Within days, Conforte was arrested and tossed into the local slammer. However, the glee savored by the feds was to be short lived at best.

In late October, the Brazilian Supreme Court reviewed the charges lodged against the fugitive. By an 8-0 ruling, they found that the narrow terms of the U.S. extradition treaty with Brazil did not cover bankruptcy fraud. In conclusion, Conforte was released from custody and allowed to remain in Brazil. He could not be forced to return to the U.S.

In November, 1999, Peter Perry, Conforte's one-time attorney who rolled and testified for the government as part of a plea bargain, was sentenced to six-months in a halfway house, six-months of house arrest, and fined $20,000. In addition, he was ordered to perform 100 hours of community service. He was also temporarily suspended from practicing law in Nevada.

In November, 2000, the Nevada Supreme Court reviewed the bar association's act to suspend the law license of attorney Peter Perry for six months.

Despite testifying for the government against Conforte, the Supreme Court took the position that Perry was nevertheless accountable for his own criminal acts. The court pointed out that according to the federal court record, Perry "engaged in a course of conduct over a period of several years in disregard of the laws.

"We conclude that the mitigating evidence presented by Perry does not outweigh the magnitude of his misconduct," the court ruled. Further, the court ruled that the bar association's six months suspension of his license was not enough.

The Supreme Court voted to disbar the attorney, and a disbarment order was issued.

Former bookkeeper, Joann Olcese, who also testified for the government, received six-months of home confinement, three-years probation, and fined $7,500. In July, 2001, Olcese won a judgment in court against Conforte in which she was awarded $226,000. Washoe District Judge Peter Breen, allowed $126,000 as payment for a "broken contract," with Conforte, and $100,000 punitive damages. It is unlikely she will ever see any of this money.

In March, 2000, A&E Television aired an hour long documentary about Joe Conforte and Nevada brothels on their "City Confidential" nighttime show. Interviewed at his lavish condo overlooking Ipanema Beach, Conforte blamed his problems on the federal government. He accused government officials of harboring a vendetta against him and anyone associated with the Mustang Ranch.

Later in the month, David Houston, attorney representing Shirley Colletti, filed pre-sentencing documents in U.S. District Court, trying to avert a prison sentence for his client.

He described her as a frail, 63 year old woman suffering from multiple health and emotional problems.

"While admittedly, her present problems have already exacted a tremendous toll on her overall well-being, it is believed a sentence of incarceration may well in fact represent more than prison, but rather the potential of a death sentence," the document stated.

Houston said he may agree to a sentence of 10 to 16 months provided the sentencing judge considered a prison alternative such as probation and home arrest.

His efforts were challenged by Assistant U.S. Attorney, Gregory Damm who made it known he would argue for "whatever sentence is factually and legally supported by a complete evaluation by parole and probation authorities.

Damm pointed out that the Federal Bureau of Prisons, maintained excellent medical facilities which were available to all federal prisoners. He said Colletti's medical problems could well be handled by the bureau. He said that in many instances, the inmates receive much better care than they did on the street.

"The same may be true for Colletti," he said.

Houston presented the court with a letter written by a Las Vegas internist explaining Colletti's health problems. In it, he said Colletti had a heart valve problem and chest pains, a claustrophobic disorder, peptic ulcer syndrome, hypothyroidism, and estrogen deficiency. The letter suggested that incarceration of even the briefest duration, could worsen her condition.

Another letter, written by a Las Vegas psychologist was also offered in her defense. In it, the Las Vegas practitioner stated that Colletti was burdened with a number of psychological problems including panic anxiety, agoraphobia, (fear of being in open or public places), claustrophobia, and depression.

If incarcerated, he said in the letter, she could suffer "very severe emotional distress to her, probably requiring inpatient hospitalization."

On Monday, April 3, 2000, Shirley Colletti stood before Judge Howard McKibben to learn her fate. Her lawyers told the judge their client was duped into helping Joe Conforte, and pointed out her position in the community.

"Ms. Colletti has devoted herself to public service and for far more reason than just the Mustang brothel," David Houston argued.

"Ms. Colletti did not have to do 90 percent of what she did as a county commissioner simply to do the bidding of Joseph Conforte," he said.

Colletti insisted she was unaware of any illegal activities at the Mustang Ranch.

"I'm devastated," she quivered, "because I'm standing here before you and I've never done anything wrong. If I'd known it was wrong, I never would have done it.

"I'd have never done anything that goes against my being a county commissioner," she said. "It's too important."

Judge McKibben listened attentively and after much thought, announced he would not hand down the maximum sentence allowable of 57 months in prison. However, he pointed out, she was certainly aware of—not duped into—assisting Joe Conforte in breaking the law.

"There is little doubt in my mind that she knew what was

going on," he told the court. "It was an elaborate plan to defraud the United States government of income."

As she stood wavering before him, Judge McKibben's words cut through her like an icicle when he sentenced her to 46 months in federal prison and forfeiture of $220,000. She was advised to get her affairs in order. The defendant glared at the judge in silence, and then began to falter, appearing momentarily on the verge of collapse.

Judge McKibben told the court the defendant could remain free on bail of $250,000 pending the appeal of both the conviction and today's sentence before the 9th U.S. Circuit Court of Appeals in San Francisco.

After regaining her composure, Colletti stormed out of the courtroom trailed by her attorneys. She had little time to respond to the clamoring media.

In mid 2001, her appeal was heard by the Ninth Circuit in San Francisco. The court ruled against her. The sentence was not to be reversed. Her only hope as of this writing, is with the United States Supreme Court. She continues to reside in Las Vegas, and remains out on bail.

The feds continue to maintain the upkeep of the Mustang Ranch, at the expense of the U.S taxpayers. This, they must do, until all appeals have been resolved.

Joe Conforte's golden years are spent indulging in the excesses of the good life in Brazil, while reminiscing about a lifetime spent peddling sex.

NOTES

Chapter One

1. The line-up displayed girls of varied ethnic backgrounds. They were also of varied shapes, sizes and ages. Anywhere from pretty 21 year olds, on up to lumpy 50 year olds. They were all expected to appear alluring, and seductive, but were forbidden to say more than their names while in line-up. They were not allowed to speak, giggle or otherwise attempt to draw attention to themselves. These procedures were in effect as a measure of fairness to all of the girls. Also, the girls in line were required to have their private parts covered. Violating any of these house rules was known as "dirty hustling," and the violators could be reprimanded by the madam (and would be despised by the others.)

2. Actually, prostitution had been widespread in Nevada since the early 1920s. A brothel in Reno, dubbed the Stockade, was a shoe box shaped structure that boasted of containing 50 cribs, and was open 24 hours a day. Each girl was checked weekly for venereal disease. The stockade ran girls from 1924, until January 7, 1942, when the U.S. Department of Defense, under pressure from wives and mothers of World War II, military personnel, coerced Nevada Governor, Edward Carville, to ban open prostitution in the state. Lt. General, J. L. DeWitt, who commanded the Western Defense Command, wrote to the governor:
"I am responsible to the parents of these splendid young men in our army for seeing to it that they are not surrounded by a vicious and demoralizing environment. I hardly need remind you that among these healthy young men of our army, venereal disease produces more disability than any other single cause, and that among industrial workers it is one of the most serious causes of disability and inefficiency, especially in the boom towns of war industry."
Carville answered the army commander, and advised him that in Nevada, each county had the option of running—or banning, legal bordellos. The governor suggested the army contact each county outlining the request.
Three of the major counties, Clark, in the south, and Washoe and Ormbsy, in the north, however, took the request under advisement.

Following a brief period of time, these three populated counties ordered all bordellos within their boundaries, to cease operations until the war's end.

What was the outcome? With the closure of the red-light districts, prostitution continued to flourish. Hustlers were driven underground. Business was now done on the streets, in back allies, and cheap hotels. But now, without weekly health checks, incidents of venereal disease among servicemen, at times, reached near epidemic proportions. This was not truly controlled, until the brothels were once again allowed to operate openly following World War II. Portions of this note printed courtesy of the Nevada Appeal Newspaper, Carson City, NV.

3. Bill Raggio, Reno native, was admitted to practice law in Nevada, in 1951. In 1952, he was accepted into the office of the district attorney. In 1958, he was elected to the post of district attorney. Attending a banquet by the Reno-Sparks Junior Chamber of Commerce, on January 23, 1960, he was named the "Outstanding Man of the Year."

4. Vagrancy as used during this period of time in Nevada, was a catch-all phrase used to roust or arrest panderers or persons who hang out or hustle around illegal red-light districts.

5. Placing of jurors in custody is sometimes effected during murder trials, especially when capital offenses have been committed, however, this procedure is rarely used in crimes of less severity. The last time this procedure had been used was more than twenty years preceding this trial.

6. In May, 1959, Raggio was fighting a legal battle to bring charges against the doctor for furnishing Scotch and champagne to an 18 year old girl in the doctor's office. Dr.Bryan's attorneys, in defense, were claiming a physician-patient relationship and had taken the matter to the Nevada Supreme Court. Raggio was still pursuing the case.

7. Black Books. Each and every casino and hotel-casino maintains a black book on all identified undesirables: persons who because of prior cheating arrests, or others of questionable character, are forbidden to enter their establishments. Photos and other forms of intelligence on these undesirables, are freely shared among the gambling security and hierarchy

CHAPTER 2, NEVADA STATE PRISON

1. During 1995, a female warden in Carson City, was caught up in this type of situation. The woman had been with the department for more than twenty years, and had promoted up through the custody

ranks, She began coming in at night to demonstrate to a male inmate (with a history of sexual assault), the finer aspects of culinary cooking. On several occasions, they were seen to go behind locked doors in the culinary, and she forbid the search and escort officers from entering during her "cooking instructions" to the inmate. When the inmate eventually paroled, he moved in with her in her Carson City home; they married, and opened a pastry business. When the relationship was discovered, she was allowed to resign. He got into more trouble and was sent back to prison which ended their relationship.

Another female warden was discovered living with a tattooed ex-prison inmate.

She, at one time, allowed the ex-inmate into the prison institution on a tour—a very serious security violation. The prison director declined to discipline her.

CHAPTER 3

1. Though brass and canvas prison exchange money was removed from the yard decades ago, the term still sticks. An inmate who has money in his prison account, can fill out a "brass slip" to make a legitimate purchase from the canteen, an outside mail order house, or to send money home.

2. Generally speaking—but not necessarily: In prison, every inmate, in his own mind, is something special. He was a successful big money crook on the outside, and never would have been sent to prison if not for his lawyer, his codefendant, his girl, his attorney, the judge, etc., etc. The point is that inmates like to brag to each other, and exaggerate their street prowess to other inmates.

    Killers are a different lot. Most of them—in their own minds, are innocent; they were set up; the witness lied; they were home in bed; Sam did it, etc. etc., ad nauseam.

    On the other hand, wife killers, for instance, do their time in abject remorse, and depression, causing few problems for staff—other than when they attempt suicide. This type of inmate may program and avoid serious trouble for years.

    Rapists, in prison, are in a world of their own. Many continue their predatory tactics when locked up, and renew their sexual predilections in prison, however; without females to prey upon, their focus changes and they target their own gender.

    Child molesters—cho-moes—along with snitches, are the lowest form of life in prison, and usually serve their sentences in protective custody.

Manicured Joe, slick, polished, generous with his money, and politically connected, fit into none of the above categories. He had no need to fabricate stories. His reputation preceded him, and he was made to feel welcome. He was Joe Conforte! And in his own mind, head and shoulders above the other cons.

3. In 1967, the stone building housing the "Bull Pen" casino, was demolished. All brass was confiscated from the inmates. Prison gambling was officially declared illegal.

CHAPTER 4

1. Nevada, the seventh largest state in land mass, has only 17 counties. Many of these counties have legalized prostitution as a source of revenue. In 1970, following favorable public opinion, Churchill, Mineral and Nye Counties enacted ordinances legalizing prostitution. In 1972, Lyon County following Storey, legalized the profession.

   Now a legitimate business owner, Conforte would flaunt his newly acquired standing in the community. He wore expensive furs, silk clothing, and large flashy diamonds, and usually had a large Cuban cigar stuck in his mouth.

   He bathed in the limelight, and could be seen around the Reno clubs nightly, accompanied by working girls from the Mustang. To drum up business, he would swagger into the local pubs with a couple of the girls and order drinks for the house. After small conversation with the patrons, he would hand out business cards, and then he and the girls would get back into a chauffeur driven limousine and head for other Reno night spots.

2. During an interview in the early 1990s, Conforte commented on these gold-colored cards calling his practice of giving them out, "professional courtesy." He said there was no expiration on these cards, that they would always be honored.

   Who were the recipients?

   He said judges, politicians, district attorneys, business persons, lawyers, doctors, people of lesser renown.

   "They all got them," he said.

3. Conforte eventually offered a reward of $20,000 for information leading to the arrest of a viable suspect.. On April 14, 1976, the arson charge against Baliotis was dismissed by Justice of the Peace Ed Colletti. Although arson was proven, the case remains unsolved. Storey County officials stated publicly that they'd cleared a total of twelve suspects.

4. On Tuesday, June 1, 1976 (in the aftermath of the Bonavena shoot-

ing, which is covered in Chapter 7), to the surprise of everyone connected with the case, Conforte did indeed sit for the polygraph which was administered by a private examiner, Jess Abel of Reno. Abel's report which was submitted to Stan Brown, Conforte's attorney, concluded by saying Conforte had no knowledge as to who started the fire at the Mustang Ranch; that he did not hire nor conspire with anyone to burn the structure, and that he was not involved in any way. No reason for the late and abrupt scheduling (not to mention the favorable conclusion) of the test was offered.

CHAPTER 7

1. Following the grand jury's report of March, 1976, Del Carlo had notified Conforte not to hire ex-felons for gun-carrying positions around the brothel. And after Brymer's most recent arrest just days earlier by the Washoe County detectives, for assault, battery and brandishing, Del Carlo had ordered Conforte "to get rid of him."

2. SK=Safe Keeper. County jails in Nevada may request the state prison system to house high profile inmates awaiting trial. Traditionally, prisoners who exhibit dangerous tendencies, or who are overly assaultive toward staff, or for other reasons that preclude their being housed in a less secure facility, are routinely slammed in the state prison in Carson City, where max lockup housing is available.

3. Seventy-two year old (in 1977) Judge, Frank Gregory, was born and raised in the mining town of Tonopah, Nevada. He had spent his entire legal career in the state, and had at various times had a private practice in Reno and Carson City. In 1953, he was elected as Disctrict Attorney, in Ormsby County (now just Carson City). In that same year, he was appointed as a district judge, and in 1954, was elected without opposition.

Stories were told about the judge's character by many who knew him. It is said at one time when he was trying a murder case and found out the defendant had a contagious disease, he moved the case outside, under a pine tree.

The stern-faced blue eyed judge became known as a no-nonsense traditionalist, and one who maintained strict obedience in his court. Judge Gregory's grandfather, Frank Bell, was governor of Nevada in 1890, and at one time was warden of the Nevada State Prison. Bell was also a first cousin to Alexander Graham Bell. With these connections, he became the first person in the state to acquire one of the new fangled communication devices, the telephone.

Gregory's mother, Fernald Bell, was born on the grounds of the Nevada State Prison, when Grandfather Bell was serving as the prison warden.

After serving for 25 years as a Storey County visiting judge, Gregory had met Conforte on various occasions. Gregory said there was a kind of mutual distant respect between the two, though they never associated socially.

At age 72 (in 1977) could he still do the work of a visiting judge? If you asked him, he'd tell you he now did five times the work that he was capable of ten years ago.

CHAPTER 9

1. On the date of this robbery, Brymer was still being held at the Nevada State Prison. However, he was released on bail on June 23, and it was after this date when he allegedly conspired to assist Mitchell in evading arrest.

CHAPTER 10

1. Over a decade ago, members of a prison gang, the Aryan Warriors, turned on each other after a gang related killing of another inmate. The leaders started rolling over on the ones who did the actual killing. A few were given pardons on their original sentences, however; the majority got no slack, indeed, they were required to move to protective custody, where many continue to serve out their life sentences.

CHAPTER 11

1. Enemy situations always existed in the fish tank. Inmates like to portray themselves as victims. They claim to have been victimized by the judge, their attorney, their spouse, or their crime partners or other law breakers or rival gang members. For this reason, during intake interviews, they are asked if they have any enemies on the wing. If they answer in the affirmative, this is noted in their C-file, and efforts are made to keep the enemies separated.

Rival gang members especially try to harm their enemies. Human waste has been washed under cell doors, and crude firebombs and caustic cleaning solutions have also been used by inmates trying to get back at each other. So, to have one inmate feed another was at best, risky because of the possibility of spitting in, or otherwise contaminating the recipient's food tray.

2. Every prison has routine body counts throughout every twenty-four hour day. This may be as few as six, or as many as twenty-four. During count, each inmate is required to be at his assigned bedside where the officers can confirm his presence. If he is not in his unit, for instance in the visiting room, or at work in prison industries, he will have been placed on out-count. Out-counts are the responsibly of the officer supervisors in the designated areas. They too, must verify all inmates under their supervision are in place during each count.

All counts are forwarded to main control where a master count is logged. When all inmates have been accounted for, the count is cleared and normal activities resume.

If there is a discrepancy and one or more inmates cannot be located, then a negative count is done. When a negative count is necessary, the housing officers visually inspect each empty bed and note the bed number. All inmates on out-count are again viewed by the officers who confirm their presence. These tallies are quickly relayed to main control. All inmates in transport (for instance out to court) are tallied into the final count. These procedures will quickly confirm the number of inmates present in the institution or in transport.

If, after this latest count, an inmate still cannot be accounted for, a yellow alert is sounded, which signals a possible escape. A yellow alert puts into motion preliminary escape procedures. All inmates on out-count are quickly sent back to their housing units where they, and all other inmates, are required to stand at their bedsides where a picture ID of each inmate is conducted by the officers.

Following these emergency procedures, the identity of the missing person or persons is quickly determined. With the exception of the roaming prison officers, all movement on the yard comes to a standstill. The institution is locked down.

Gun tower officers scan the yard and perimeters with binoculars. Search and escort officers begin to scour all areas in the facility where an inmate could hide. Local law enforcement agencies, the Highway Patrol, and designated security personnel at railway, bus and airline terminals, are notified of a possible escape, and a brief description of the suspected escapee is given.

If the facility search teams still fail to locate the missing person or persons within the institution, a probable escape is assumed and the prison is put on a red alert. A red alert puts into action many time tested procedures.

Outside law enforcement and other involved security personnel, are again contacted and advised the escape is now confirmed. A detailed description of the escapee is described. Armed Search teams from the prison are assembled and assigned to mobile or fixed positions outside of the prison. Couriers deliver ID pictures of the suspected escapee to all involved outside agencies.

Visiting records are scanned by the prison investigators which reveal the identity of persons who have visited the inmate in prison. The inmate's personal property and clothing, bedding, correspondence, photos, and other tangibles at his bedside are seized and sent to investigations for evaluation. His known inmate associates are interviewed (though it's doubtful they would reveal anything).

Prison investigators will assess the information gleaned, and share this intel with outside law enforcement agencies. Stake-outs near the homes of the inmate's visitors may be put in place.

Radio and television stations will be notified, which may broadcast or post photos of the suspected escapee during their news briefs.

Until located, the inmate is carried on escape status.

3. During this period of time, the prison had not yet been furnished with the taser nor OC gas. The stun gun—not to be confused with the run-of-the-mill shocking devices seen today—was a 30" long lethal appearing metal cylinder that fired a heavy canvas bean bag with sufficient force to drive an inmate up against the wall leaving him well bruised. Occasionally, an inmate would use his mattress as a shield. When this happened, a high powered charge was used which would plaster the mattress and inmate with enough force to disable him temporarily (this was the author's favorite weapon when dealing with an unruly inmate, much superior to today's pepper gas and tasers). Was this excessive? Absolutely not. During orientation, the inmates were told to behave. It was impressed upon them, that if they caused trouble, force would be used against them, sufficient to gain compliance. We never went back on our word.

4. This career criminal, now in his fifties, has been locked up for most of his adult life. During an attempted takeover of the old Clark County Jail, in Las Vegas, he led others on a destructive rampage that resulted in the death of two other jail prisoners.

Another time, while he was housed there, he killed his cell mate, he said, over a chess game. This incorrigible career criminal now languishes on death row at the Ely State Prison, Nevada.

5. Every prison has its Programs Division and its Custody Division. Programs consists of non-uniformed personnel who supervise prison industries, the medical and psychological departments, food preparation, the athletic department, the educational system, and all counselors.

Custody refers to the uniformed personnel, who have the responsibility of supervising and maintaining security at the prison. Custody personnel man the gun-towers, work the housing units, patrol the grounds and are responsible for ensuring the security at the work places and schools which are run by the Programs Division. They are responsible for preventing escapes, subduing violent inmates, and ensuring that the orderly day-by-day functioning of the prison is not compromised. From these two examples, the reader can see that generally speaking, programs personnel are there to assist the inmates in their prison adjustment. They are regarded as more inmate friendly than are the custody officers. The custody staff are there to maintain discipline. Inmates have learned to play members of one group against the other.

6. A legitimate cash flow of $2,500 a week coming into the yard from the plasma center, along with an undetermined amount of money coming in through visiting and other illegal avenues, is serious in itself. However, coupled with the administration's policy of allowing prisoners to keep and wear civilian clothing, was an open invitation for a prisoner to attempt an escape.

A lot of prisoners tried, and many succeeded. Most of those who were successful, simply donned civilian clothing, stashed their pockets with money, and climbed over one of the fences. Youthful David Lani, a Reno cop killer was one who did just that.

Richard Bryan, then the governor of Nevada, was quoted in the local paper, saying escapes and hostage taking incidents occurred so frequently, that "local wags suggested we ought to post a sign out by the prison that would say 'Drive Slowly, Prisoners Escaping.'"

The folly of this administration's questionable supervision of inmates blew up in their faces on the dark night of December 29, 1981. Warren Standen, an overweight killer, serving a sentence of life without parole, and who had been allowed to drive a station wagon around inside the prison grounds, drove the vehicle toward the first gate of a two-gate chain link sally port. The first gate was opened for him so he could enter and park the vehicle in the sally port, something he'd been permitted to do only recently. After parking, he was supposed to get out and walk back to his housing unit.

That fateful night, however; he had other plans. Once inside the sally port, the only obstacle between him and freedom, was the second chain link sally port gate. And with a sentence structure of life with no chance of parole, he knew he had little to lose. He glared at the gate house officer who was sauntering over towards him, and screamed obscenities as he slammed his foot to the floorboard. The sudden shrillness of the engine and screaming tires caught the startled officer completely off guard. He jumped back out of harms way, as Standen tore through the outer gate and roared down the prison road amid clouds of billowing smoke and dust. The officer in two-tower sprang to his feet and fired the 30.06 rifle toward the fleeing station wagon, but without visible impact.

A red alert was issued immediately alerting all outside law enforcement agencies of the escape, at the time, thought to be the work of one lone inmate, Warren Standen. However, following an emergency count, three other hard-core prisoners could not be accounted for: William Clayton, 31, serving a sentence of life for sodomy and homicide; Robert Nank, 34, serving 100 years for rape and murder; and Peter Huertas, 31, serving life for first degree murder. It was later determined that these three had hidden in the back of the station wagon, and along with Standen, had planned the escape for days. This was also the fourteenth successful escape from this facility in one year. (One has to question why these four killers with such stretched out sentences, should have been housed in a medium security prison at all.)

All available prison personnel along with the local law enforcement agencies were pressed into the hunt for the four killers. Deputies went house to house warning residents; roadblocks were set up from Carson City to the California border. The sheriff's mounted posse, tracking dogs, and a helicopter were also mobilized. Clayton, was the first to be apprehended. He was taken down before midnight in the Sierra Nevada foothills; Standen, not far away, was taken about 8:00 a.m., the next morning. Nank and Huertas were captured in Bishop, California, late Thursday night, just before the New Year rang in.

Just prior to this breakout, a tough-as-nails career warden from San Quentin, George Sumner, was appointed warden at Nevada's maximum security prison in Carson City. Sumner was faced with the challenge of cleaning up a yard where gang members were running rampant, where serious hostage taking incidents had occurred, and where only a couple of months earlier, three correctional officers had been ambushed, beaten and stabbed by members of the Black Warriors prison gang. Prison murders which had gone unsolved were also thrust upon the new warden to clear up.

Although, he had been hired to clean up max, the experienced warden from California, was asked to help tighten up security at NNCC. Less than a week later, at Sumner's insistence, 25 hardcore inmates at NNCC were gaffed up and transferred to max (the author was part of the team that was assigned the job of rounding them up, placing them in shackles, and loading them onto the transportation vans). Once these career criminals had been removed from the medium security prison, Sumner concentrated on correcting the problems at max.

Appearing before the legislature, Sumner was successful in convincing the law makers that he had to have money to restructure the max prison in order to curtail gang activity and reduce violence. Without adequate funds, he told them, conditions would only worsen. They were swayed by his sincerity, and came up with funding.

Sumner got right to work at max installing rows of inside fencing, isolating housing units. A gun-rail to cover main street and the exterior of the housing units was constructed, as was a culinary gun-cage, and a 40-cell, max lockup block, designed to house the most dangerous inmates in the system. Additional funds were allotted to form a security squad.

Within a few years, the success of his efforts had drawn the attention of the law makers. Sumner had locked up all the major gang leaders, sent many others out of state, had solved previously unsolved murders, and had severely curtailed the violence and hostage incidents so prevalent in the past. Governor, Richard Bryan, one of his strongest supporters, asked him to take control of the entire prison system. In May, 1985, Sumner was appointed director of the Nevada Department of Prisons.

He cast a wary eye on inmate friendly NNCC, and the administrative staff. He put a stop to inmates wearing civilian clothing and dressed them all in prison dungarees. He then pointed out the absurdity of inmates possessing money on the yard, and made them surrender all moneys which was placed in their individual inmate accounts. And his final effort to establish security at NNCC was to disband the plasma center. All of these changes, long overdue, were warmly received by the custody officers (but not necessarily by the programs people who lamented the loss of revenue with the closure of the plasma center).

7. A lawsuit challenging the prison's psychiatric care was initiated in 1979 by inmate Allen Taylor, a psyche patient. Taylor, who was doing nearly a hundred years for a sadistic sexual assault on a taxi driver, had, for years, fought the officers using hands, feet, and whatever other weapons were at hand. Over the years, he had injured more officers than any other inmate in the prison system. The other prisoners, who regarded him as a legend, always gave him plenty of room.

The suit, among other things, accused the prison officials of such practices as "four-pointing," a term used when the inmate was chained hands and feet to the steel beds, or in some cases to the floor. Other challenges were directed at the practice of forced medication.

In 1982, U.S. District Judge, Edward Reed, granted the inmates' request to give the suit "class action status," and a negotiated settlement was worked out between the plaintiffs and the attorney general's office.

An auditor was appointed to monitor the psychiatric division for a period of 18 months. The end result of all this was to demand replacement of the chains used in four-pointing violent inmates. Leather restraints would have to replace the chains. A psychiatric panel was formed to assess the need for forced medication on an individual basis, and the practice of using inmate psyche techs, was eliminated. This forced the prison system to employ civilian "forensic techs." The agreement also adopted the American Correctional Association's standards for mental health services. Claims for damages sought by Taylor and other inmates, were left unsettled.

8. All new commitments have their blood drawn as a routine check for contagious diseases. They are also given a skin test for tuberculosis. Until cleared, the prisoners are confined to their cells. After clearance, which usually takes about three days, they are allowed out to begin the routine fish-tank processing, and as in the case of Ross Brymer, to work as tier runner.

9. Pin rolls : slim marijuana cigarettes, during this period of time that usually sold for $10.00 each on the yard.

10. Pruno: Illegal, prison made liquor. To make pruno in a prison cell, one vital ingredient is necessary: yeast. Other items may be fruit juice, fresh or canned fruit, sugar, or jams, and jellies containing sugar. Potatoes or gains are also used.

Yeast is kept under lock and key in most prison bakeries. To substitute, inmates use a slice or two of yeast bearing bread compressed tightly into a ball and held together in a piece of torn cloth. This and the other ingredients are blended with water in a common container, and left to ferment. After a few days, the concoction will have matured into a mixture containing an ample amount of drinkable alcohol, weak, but acceptable.

Often, when a large amount, say four or five gallons is brewed in a single container, the odor released from the fermentation is inescapable. To mask this odor, a sealed container with an outlet made from rubber or plastic tubing is used. Gasses flowing out this tube are directed into another container containing household bleach. Filtering through this bleach effectively masks the telltale pruno odors.

11. Observation windows are supposed to be kept clear. Inmates trying to hide their illicit activities will cover the window with a sign saying, "Taking A Shit," or something similar. This may buy them a little time from the prying eyes of the unit officers.
12. Toothbrush shank: made by heating the handle end of a toothbrush with matches, and when the plastic is pliable, imbedding a razor blade into the end. When cooled, the inmate has a razor-tipped shank which is capable of inflicting deep, incised-like, painful cuts.
13. Inmates housed on death row (Condemned Men's Unit—CMU), are isolated from the general population. However; there are many ways they communicate with general population inmates: They may see each other in the infirmary or on the same transportation vehicles. They shout to each other from yard to yard, or hold up papers at the barred windows with scribbled messages. Many have learned to sign with their hands. Friendly officers carry messages; food service workers, law clerks, and other general population inmates whose duties carry them into CMU, pass messages. The most skillful inmates have learned to fish.
    Fishing on the tier: A scribbled message on paper is wrapped in plastic and secured to a line which is held by the sender. The person who is to receive the message fashions a similar package. Next both of these small lumps are placed in each individual's toilets which are flushed simultaneously while each inmate hangs on to his line. The two bundles will tangle together inside the sewer pipe that runs the length of the tier. The receiving inmate will then reel in his line with the other's message attached. This may take several attempts.
    Another method of communicating on the tier is by using a "cadillac." A cadillac is a line attached to a message or small item such as a bar of soap or piece of fruit. A skillful inmate can whip this outside of his cell door, and up or down the tier to another cell.

CHAPTER 13

1. In 1972, a landmark decision handed down by the United States Supreme Court, voided 40 death penalty statutes nationwide, effectively suspending capital punishment. In Nevada, all death row inmates' sentences were commuted to life without possibility of parole, and the death row inmates were moved to general population. Death row cells were put to use housing psychiatric patients, and the observation room (where witnesses congregated to view past executions) was used by the prison psychologist for group ther-

apy sessions.

In 1973, the Nevada Legislature changed its laws to meet the new guidelines of the Supreme Court's ruling. And again, in 1977, wrote a new death penalty law to comply with the federal court's decision, providing for a separate hearing to set the penalty for persons convicted of first-degree murder.

2. Under Nevada law, a person with three felony convictions can be sentenced as an habitual criminal and sentenced to life in prison. This can be a life sentence without possibility of parole, (the big bitch), or life with the possibility of parole (the litte bitch)

CHAPTER 14

1. The Starlight's license was in the name of Gloria Elliot, aka: Kitty Bono. Conforte was alleged to have held a hidden majority partnership with her. When Elliot, aka: Bono, pulled out, she took the license with her leaving the place unlicensed. Joe was furious.

1. The main Mustang Ranch building with the newly affixed sign reading "CLOSED."

2. Nevada State Prison Cell House under construction (Nevada State Library and Archives).

3. Aerial view of the Nevada State Prison
(Nevada State Library and Archives).

4. Nevada State Prison, East facing Lower Yard (Nevada State Library and Archives).

5. Looking west from the cell house toward the activities and education block. Main control is seen at the far right, circa 1940 (Nevada State Library and Archives).

6. "Chow down," in the prison culinary, circa 1940 (Nevada State Library and Archives).

7. "Modern" cell in cell house, circa 1940
(Nevada State Library and Archives).

8. Steel-walled disciplinary cells, circa 1950 (Nevada State Library and Archives).

9. Disciplinary detention cell on the east-facing, lower tier of C-Block. Note the "honey bucket" sunk into the concrete floor, circa 1960 (Nevada State Library and Archives).

10. Intake photo of Leonard Fristoe, circa 1920 (Nevada State Library and Archives).

11. Leonard Fristoe, on the yard of the Nevada State Prison, prior to his escape, circa 1923.

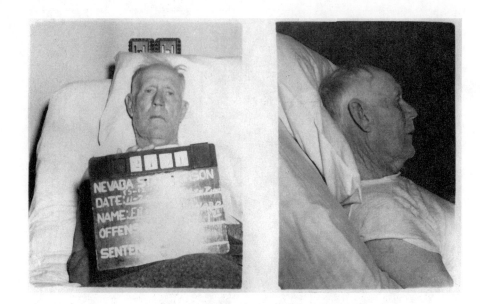

12. Leonard Fristoe, after being returned to the Nevada State Prison following his lengthy escape, circa November, 1969 (Nevada State Library and Archives).

A PROCLAMATION BY THE GOVERNOR

Whereas, LEONARD W. FRISTOE and ELWELL L. HOLT escaped from confinement in the Nevada State Prison on December 15, 1923, and satisfactory evidence has been presented to me that each of them was duly charged with murder, was guilty of the crime of murder, and duly sentenced to confinement in the State Prison by a court having competent authority within this State:

Now, Therefore, I, **James G. Scrugham,** Governor of the State of Nevada, under the authority vested in me by the Constitution and laws of the State of Nevada and particularly Section 2831, Revised Laws of Nevada (1912), do hereby offer and proclaim a reward, in the name of the State of Nevada, of

FIVE HUNDRED DOLLARS FOR THE CAPTURE (DEAD OR ALIVE)

of the said Leonard W. Fristoe and Elwell L. Holt, or either of them.

Satisfactory proof will be required by the Board of Examiners as to the title of any person to said reward or any share in the same. No Sheriff, Constable, Marshal, State Police, or other police officer, who shall make such capture in the performance of the duties of his office in the State, or any county, of Nevada, where such officer resides or in which his duties are required to be performed, shall be eligible to receive such reward. No assignment of claims for reward will be honored.

Given under my hand and the Great Seal of the State of Nevada, at the Capitol, in Carson City, this 21st day of December in the year of our Lord one thousand nine hundred and twenty-three.

J. G. Scrugham
Governor.

By the Governor:

W. G. Greathouse
Secretary of State.

13. Leonard Fristoe Arrest Warrant

14. The author on patrol in C-Block circa 1997.

15. Prison brass which was used as the legal medium of exchange at the Nevada State Prison, circa 1930-1960. The obverse and reverse sides of each coin are shown. At the top is a one-dollar canvas bill (Nevada State Library and Archives).

16. "Low Ball" card table, in use at the Nevada State Prison, circa 1950-1960 (Nevada State Library and Archives).

17. Fully operational craps table in use by NSP inmates (Nevada State Library and Archives).

18. Baseball and horse race betting area
(Nevada State Library and Archives).

19. Joe Conforte, chomping on the ever present Cuban cigar, ready to throw the dice, circa 1962-1963 (Nevada State Library and Archives).

20. Oscar Bonavena was slain outside this gate, the customer entrance into the Mustang Ranch bordello.

21. The one-lane bridge that leads into and out of the Mustang's parking lot.

22. Figures seated at a Lake Tahoe Hotel-Casino watching a Frank Sinatra stage event. Third from the bottom on the left, and with a cigar, is Oscar Bonavena. Behind him is Ross Brymer. On the right, third from the bottom, is Joe Conforte. Behind him is Johnny Colletti, a onetime Conforte bodyguard. The other persons are unidentified (photo courtesy of Ross Brymer Jr.).

23. Entrance to the Storey County Courthouse and jail which was completed in 1876, and where the two Ross Brymer trials were held.

24. The once elegant, but now boarded up, Cabin in the Sky Restaurant, in Gold HIll, once owned by Joe Conforte, and for a short while, his partner, Storey County Sheriff, Bob Del Carlo. In 1976, Conforte put up this restaurant as collateral to bail out Ross Brymer on the Bonavena murder charge.

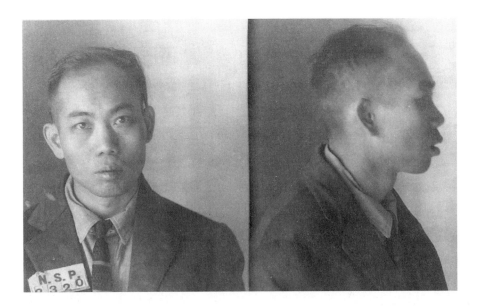

25. ID photo of Gee Jon when he arrived at the Nevada State Prison in 1921 (Nevada State Library and Archives).

26. Strap-iron gate securing the entrance to the isolation cave used as disciplinary housing of recalcitrant inmates at the Nevada State Prison, circa 1920-1960 (Nevada State Library and Archives).

27. View from inside the cave. The imprints on the rock floor are those of prehistoric animals that once roamed the region (Nevada State Library and Archives).

28. Drawing of the firing squad "killing machine" which was used to execute Andriza Mircovich, on May 14, 1913 (drawn by C/O Robert Schobert, from a sketch provided by the Nevada Historical Society).

29. The stone building built in 1888, on the grounds of the Nevada State Prison, and which was used as the world's first legal gas chamber The high rising exhaust pipe on the roof, was put there to exhaust the gas used for the second execution (Nevada State Historical Society).

30. The first building designed for, and constructed specifically for, a lethal gas chamber, on the grounds of the Nevada State Prison (Nevada State Historical Society)

31. Witnesses crowded around the observation windows viewing an execution by lethal gas (Nevada State Historical Society).

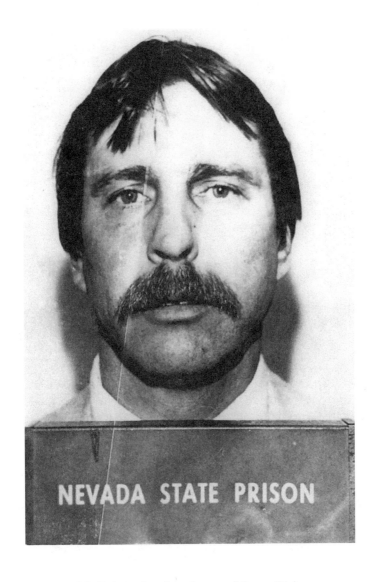

32. Prison intake photo of Jesse Bishop (Nevada State Library and Archives).

33. The two-chaired gas chamber at the Nevada State Prison, where Jesse Bishop took his last breath (Nevada State Library and Archives). Bishop was the last person to be put to death by lethal gas in Nevada.
Following his death, the prison adopted lethal injection. When a gurney replaced the death chairs, the chairs were moved over to the office of the Inspector General, where they found use as novelty seats.

34. Entrance into the lethal gas chamber through the air-lock door that was once part of a naval vessel (Nevada State Library and Archives).

35. Ross Brymer being subdued by officers in the parking lot of the Nevada State Prison the night Jesse Bishop was executed (Nevada State Library and Archives).

36. Ross Brymer pictured with Willie Nelson (photo courtesy of Ross Brymer Jr.).

37. Ross Brymer pictured with another musician (photo courtesy of Ross Brymer Jr.).